(*Continued from flap*)

his Marxist opponents. This study, clearly written and clearly argued, will fill a significant gap in the historiography of the Russian revolutionary movement.

Ronald I. Kowalski is Senior Lecturer in Russian History at Worcester College of Higher Education in England.

# The Bolshevik Party in Conflict

## The Left Communist Opposition of 1918

Ronald I. Kowalski

University of Pittsburgh Press

Series in Russian and East European Studies No. 14
Published in the U.S.A. by the University of Pittsburgh Press, Pittsburgh, Pa.
Published in Great Britain by The Macmillan Press Ltd.
© 1991, Ronald I. Kowalski
All rights reserved
Printed in Great Britain

Library of Congress Cataloging-in-Publication Data
Kowalski, Ronald I.
    The Bolshevik Party in conflict : the left communist opposition of
1918 / Ronald I. Kowalski.
        p.      cm. — (Series in Russian and East European studies)
    Includes bibliographical references and index.
    ISBN 0–8229–1161–2 (cloth)
    1. Communism—Soviet Union—History—20th century.  2. Soviet
Union—Politics and government—1917–  3. Kommunisticheskaîa partiîa
Sovetskogo Soîuza—History.  I. Title.  II. Series.
HX313.K674   1991
324.247′075—dc20                                                    90–21259
                                                                          CIP

To my mother and father

# Contents

# Acknowledgements

As this work neared completion my realisation of the mani-fold debts that I had incurred grew. My colleagues in the History Department at Worcester College of Higher Educa-tion have tolerated with patience and good humour my frequent frustrations. In particular, I am indebted to my head of department, Ted Townley, for his consistent sup-port, and to Dil Porter for his comradeship throughout this project. The History Department of Indiana University of Pennsylvania where I spent the academic year of 1988–9 as a Fulbright Exchange Teacher provided me with the practical facilities with which to finish this work. To the many libraries and their staffs that placed themselves at my disposal I am also grateful, but to none less than Kate Gardner, former deputy librarian at Worcester, whose uncomplaining pursuit of numerous rare materials is greatly appreciated. My thanks also must go to the British Academy, under whose auspices I was able to spend a fruitful two-month period of research in Moscow where I had the good fortune to unearth numerous local and regional newspapers unavailable in the West; and to the Twenty-Seven Foundation for a small grant which helped me in my study of the Moscow Left Communists. To the participants of a Soviet Industrialisation Project Seminar (SIPS) of the Centre for Russian and East European Studies (CREES) in the University of Birmingham in March, 1985, and of the Twelfth Conference of the Study Group on the Russian Revolution (SGRR), I owe a collective debt, for their critical yet encouraging response to the papers on the Left Communists that I presented. Maureen Perrie read and commented on part of this work, while Evan Mawdsley scrutinised a briefer exposition of the basic theses presented in it. Their help, and that of Professor R. W. Davies and, in particular, of Richard Sakwa for their critique of the entire manuscript, enabled me to expunge a number of historical, and verbal, atrocities that otherwise would have eluded me. Needless to say, they do not necessarily agree with my conclusions which together with whatever other shortcom-ings are to be found are my own. Chapters 1 and 7 in large part are based on an earlier paper, 'The Left Communist Movement of 1918: A preliminary analysis of its regional strength', published in the journal of the SGRR, *Sbornik* (now renamed *Revolutionary Russia*), 12 (1986). I am obliged to the editor of this journal for permission to reproduce much of this material here. Finally, I thank my family: my parents, for their support and encouragement over many years; my children, Anna and Helen, for their forbearance in the last few years as I strove to come to terms with the Left Communists; and above all to Jenny, without whose constant support and understanding this book would never have been completed.

R.I.K.
Indiana, PA

# Introduction

It remains rather surprising that some seventy years after its appearance the Left Communist movement, in Stephen Cohen's view perhaps 'the largest and most powerful Bolshevik opposition in the history of Soviet Russia',[1] should have suffered from such relative neglect. In the West, admittedly, historians often have discussed the conflict within the party in the first half of 1918 between Lenin and his faction on the one hand and the Left Communists on the other, but invariably in the context of more general studies, of the revolution, the party, or its leaders.[2] In consequence, our understanding of the Left Communist movement continues to be partial, lacking the breadth and depth of treatment that its importance seemingly warrants. For example, almost all that has been written about it has been confined to examining the conflict at the centre, within the leading echelons of the party. The nature of the movement at the regional and local levels has not been examined in any systematic way, although general allegations that the Moscow region, the Urals and Ukraine were bastions of Left Communism have received widespread currency.[3] Moreover, there has been an over-emphasis on the Left Communists' clash with Lenin on the questions of separate peace with Germany, and, subsequently, of the organisation of industry. This has occurred at the expense, certainly, of any sustained discussion of their bitter disagreements over agrarian policy (a remarkable omission given the significance of this issue in what was still a predominantly peasant society) and, to a lesser extent, their conflict concerning the structure of the revolutionary state.

Despite the absence of an adequate study of the Left Communist movement itself, Western historiography has witnessed several bold attempts to provide a theoretical framework in which to situate not just Left Communism, but the various other factions which emerged in the Bolshevik party, before the iron heel of Stalinism descended upon it. In his pioneering work on Communist opposition Robert Daniels argued that by 1917 two distinct currents existed within the party, the 'Leninists' and the 'Leftists', the former

1

emphasising 'power' and 'revolutionary pragmatism', the latter 'principle' and 'revolutionary idealism'. He continued, however, that it was rather misleading to attempt to differentiate them solely by reference to traditional distinctions between the political right and left on 'a simple unilinear scale'. Both factions after all were clearly on the left of such a scale, inasmuch as they both aspired to radical, nay revolutionary, political, social and economic change.[4] To understand the distinctions between them he suggested that it was necessary to refer to another scale, measuring degrees of hardness and softness. The 'Leninists', he contends were 'hard', in the sense of being 'the most aggressively power conscious and tough-minded people'. The 'Leftists', on the other hand, were located on the soft side of the scale, albeit divided into two groups: the 'Ultra-Left', such as the Workers' Opposition, and even the Democratic Centralists, the 'more utopian and emotionally democratic' of them; and the 'moderate Left', Leon Trotsky and his supporters, 'less carried away by enthusiasm and more prepared to resort to force'. He appears to be uncertain on which side of this scale to locate the Left Communist movement itself, assigning it to the mid-point of his hard-soft axis.[5]

While recognising Daniels' 'important contribution to the understanding of early Bolshevik thought', more recently James McClelland has argued that his model has tended to obscure the fact 'that there were *two* Bolshevik positions which were *equally* leftist, idealistic and bold, but which were diametrically opposed to each other in the content of their programs as well as their methods'.[6] He submits that both leftist currents envisaged radical socio-economic transformation, leading to similar 'anticipated utopias', yet differed fundamentally 'in the routes they proposed to travel in order to reach them'. One current, the utopian, 'argued for immediate and drastic changes in the existing culture and social structure on the premise that socialism could be built only after the masses, through widespread autonomy and crash educational and cultural programs, had acquired a truly proletarian class-consciousness'. The other, 'revolutionary heroic', current 'maintained that ... a massive build-up of the economy, rather than the psychological transformation of the masses, was the most urgent prerequisite for the

construction of socialism'.[7] In other words, the utopian Left
gave priority to 'proletarian cultural revolution' as the essential prerequisite for the construction of socialism, while the
'revolutionary heroic' Left emphasised the prime necessity of
industrialisation *per se*.[8]

McClelland does not attempt to apply his model to the Left
Communist movement itself, alleging that the distinction
between these two leftist currents only crystallised fully
during the civil war.[9] His conclusion seems to be confirmed
by Thomas Remington, whose own analysis of the phenomenon of Leftism within the Bolshevik party echoes that
of McClelland. Remington also divides the Left into two
currents: the 'technocratic', which stressed the need for the
'scientifically planned transformation of society', even at the
expense of workers' democracy, if socialism was to be built;
and the 'democratic', which continued to defend the 'popular
participation' of the workers in government and economic
administration as the most vital precondition of socialist
construction.[10] The Left Communists, he contends, 'advanced both themes' in the first half of 1918. Subsequently,
the Left split into distinct factions, with the Democratic
Centralists, the Military Opposition and the Workers'
Opposition continuing to defend 'democratic values' against
'the progressive centralisation of power' championed by the
technocrats.[11]

The strength of these interpretations lies in their recognition that the Left in the Bolshevik party was not a monolithic
tendency. Certainly, the leading protagonists of the Left
Communist movement found themselves at odds in the years
after 1918, occupying divergent and often shifting positions.
During the civil war, for example, Nikolai Bukharin, while
not abandoning his commitment to cultural revolution, gave
staunch support to Trotsky, the symbolic leader of the
'revolutionary heroic' tradition, 'in defending the need for
the mobilisation of labor and the "statification" of trade
unions'. Thereafter, he 'decisively part[ed] company with the
principles of revolutionary heroism' and moved to the Right
of the party where he became the principal advocate of
'much more pragmatic, cautions and moderate policies . . .
which found their fullest embodiment in the NEP'.[12] He now
found himself in opposition to his old Moscow comrades and

former fellow thinkers, Valerian Osinskii and Vladimir Smirnov. With Timofei Sapronov, they were the founders of the Democratic Centralist movement which took up the anti-bureaucratic mantle of the Left Communists. Thereafter, this *troika* itself split. After participating in the group of the 'Forty-Six' in 1923 Osinskii abandoned the Left, only to appear on the Right of the party at the end of the 1920s.[13] Sapronov and Smirnov, 'the two irreconcileables' according to Victor Serge, apparently remained committed to the democratic Left, bitterly opposed to what they saw as the continued growth of 'a bureaucratic police regime'.[14] Few, however, joined the Workers' Opposition which defended 'proletarian consciousness ... as the driving force in the establishment of the economic foundations of communism'. The most prominent exception was Alexandra Kollontai, though rather ironically her then partner and co-leader was Aleksandr Shliapnikov, himself a critic of untramelled workers' democracy in 1918.[15] Evgenii Preobrazhenskii subsequently followed a somewhat ambivalent path. While continuing to defend 'freedom of party criticism and conciliation of opposition' during the civil war, he did gravitate to the 'revolutionary heroic' or technocratic wing of the Left Opposition. Continuing for much of the 1920s to argue for greater intra-party democracy, at the same time he elaborated the concept, first proposed in a more rudimentary form by Smirnov in 1918, of 'primitive socialist accumulation', the theoretical foundation for the rapid industrialisation of Soviet Russia advocated by the Left Opposition in the 1920s. Indeed, he forsook the opposition in 1928 when Stalin effectively abandoned the gradualism of the NEP in favour of a 'revolutionary heroic' campaign for the rapid industrialisation of the country.[16]

However, what still remains unexplained are the reasons for this fracture within the Left, the reasons why some former Left Communists continued to stress democratic principles while others embraced the 'revolutionary heroic' or technocratic solution – and some, such as Emelian Iaroslavskii and Valerian Kuibyshev, deserted the Left entirely, to become 'pillars of orthodoxy' within the party.[17] There is no obvious answer to these questions. It is tempting to seek the inspiration for the democratic Left in the work of Aleksandr

Bogdanov, '[t]he most profound theorist of proletarian culture', and in the *Vpered* group which embraced 'the concept of proletarian culture'.[18] Tempting or not, given the present state of knowledge such a conclusion could well be misleading. As Zenovia Sochor has cautioned regarding the influence of *Proletkult*, the spiritual heir of Bogdanov and the *Vpered* group, 'direct ties between, or even a common intent of, Proletkult and the Workers' Opposition are difficult to substantiate'.[19]

The same caution seems broadly applicable in the democratic Left as a whole. Some prominent *Vperedists*, such as Ivan Skvortsov-Stepanov and Mikhail Pokrovskii, did join the Left Communist movement, yet played no role in future oppositions. Bukharin, admittedly, seems to have been supportive of concepts of proletarian culture, yet he himself had not been a *Vperedist*, nor was he simply 'Bogdanov's disciple'.[20] Osinskii, Sapronov and Smirnov had no obvious connections with Bogdanov or *Vpered*, and in fact Osinskii, while agreeing with Bogdanov and the Otzovists in demanding the recall of the Bolshevik deputies from the State *Duma*, denied that he had ever been a Bogdanovist. Kollontai herself had lectured at the party school in Bologna set up by the *Vpered* group, and, according to one of her recent biographers, Barbara Clements, her ideas on proletarian ideology were informed by those of Bogdanov.[21] Yet Aleksei Gastev, for a time in the vanguard of the *Proletkult* movement, became a champion of the 'technocratic' Left.[22] Only a detailed and exhaustive study of the Left Oppositions after 1918, perhaps a prosoprographic analysis, may allow us to arrive at a fuller understanding of why the Left fractured. Such a task, however, lies beyond the scope of this particular work.

Soviet historiography, unsurprisingly, has endowed us with a considerably less subtle analysis of the various intraparty oppositions. Yet with respect to the Left Communist movement itself it has done somewhat better, providing two useful monographs and a number of more limited studies which still manage to throw much light on the support that it enjoyed at the regional and local levels. The first major Soviet study, that of Vladimir Sorin, a former Left Communist himself, appeared in 1925. Not itself a product of 'the

Stalin school of falsification', nevertheless it must be seen in the context of the intra-party struggle of the mid-1920s. As Sorin confessed in his preface, his primary objective was not to provide an exhaustive history of the movement *per se*. Rather, he had an overt political purpose in mind, to demonstrate the links, ideological and personal, between the Left Opposition of the mid-20s and the Left Communist 'deviation' of 1918.[23] Whilst self-professedly Leninist in spirit,[24] Sorin's interpretation, compared to subsequent accounts, was remarkably free of vilification.

Conceding that the Left Communists were genuine Marxist revolutionaries, he explains their opposition on two main grounds. First, their analysis, a mistaken analysis according to Sorin, of imperialism led them to exaggerate the prospects for immediate socialist revolution across Europe and, in turn, this conditioned their rejection of separate peace with Germany as unnecessary. Second, they were allegedly influenced by the aspirations of the petty-bourgeoisie, that is, the peasants and the Left Social Revolutionaries (Left SRs), their intellectual leaders. Their influence is said to have driven the Left Communists in the direction, on the one hand, of patriotism, viz., their opposition to peace on German terms, and, on the other, of a typical petty-bourgeois form of 'ultra-revolutionism' which prevented them realising the necessity of retreat, both at home and abroad, in the first half of 1918, when radically changed circumstances no longer favoured the advance of the revolution.[25] Paradoxically, elsewhere they were condemned for their failure to understand the peasants and their aspirations![26] Sorin's study is also noteworthy for the distinction that it continued to draw between the Left Communists and Trotsky and his followers. Both, of course, adopted incorrect, non-Leninist positions. Yet Sorin was less scathing in his treatment of the Left Communists, understandably perhaps as an erstwhile member of the movement himself and more certainly in the context of the mid-1920s when Trotsky was the main target of the party leadership. For Sorin, the Left Communists at least consistently defended a clear-cut policy in favour of revolutionary war. Trotsky, on the other hand, while correct in dragging out the negotiations at Brest-Litovsk as a propaganda device to mobilise the European proletariat, had wrought great harm by advocating the ultimately groundless policy of 'no war, no peace'. This attempt to find a third way, between peace or revolutionary war, simply confused and prolonged the debate within the party and allowed the Germans to impose more Draconian terms on Soviet Russia.[27]

The wilful falsification of the history of the Left Communist movement that followed in the 1930s is quite familiar, having been ably charted by Daniels and Leonard Schapiro.[28] The distinction between the Left Communists and Trotsky that Sorin had emphasised became elided in the history of the party written in 1931 by another former Left Communist, Andrei Bubnov.[29] In the 1933 edition of his work on party history, Iaroslavskii distorted the picture even more wildly, alleging that Left Communism was nothing but a petty-bourgeois phenomenon, encompassing the unlikely combination of anarchist, Menshevik, Trotskyist and anarcho-syndicalist ideas which had typified all subsequent 'anti-party groups'.[30] What also emerged in the early 1930s was the charge that the Left Communists had entered into some compact with the Left SRs to overthrow Lenin's government.[31] This accusation re-emerged in the show trials of the later thirties and in the culmination of Stalinist rewriting, the infamous *Short Course*. The Left Communists, quite grotesquely, were now depicted as the witting accomplices of Stalin's *bête-noire*, Trotsky, who together had conspired to oust Lenin, even to assassinate him, and to form a new government with the help of the Left SRs.[32] Sufficient has been written already to refute this outrageous slander. That some discussion of a coalition to oppose peace, perhaps even to set up a new government, took place between the Left Communists and the Left SRs is well-established. But the Left Communists, ultimately, baulked at the prospect, not simply because they suffered a failure of nerve. As we shall see, their antipathy to the peasants, as well as their understanding of what proletarian politics meant, made the prospect of any lasting alliance with the Left SRs highly improbable – and indeed, in July, when the latter launched their abortive coup in Moscow the Left Communists showed no qualms about the measures taken to suppress them.[33]

This crudely distorted picture of Left Communism remained dominant within Soviet historiography for twenty years, until the Soviet historical profession was freed in part from its Stalinist straitjacket in the era of reform introduced by Nikita Khrushchev. In turn, some advances in our knowledge were made. The most significant of them was the admission that for a time Left Communism in fact was a popular, broadly-based movement with considerable support at lower levels within the party. A number of detailed studies have cast much light on the sources of Left Communist strength.[34] The extent of this rank-and-file support is explained by reference to a combination of the anger at the crippling peace terms proposed by the Germans; of euphoria produced by the swift and relatively bloodless triumphs in October and over subsequent feeble counter-revolutionary assaults; and of faith in the imminence of revolution in Europe. Once set right by the efforts of Lenin and the party centre, however, many of those who had been seduced by the appeal of Left Communism, including a considerable number of its leaders, worked hard and honourably to carry out party policy.[35]

The weakness of these studies, however, is that they offer no convincing explanation for the persistence of grass-roots sympathy for Left Communism in the spring of 1918. Equally, the fiction of a Left Communist/Trotskyist/Left SR/anti-socialist conspiracy became muted, although many prominent Left Communists, as other eminent oppositionists, did not yet receive full and public rehabilitation.[36] Finally, the last year of the Khrushchev era saw the publication of one purportedly comprehensive study of Left Communism, that of K. I. Varlamov and N. A. Slamikhin. As well as re-examining the conflict over the Brest peace and providing a partial survey of the areas of Left Communist strength, it also, as the authors stress, seeks to analyse the debates on socialist economic construction in Russia in the first half of 1918 in a detail hitherto lacking.[37] Whatever virtues this work possesses (for example, it does address the much neglected clash over agrarian policy), it is weakened by rather glib and sweeping assertions that purport to explain Left Communism by reference either to an alleged affinity with Trotsky on the issue of 'permanent revolution' and the impossibility of socialism in one country; or to a 'petty-bourgeois fanaticism' which precluded them from responding in a creative Marxist manner to changing circumstances and new tasks; or to anarchist or anarcho-syndicalist influences.[38]

Little of import was contributed in the Brezhnev years which, according to Lewis Siegelbaum, witnessed the reestablishment of 'an historical orthodoxy that had been breached during the Khrushchev years'. Now, however, the penetration of *glasnost*' into the realm of the historical profession promises some hope of renewed advances. For instance, leading Left Communists such as Bukharin, Iurii Piatakov and Karl Radek have been legally exonerated of all criminal charges laid against them. Moreover, a new study of Bukharin, by I. E. Gorelov, has been recently published, with the aim of redressing the falsifications of the last fifty years concerning his life and work, and at a round-table of historians which met in May 1989, Professor A. A. Chernobaev called for a new, dispassionate treatment of the Left Communists' opposition to the peace of Brest-Litovsk.[39] The portents are encouraging, and one hopes that in the near future Soviet historians will be able to offer more honest and empirically-grounded accounts of the Left Communist movement. But, as Siegelbaum has also reminded us, it is unrealistic to anticipate that the legacy of decades of conformity can be overcome overnight.[40]

In the meantime, many *lacunae* and misconceptions concerning the Left Communists continue to prevail. This study will attempt to rectify them, at the risk of being overtaken in the foreseeable future by new research emanating from the Soviet Union itself. No doubt any work of history faces such a prospect, but the hope remains that whatever new evidence may be forthcoming will not refute substantially the conclusions drawn in this book. They will, I fear, be contentious, which itself is inescapable when dealing with such a politically emotive subject. As an apostate myself, one who once believed that the Left Communists offered a democratic socialist model for revolutionary Russia that was never implemented, perhaps my treatment of them on occasion may seem to be over-critical, even harsh. Yet I have sought to present their ideas as fully and accurately as possible, so that the reader may arrive at his or her own judgement of them.

The study will proceed in a number of discrete, yet linked stages. The first step will be to demonstrate that the Left Communists did operate within a common theoretical framework, not necessarily of shared commitment to democratic principles, but one based fundamentally, as Sorin, Varlamov and Slamikhin, among others, have suggested, on an essentially common analysis of imperialism. Their conclusions regarding the prospects for socialism within and without Russia appear to have been derived from this analysis. In turn, it also helps to explain to some degree their opposition to Lenin on the question of a separate peace with Germany. A detailed treatment of this issue, which precipitated the formation of the Left Communist movement, will form the next stage. Moreover, it also helped shape their own programme for the transformation of agriculture, industry and the state on socialist principles. A re-examination of this programme, which demands a much more systematic and critical exposition than it has received thus far, will comprise the further stage in the study. Finally, it will conclude with a detailed investigation of the support which the Left Communists in fact were able to muster in their alleged strongholds, the Moscow region, the Urals and the Ukraine. Clearly, they did win much sympathy there, as elsewhere, for their advocacy of revolutionary war, at least until the renewed advance of the Germans demonstrated that such a policy simply was not feasible. The majority of Russians ultimately would not fight! Thereafter, their support rapidly dwindled. Even the Moscow region, supposed to have been a bastion of Leftism, on closer examination proves to have been no such thing. In their other alleged strongholds, the Urals and the Ukraine, support survived in varying degrees even after the peace was signed. What remains at issue here are the reasons why this was the case. However, before embarking on this complex (but let us hope not convoluted) path of inquiry into the nature of Left Communism it will be prudent, first of all, to review how the movement emerged, rose and, rather quickly, fell. The next chapter will be devoted to preparing the ground for the reconstruction which follows.

# 1 The Rise and Fall of the Left Communist Movement

The first portents that the question of peace or war would prove to be a source of bitter controversy within the Bolshevik party emerged in November, 1917. The failure of the Decree on Peace of 26 October, which called for a general democratic peace, to evoke any response impelled the Soviet government to initiate negotiations for an armistice with Germany on 14 November. In response, an influential group in the powerful Petersburg Committee, led by by G. E. Evdokimov, Ia. G. Fenigshtein (Dolecki), V. N. Narchuk and Karl Radek, opposed the idea of peace treaties with any of the imperialist states, calling instead for an international civil war against world capitalism.[1]

A week after the armistice came into force, negotiations with the Germans for peace began at Brest-Litovsk on 3 December, with Adolf Ioffe leading the Soviet delegation. Suspended on 15 December, apparently on the Bolsheviks' suggestion, to allow time for the Allied powers to enter into them and so conclude a general peace, they were renewed on 27 December. Leon Trotsky now headed the Soviet mission, with the task of dragging out the talks in the belief that world revolution would soon intervene and render the need for a separate peace redundant. It was at this point that the Left Communists coalesced as a distinct faction, previously having only made separate statements condemning the Soviet government's conduct of foreign policy. On 28 December Nikolai Osinskii (V. V. Obolenskii), A. Lomov (G. I. Oppokov) and Innokentii Stukov issued a resolution, adopted the same day by a plenary session of the Moscow Regional (*Oblast'*) Bureau, the organisational centre of Left Communism according to Z. L. Serebriakova. It demanded an end to negotiations with Imperial Germany, and the rupture of all relations with the other imperialist 'robber' states. Instead Soviet Russia must declare revolutionary war against world imperialism. Previously, even Lenin had concurred with this policy, Osinskii claimed, insisting that he was doing no more than defending 'Lenin's old position'. On the same day, so F. N. Dingel'shtedt recalled, the Petersburg Committee, goaded by Fenigshtein, S. N. Ravich and V. Volodarskii (M. M. Goldstein) and others, came out in support of this policy, the so-called 'Moscow point of view'.[2]

Soon many leading Bolsheviks, including the cream of the party intelligentsia, rallied in support of revolutionary war (see appendix A). Yet the Left Communist movement was not just one of disgruntled intellectuals, isolated from and unrepresentative of the views of the rank and file throughout the country, as Lenin's polemic on occasion implied.[3] On the contrary, throughout January and February widespread opposition to peace existed in the lower reaches of the party, and beyond. A majority of local party organisations, and local soviets too, in which the Mensheviks and SRs added their voices to those of the dissenting Bolsheviks, opposed separate peace with Imperial Germany. 'Most town committees and nearly all regional committees', Robert Service has argued, 'were sternly declaring that revolutionary war was the only possible option for the party if the truce should break down . . .'.[4] Moscow and Petrograd were cases in point. The leading party organisations in Moscow – the Regional Bureau, the District (*Okrug*) Committee and the City Committee – consistently opposed the continuation of negotiations for peace with the Germans.[5] The Petersburg Committee adopted the same position, endorsed by the majority of party activists at a meeting on 18 January.[6] The renewed German offensive on 18 February, eight days after the negotiations at Brest had broken down when Trotsky declared that Russia would neither continue the war nor sign peace on German terms, certainly raised doubts in the minds of many in the capital about the feasibility of waging revolutionary war. On 21 February the majority Bolshevik fraction of the Petrograd Soviet, with apparently only four dissenting voices, changed tack, to support the decision of the Council of People's Commissars (*Sovnarkom*) to accept peace on German terms.[7]

However, at the grass roots across the city militancy, it would seem, continued to prevail. In face of the dire threat posed by the German advance, many district (*raion*) soviets, as well as individual factories and plants, passed resolutions in favour of revolutionary war. They echoed the despairing plea of the Okhta district soviet which proclaimed that it was preferable to die fighting for international socialism than to wait to be crushed by the forces of international imperialism.[8] At this time words appear to have been matched by deeds, as many Bolsheviks and ordinary workers mobilised to defend the capital – 500 from the Vulcan and 600 from the Sestroretsk works, all those under the age of fifty from the Baltic shipyard, 2000 from the Second City district, and 3000 from Vyborg. In all, David Mandel concludes that in the final days of February 10 000 volunteered for the Red Army, others joined the Red Guards, while additional workers' detachments were set up.[9] The Fourth City Conference of the party, which reconvened on 1 March after adjourning in face of the emergency precipitated by the German advance, reflected these sentiments. Delegates from the districts – with the exception of Vyborg which was split on the issue – were reported to have opposed any fresh overtures to the Germans.[10] Other major towns in north Russia, such as Archangel, Murmansk, Novgorod and Vologda, followed the lead given by the two capitals, as did the naval base of Kronshtadt, where, according to Israel Getzler, it was the Left SRs who were chiefly instrumental in raising opposition to a separate peace.[11]

A similar pattern was to be found in the Volga region. Urged on in particular by V. P. Antonov-Saratovskii, I. Vardin-Mgeladze and M. V. Vasil'ev, chairman of the Bolshevik city committee, both the leading party organisations and the Bolshevik-dominated city and provincial Soviets in Saratov repeatedly rejected separate peace with Germany. Meetings of the party rank and file and other workers' organisations – but not the peasants – from January until late February and early March consistently endorsed this position, lending credence to the claim of Vardin-Mgeladze, the delegate from Saratov at the Seventh Extraordinary Party Congress, that the majority of workers remained opposed to peace.[12] Counter to the decision of this Congress, on 9 March, the executive committee of the Saratov Soviet mandated its delegates to the forthcoming Fourth All-Russian Congress of

Soviets to resist ratification of the Brest peace.[13] A comparable correlation of forces existed in Samara. Leading party organs and much of the rank and file supported the Left Communists. The executive committees of the city and provincial Soviets, then dominated by the Left Communists, also mandated their delegates to the Fourth Congress of Soviets – Kuz'min and Kazakov from the provincial Soviet and Valerian Kuibyshev and I. Krainiukov from the city – to reject ratification of the peace.[14] This situation was mirrored elsewhere in the region. In fact, in February all the provincial Soviets in the region had adopted a Left Communist position, although at the *uezd* and *volost'* level, so V. I. Tkachev has recently claimed, support for revolutionary war appears to have been much less certain. In the first half of March hostility to peace remained widespread both in the party and the Soviets in Astrakhan, Penza, Simbirsk and Tsaritsyn.[15]

Further east, in the Urals and beyond, the Left Communists also gained considerable support. Siberia was a case in point. The West Siberian Regional congress of Soviets on 19 January; the Second Congress of Soviets of Siberia which met in Irkutsk in the last week of February; the first Siberian peasants' congress on 1 March; the Krasnoiarsk party which, in the opinion of Russell Snow, was the strongest bastion of Left Communism in the region; and the Soviets in Eniseisk, Khabarovsk, Omsk and Vladivostok all opposed negotiations with Germany in the belief that only the struggle for international revolution could secure a lasting peace. Moreover, Left Communist sympathisers who dominated the Far Eastern Regional Bureau of the party, so Paul Dotsenko has alleged, appear to have been prepared to split Siberia from the Russian Republic should the latter consent to peace.[16] On 22 March, after the Fourth Congress of Soviets had voted to ratify the peace, the executive committee of the Siberian Soviet continued to refuse to countenance this course of action, while 'the Siberian Council of People's Commissars even declared itself still at war with the Central Powers'.[17] Finally, Left Communist strength was also pronounced in the Urals itself in the winter of 1918, as it was in the south of the country, in Kursk and especially in the Ukraine and the Donbass.[18]

Only in the west of the country, in provinces such as

Vitebsk and Smolensk, most immediately threatened by the renewed German offensive, and within the Western Regional Committee, did support for peace at virtually any price rapidly swell in the last third of February. Even here, however, instances of grass-roots militancy in face of German depredations were reported, but they appear to have been largely ineffectual in checking the advance.[19]

Local soviet responses to the Central Executive Committee's (CEC) circular of 26 February seeking to determine their position on the Brest peace appeared to confirm the extent of opposition to peace. Lenin himself conceded that of the 200 replies received in the first ten days of March a small majority – 105 to 95 – favoured revolutionary war. The Left Communists gleefully exploited these results for their own factional ends. In the first issue of *Kommunist*, the daily newspaper issued by the Left-dominated Petersburg Committee and Petersburg District Committee to mobilise popular support for revolutionary war, Lomov argued that the responses to date confirmed the Left's contention that the major proletarian centres of the country remained opposed to separate peace on German terms. With the partial exceptions of Petrograd and Sevastopol, he continued, pressure for peace had come mainly from peasant-dominated *volost'* and *uezd* soviets, so bearing out the Left's repeated assertion that Lenin and his faction had abandoned revolutionary war in response to reactionary peasant aspirations.[20]

Evidently the renewed German offensive had not produced a complete collapse of the will to resist. In fact, the German ultimatum of 23 February containing even harsher terms for peace than previously – in addition to Poland, Lithuania, western Latvia and the Moon Sound Islands, Russia was now to surrender eastern Latvia, Finland and the Ukraine – provoked, for a time, a stiffening of resolve across Russia to fight. As even Lenin admitted, 'from everywhere [it generated] a readiness to rise in defence of Soviet power and to fight to the last man'.[21] Yet enthusiasm itself, he hastened to add, without an organised and equipped army, was totally incapable of halting the German juggernaut. Convinced of Soviet Russia's military exhaustion, of its inability to defend itself effectively, Lenin uncompromisingly resisted all pressures to continue the war, however widespread they seemed to be. His intransigence threatened to split the party, at least at its highest levels. At the session of the Central Committee (CC) held on 23 February, when the revised German peace terms were communicated to its members, Lenin threatened to resign if 'the policy of revolutionary phrase-making', as he derisively termed it, did not cease at once. The Left Communist die-hards on the CC, Andrei Bubnov, Bukharin, Lomov and Moisei Uritskii, were equally unyielding in their opposition to acceptance of peace, with Lomov sanguinely predicting that further resistance was 'certain [to cause] demoralisation among the German troops' and so halt their advance.[22] Yet the real state of affairs – the continuing absence of revolution within Germany and the rapid disintegration of Russian forces at the front – undermined their position and produced a realignment within the CC. Trotsky now abandoned his obdurate opposition to peace, arguing that the deep divisions in the party precluded the possibility of successfully waging revolutionary war in any shape or form. Yet, still unable to steel himself to vote for peace, he abstained, as did Feliks Dzerzhinskii, Ioffe and Nikolai Krestinskii who shared his point of view. Their abstentions, however, enabled Lenin, with the support of Ivan Smilga, Grigorii Sokol'nikov, Joseph Stalin, Elena Stasova, Iakov Sverdlov and Grigorii Zinoviev, to gain a majority in favour of peace when the question was put to the vote. This decision in turn provoked the resignation of Bukharin and his co-thinkers from all positions of responsibility in the party and government, with the added threat that they would campaign openly against peace.[23] After an all-night session on 23–4 February the CEC was won round to accept the now more punitive peace terms offered by the Germans.[24]

In early March, despite an intense grass-roots campaign of opposition to Lenin's policy, the tide clearly turned against the Left Communists. At lower levels within the party and soviets, sympathy for revolutionary war rapidly began to erode. This was soon apparent in the capitals. In Moscow, the Soviet, closely followed by a City Conference of the party, overwhelmingly adopted resolutions in favour of peace on 3 and 4 March. In Petrograd too, the groundswell of militancy evident across the city in the last week of February began to disintegrate in early March. The Left Communists themselves grudgingly conceded the erosion of their support amongst the rank-and-file, alleging, however, that it was in large part the product of the demoralising impact of the government's peace policy itself, as well as of the mobilisation of the more politically-conscious and militant workers to the front. On 5 March the Petrograd Soviet reaffirmed that peace was inevitable, given the unwelcome delay in the outbreak of revolution in Europe and Russia's own military and economic weakness.[25] Bolshevik organisations in the First and Second City, the Moscow, Vyborg and Vasil'evskii districts soon followed suit, as did the Petersburg District Committee. Aware of these realignments, the Left-dominated Petersburg Committee convened an Extraordinary City Conference of the party, to ascertain precisely what the attitudes of the rank-and-file in the city were. When it met on 20 March, the answer was clear. The Left Communists lost their majority on the Petersburg Committee, with only the Narva district continuing to support them. Moreover, *Kommunist* was condemned for its splitting tactics and closed down.[26] Even more tellingly, at the session of the Seventh Party Congress held on 7 March Radek candidly admitted that 'now we [Left Communists] are the minority'. By mid-March, when delegates to the Fourth All-Russian Congress of Soviets gathered in Moscow, his assessment of the situation was apparently confirmed. At the Bolshevik caucus preceding the Congress they could only muster thirty-eight votes in support of revolutionary war, against 453 in favour of accepting the Brest peace.[27] At the Congress itself, of the 814 Bolshevik delegates present, only sixty-five refused to sanction ratification of the peace but, rather than split the party by voting against it, they abstained (see appendix B).

Arguably, these figures exaggerate the decline of the Left Communist movement. The reports of delegates to the Fourth Congress of Soviets suggest that in some regions support for peace was still far from assured. In the Volga region, particularly in Saratov, many doubted if the Brest peace would in fact provide Russia with any respite in which to recover, and then to proceed with the construction of socialism. Substantial Left Communist enclaves also continued to exist in Simbirsk and Samara, within both the party

and the soviets.[28] In the Urals, too, especially in Perm'
province, support for revolutionary partisan war remained
strong. but it was from the south most of all that voices in
favour of continued resistance were to be heard most
vociferously, from the provinces of Poltava and Taurida,
from the city of Sevastopol, where there appears to have
been a dramatic change of mood, and from the Donbass.
There, where there had been no lull in the war, the continuing advance of the Germans threatened all the gains that
the workers and peasants had made during the revolution.
Even the Don Cossacks, fearful of German intentions, were
reportedly ready to wage a partisan war.[29] For their part, the
Left Communists in the south tried to capitalise on this
sympathy for their position by attempting to unite these
disparate forces into a single military organisation which
would be better able to resist the Germans. In late March and
early April S. I. Syrtsov and his fellow-thinkers in the Don
Soviet Republic won considerable support for the idea of a
military union with what remained of Soviet power in the
Ukraine. This plan, however, came to naught. At the Congress of Soviets of the Don Republic which convened in
Rostov on 9 April, Lenin's allies, afraid that such a union
would provide the Germans with a *casus belli* for a fresh
assault on the Russian republic, thwarted this scheme. Under
the leadership of Sergei Ordzhonikidze they secured a
sizeable majority for ratification of the Brest peace.[30]

These reservations notwithstanding, it seems clear that
soon after the renewed German offensive the Left Communists in the main were fighting a losing battle on the question
of peace or revolutionary war. Three factors appear to have
been primarily responsible for their defeat. First, and, in
Service's view, most important, Soviet Russia's inability effectively to resist the advancing German forces made Lenin's
ruthless and insistent logic that there was no alternative but
to sign the peace appear more and more irrefutable, as the
rank-and-file within the party and the soviets increasingly
realised. Second, Lenin and his lieutenants conducted their
own grass-roots campaign of agitation and persuasion, most
vociferously in Petrograd and Moscow, to persuade the rank
and file of the rectitude of their policy. Third, the machinations of Sverdlov, the Central Committee secretary, and

according to Leonard Schapiro 'the main power behind the party organisation', ensured that Lenin's supporters were in a majority at the Seventh Party Congress – provincial organisations opposed to peace were deliberately under-represented. At the Fourth Congress of Soviets his manipulation of procedures, as Iu. O. Martov caustically remarked, combined with his emphasis on party discipline, facilitated ratification of the peace there.[31]

Even after their defeat on the issue of peace the Left, or 'proletarian' Communists as they increasingly called themselves, did not disband. However, with the ratification of the Brest-Litovsk treaty the focus of their opposition shifted. While continuing to carp at the foreign policy of the dominant Leninist faction, and even to revive the call for revolutionary war in May, after the Germans had installed the reactionary Skoropadskii regime in the Ukraine the burden of their attack was directed against what they perceived to be Lenin's compromises and retreats in internal policy. At the beginning of 1918, in January and February, they had castigated Lenin for his willingness to appease the peasants by sanctioning the division of the land amongst them. Not only was such a policy contrary to the demands of socialism but potentially fatal to it. The peace itself had been in large part another concession to peasant pressure. If continued, this path of conciliation would have grave consequences, leading to 'the political supremacy of the semi-proletarian, petty-bourgeois masses and prove to be only a transitional stage to the complete domination of finance capital'.[32] In the spring they repeatedly asserted that evidence of such degeneration towards state capitalism was at hand, manifest in Lenin's willingness to collaborate with the remaining capitalists as a means of restoring Soviet Russia's fast-disintegrating industrial base. Parallel and quite consistent with this development, Soviet democracy, conceived in terms of a '"commune state" ruled from below', was increasingly being supplanted by an authoritarian, centralised, bureaucratic state.[33] At a meeting with Lenin and his faction on 4 April Osinskii presented their *Theses on the Current Situation*, in which these concerns were articulated fully. Subsequently, the *Theses* were published in a new, short-lived, theoretical journal, named like its predecessor, *Kommunist*, edited by Bukharin,

Osinskii, Radek and Vladimir Smirnov. Published under the aegis of the Moscow Regional Bureau, until they lost control of it at the Fourth Moscow Regional Conference held between 14 and 17 May, it was composed largely of a series of polemical articles debunking the domestic policies then defended by Lenin and the majority of the party and sketching out their own, more radical programme for the construction of socialism.

During this phase of their opposition the Left Communists continued to garner some grass-roots support for their views. Never as extensive as in the debate over peace, it remained limited almost exclusively to the Moscow region, the Ukraine and the Urals, as well as Krasnoiarsk.[34] They also found some support within the *sovnarkhoz* structure, from where they opposed in particular Lenin's programme for industrial reconstruction.[35] Yet by the end of May their bases within the party had been recaptured by Lenin's allies, and as a faction the Left Communist movement disappeared – although not without trace. At the end of August Evgenii Preobrazhenskii attempted, vainly, to win over the regional party committee in the Urals to Left Communist policies, while at the Second Congress of Economic Councils in December, as Samuel Oppenheimer has noted, vestigial voices from the Left were heard, bitterly criticising the continued drift to bureaucratic centralisation within the economy at the expense of workers' control.[36]

The eventual demise of the Left Communist movement is not reducible to any single or simple cause, such as the failure of its leadership, as Stephen Cohen among others has suggested.[37] Circumstances within and without Russia in the first half of 1918 militated against its survival. First, its policies rapidly lost credibility. Just as revolutionary war had come to appear impractical, so too its defence of the commune state, in which economic and political power would be diffused to the local soviets and other elected workers' organisations, seemed to offer no realistic solution to the chaos gripping the country. In particular, many within the party, the trades unions and, to a lesser extent, the leadership of the factory-plant committees, agreed with Lenin that workers' control was exacerbating economic dislocation and had to be curbed if industry was to be revived. His arguments in favour of a return to tried-and-tested methods of centralised economic control, one-person management, and traditional means of discipline and incentive were gaining ground even before the renewed outbreak of civil war in May. Then the very survival of Soviet power ever more insistently demanded the speedy restoration of order in industry to increase the production of war *matériel*. To many Lenin's prescriptions seemed best able to produce such results, while the majority of the Left Communists were prepared to suspend their opposition in view of the growing military threats to Bolshevik rule.[38]

Second, in the latter half of May the CC acted to establish a more rigid form of party discipline, threatened both by the influx of new, politically-untempered recruits and by the exodus of many experienced activists to take up administrative positions within the state and economy or to join the newly-forming Red Army. Moreover, the overt and strident opposition of the Left Communist faction, the CC continued, had undermined discipline further. Sverdlov's machinations notwithstanding, hitherto the debate with the Left Communists had been conducted fairly openly and democratically, even harmoniously. At the session of the CC on 23 February Lenin had conceded that they had the right to agitate openly against acceptance of the peace; at the Seventh Party Congress he had referred to them as 'our young Moscow friends'; while *Pravda* called them 'our friends from *Kommunist*'.[39] The critical situation now facing the revolution led to a change in the CC's attitude. Lenin and his allies sought a more compliant party in which all decisions, once taken, were to be implemented without further discussion.[40] This requirement appears to have been directed specifically against the Left Communists, as Varvara Iakovleva implied when she accused the CC of aiming to eliminate independent thought within the party.[41] Indeed, the entire campaign to raise party discipline was used as a stick with which to beat the Left Communists. Some were expelled, though how many suffered this fate and how crucial such a purge was to their eventual defeat is difficult to gauge with any accuracy.[42]

Third, certain changes in policy, while not introduced solely in response to Left Communist criticisms, may have gone some way to appeasing them. In late April and May

Lenin's hopes of running industry in collaboration with the indigenous capitalists collapsed, to be superseded by a more thorough and extensive nationalisation of large-scale industry. By mid-May Lenin himself was calling for 'the most decisive measures against our bourgeoisie'.[43] Moreover, the worsening food crisis in urban Russia compelled him, so Silvana Malle has concluded, to sanction an assault on the peasants (in theory only the rich peasants) and to encourage the more rapid establishment of communal agriculture, as the Left Communists had sought.[44]

\*          \*          \*

Towards the end of this study we shall return to re-examine in detail certain regional manifestations of Left Communism, specifically, in Moscow, the Ukraine and the Urals, to discover if the existing assumptions that they were Left Communist strongholds are tenable. First, however, it will prove fruitful to return to somewhat more familiar territory, and once again to map out the nature of the conflict between Lenin and the Left Communists, on the issue of peace and war, and on the methods to be employed in the construction of socialism in Russia. The purpose of so doing will emerge in the following chapters which will seek to demonstrate that while the terrain may be familiar, to date it has been ill-charted. But before a more accurate map can be drawn, it will prove necessary to consider the implications of Bukharin's defence of the Left Communists' position at the Seventh Party Congress. He protested against the accusations levelled at them by Lenin (in his *The Revolutionary Phrase*, for instance, and in his speech at the Seventh Party Congress) that carried away by the 'triumphal march ... of Soviet power' they had become intoxicated by a youthful romanticism or idealism which had led them to indulge in an orgy of radical sloganising, with no regard for the 'objective circumstances' of the moment.[45] On the contrary, he insisted that the reasons for their opposition to Lenin were 'much more profound':

> Our disagreements, comrades, are not at all reducible to the fact that some of us stand for a phrase, others for a business-like approach. This is complete nonsense. Our

disagreements lie in another plane – in a different evaluation of the international situation, and also ... of our
internal situation.[46]

The task of the following chapter will be to explore in detail
Bukharin's defence since, as we shall discover, there are good
grounds for supposing that the Left Communists and Lenin
did in fact have differing assessments of the prospects for
socialist revolution within and without Russia. But to fulfil
this objective, it will be necessary first of all to determine the
competing theoretical frameworks within which they operated. Such a task requires that we return several years before
1918, to analyse how the Bolsheviks conceptualised the
imperialist world in which they lived.

# 2 The Debate on Imperialism

It is an axiom of Soviet historiography that 'proletarian revolution [was] not simply the product of the good intentions of the ideological leaders of the proletariat, but rather [was] . . . an objective phenomenon determined by the laws of historical development (*zakonomernost*'). The Bolshevik-Leninists derived this conclusion from their analysis of imperialism. . . . Their theoretical investigations served their revolutionary practice'.[1] More pertinently, it has also long been axiomatic that the analyses of imperialism developed by Lenin and the Left Communists respectively differed in certain key respects. As David Baevskii argued some sixty years ago, a fundamental source of the disagreements between them lay in 'a different conception of the epoch of imperialism and of socialist revolution'.[2] The two most substantial Soviet studies to date of Left Communism, those of Vladimir Sorin and of K. I. Varlamov and N. A. Slamikhin, both posited that competing theorisations of imperialism underlay the conflict between Lenin and the Left in 1918.[3] Equally, a number of Western historians have recognised, if not always sufficiently emphasised the fact, that Lenin and the Left Bolsheviks did not elaborate identical theories of imperialism.[4] Admittedly, certain of their theoretical divergences have been analysed closely. Stephen Cohen, for example, has reconstructed in some detail the debate between Lenin and Bukharin during World War I on the nature of imperialism, particularly as it related to the questions of national self-determination and the state.[5] However, there has been a tendency, not without some foundation, as we shall see, to minimise these divergences, especially during 1917 itself. For instance, in his much lauded study of Lenin's political thought, Neil Harding has argued that Bukharin's 'views on imperialism generally came . . . close' to those of Lenin, cautioning, however, that their convergence was not quite complete.[6] Even more significantly, perhaps, during the debate over the revision of the party programme in the late summer and autumn of 1917 Lenin himself conceded that

> on the question of imperialism there is apparently complete agreement *in principle* within our Party – as was to be expected, for the practical propaganda of our Party on this question, both oral and printed, has long since, from the very beginning of the revolution, shown the complete unanimity of all the Bolsheviks on this fundamental question.[7]

But, he continued, '[w]hat remains to be examined is the differences in the way the definition and characterisation of imperialism are formulated'.[8]

The task then is to elucidate these remaining differences, with special reference to two issues of crucial importance for this study: first, their visions – competing visions – of how socialist revolution would unfold internationally; and second, their respective assessments of the maturity of conditions within Russia itself for socialism. The third important issue, that of the relationship between imperialism and the state, will be considered more fully in Chapter 6.

The majority of Bolsheviks were indebted in their studies of imperialism to the pioneering work of Rudolf Hilferding.[9] His seminal study, *Finance Capital*, had focused chiefly on elucidating the internal changes experienced by the leading capitalist economies since Marx's own time. The essential features of his analysis are by now quite familiar, since, as Cohen, among others, has pointed out, 'Lenin prefaced his discussion of imperialism and colonialism with an analysis of monopoly capitalism . . . , briefly and without any notable additions to Hilferding'.[10] As capitalism grew, Hilferding had argued, production – and capital itself – had increasingly become concentrated in ever larger units, initially in joint-stock companies instead of individual enterprises, then in cartels and trusts. In large part this process was the result of the destruction of smaller, less efficient enterprises during the periodic crises of over-production that, to him, were an inalienable feature of capitalism. Eventually, monopolies in individual branches of industry had emerged, by the amalgamation of the surviving firms within them into cartels and trusts. Their purpose was to eliminate competition within their own industries, regulate output and, consequently, prices, and in this way to preserve profitability. Cartels, however, bred cartels. Still-competitive industries dealing with cartels either would fall under the control of the latter, far stronger financially, in some form of vertical combination, or they would be forced to cartelise themselves to avoid such a fate.[11]

A similar concentration had taken place within banking, culminating in the formation of a few banks of great wealth and power in each capitalist country. Moreover, these banks had become the chief financiers of industry, so that in effect a merger, or fusion, of industrial and banking capital had occurred, to form what Hilferding called finance capital.[12] In turn, this fusion of capital had led to a considerable degree of regulation of production within each national economy. It was in the interests of the banks to limit competition amongst the various enterprises in which they had invested capital, in order to avoid their potential bankruptcy and to maintain their profitability, and to encourage either the merger of less profitable firms with more profitable partners, or even their closure.[13]

The bulk of Hilferding's *magnum opus* was devoted to analysing and articulating these changes within each capitalist state. The increasing organisation of production within each economy which had resulted from the evolution of finance capitalism led him to posit that much of the hitherto anarchic and contradictory nature of capitalism itself had been eliminated. This characteristic of finance capitalism, termed by him the 'socialisation of production', was creating the economic framework upon which socialism could be built. Hilferding concluded, quite unequivocally, that 'the development of finance capital itself is resolving more successfully the problem of the organisation of the social economy'.[14]

However, Hilferding continued, the contradictions of the capitalist system had by no means all been removed. Rather, finance capitalism had intensified the polarisation between capital and labour and itself remained 'an antagonistic form of socialisation, since the control of social production remains vested in an oligarchy'.[15] Consequently, to realise the potential for socialism created by it, it was first necessary for the proletariat to 'conquer' the state, a task which he believed could still be achieved by parliamentary means. Having conquered state power, it should use it to take over and administer what he believed to be the key sectors of the economy, whereafter the transition to socialism could take place, to borrow Cohen's phrase, 'relatively painless[ly]'.[16] Citing Germany as an example, Hilferding described how he envisaged this transition would occur:

> Taking possession of six large Berlin banks would mean taking possession of the most important spheres of large-scale industry, and would greatly facilitate the initial phases of socialist policy during the transition period, when capitalist accounting might still prove useful. There is no need at all to extend the process of expropriation to the great bulk of peasant farms and small businesses, because as a result of the seizure of large-scale industry, upon which they have long been dependent, they would be indirectly socialised just as industry is directly socialised. It is therefore possible to allow the process of expropriation to mature slowly, precisely in those spheres of decentralised production where it would be a long drawn-out and politically dangerous process. In other words, since finance capital has already achieved expropriation to the extent required by socialism, it is possible to dispense with a sudden act of expropriation by the state, and to substitute a gradual process of socialisation through the economic benefits which society will confer.[17]

While Hilferding remained most concerned to explain recent developments within advanced capitalist economies, his studies quite logically led him to conclude his analysis with a relatively brief discussion of contemporary imperialism. He began by outlining the new pressure for protectionism within finance-capitalist states. Tariffs, he argued, benefited the cartels by shielding them from foreign competition and the pressure of world prices, consequently allowing them to charge monopoly prices in their home markets. Hence they would gain super-profits on their domestic sales. Their problem, however, was that the fixing of monopoly prices meant that they would be able to sell less domestically, which would reduce their scale of production, raise their costs and so threaten their profit margins. One solution to this dilemma was for the cartels to expand their export markets, in order to maintain production and profit levels, a solution facilitated by their ability to apply the super-profits acquired from the domestic market to dump their goods overseas.[18]

But the essence of modern imperialism for Hilferding did not remain rooted simply in the pursuit of markets, or for that matter of raw materials to fuel large-scale industry. What distinguished it was the export of capital. He conceded that this phenomenon was in part determined by the opportunities for higher returns on capital in less developed regions of the world where the organic composition of capital was low and, according to Marxist economic theory, interest rates high, wages low, land cheap and the raw materials required by modern industry abundant.[19] However, the export of capital had also been precipitated by the recent wave of protectionism. While designed to safeguard the home market for the native monopolies, at the same time it placed obstacles in the way of their exports to similarly-protected foreign markets. One method of hurdling these tariff barriers was for the cartels to export capital and set up production within foreign markets themselves.[20] Equally, the monopoly profits which had accrued from the whole process of cartelisation and protectionism had led to the very rapid accumulation of capital. The problem, as he saw it, was a dearth of domestic investment opportunities given the cartels' concern, first, to limit domestic production to maintain high price levels and, second, to lower profits in any remaining competitive branches of industry.[21] Again, the export of capital appeared to be the only solution.

Moreover, the development of finance capitalism, Hilferding continued, had distinct political as well as economic ramifications. Domestically, the divisions between large industry on the one hand and large agrarian interests and the petty-bourgeoisie of the towns and countryside on the other were increasingly being overcome, to create a relatively unified ruling bourgeois class, albeit one in which 'the leadership ... [had] long since passed into the hands of big business'.[22] The bourgeoisie was bound together in the first place by its antipathy towards, and fear of, the rapidly-developing organised workers' movement, and in the second place by protection and the overseas economic expansion from which it benefitted in varying degrees.[23] However, to ensure its survival the 'capitalist oligarchy' had been compelled to take 'possession of the state apparatus in a direct, undisguised and palpable way', and to establish what Hilferding termed 'the dictatorship of the magnates of capital'.[24] It employed the might of the state for two main purposes: internally, to counter the growing power of the proletariat;[25] and, externally, to pursue successfully a predatory policy of territorial annexation.[26] In an increasingly competitive and hostile world, annexation alone seemed able to guarantee the continued expansion on which finance capitalism was ever more dependent. By incorporating territory within the protective shield of the metropolitan economy, it provided a stronger defence against penetration by rivals. In addition, in backward societies where either legal and political fragmentation or the emergence of indigenous opposition to imperialist exploitation threatened the designs of finance capitalism, forcible annexation and the imposition of order again presented itself as the only solution.[27] In rudimentary terms, as Harding has pointed out, Hilferding was essentially arguing that finance capitalism was breeding what later was to be termed, by Bukharin and Lenin among others, state capitalism.[28]

These same developments, he conceded, had intensified 'competition for the newly-opened spheres of investments [which had] produce[d] further clashes and conflicts among the advanced capitalist states themselves'.[29] In all probability such conflicts would have resulted in war but for the 'countervailing forces at work'.[30] The most important of these forces were: first, the interweaving of national capitals, for example, France and even Britain had loaned capital to German industries, which meant that they all had much to lose by any resort to war to settle their differences; and, second, 'the socialist movement [which] has inspired a fear of the domestic political consequences which might follow from a war'.[31] War, for Hilferding, was not an inevitable consequence of imperialism, nor would it be the midwife of socialist revolution, as the Bolsheviks later were to insist. If anything, he appears to have feared that the economic collapse which would result from war would make socialism unrealisable.[32]

The Bolsheviks' own interest in imperialism was rather different from that of Hilferding. They were not primarily concerned with explaining developments within each capitalist economy, but rather with the increasing tensions in the early twentieth-century capitalist world and, in particular, the causes of World War 1.[33] In doing so, they built on Hilferding's pioneering work. While accepting that the development of finance capitalism had laid the basis for the creation of a socialist economy, their own analyses nevertheless led them to conclusions at variance with those of their mentor regarding the inevitability of revolution. Equally, their studies led them, including Lenin for a time, to the belief that the continued growth of imperialism meant that socialist revolution, when it broke out, would inevitably do so on an international scale.

Of the Bolsheviks, Nikolai Bukharin was the first to produce a systematic account of the nature of modern imperialism. His starting-point, as Michael Haynes has stressed, was the world economy.[34] The growth of industrial capitalism into finance capitalism, he argued, with its inherently expansionist tendencies, had dramatically accelerated the integration of the world economy. In consequence, the first decade and a half of the twentieth century had witnessed the development of 'an extremely flexible economic structure of world capitalism, all parts of which are mutually interdependent. *The slightest change in one part is reflected in all*'.[35] As Hilferding had earlier, he also emphasised the growth-inducing impact of imperialism.[36] 'The tendencies of modern development', he contended, 'are conducive to the industrialisation of the agrarian and semi-agrarian countries ... at an unbelievably quick tempo....'[37] This process, he added, also tended to counteract the fact that, hitherto, different countries had developed unevenly. Imperialism, as well as fostering the internationalisation of economic life, was bringing about 'the levelling of economic differences....'[38] Indeed, this emphasis on the tendency of modern imperialism, so Haynes argued, 'to even out differences in levels of development'[39] appears to have been the theoretical basis of his conclusion that 'as far as the possibility of social production is concerned, the foremost countries are all on a comparatively equal level'.[40] Applying Hilferding's conclusions regarding the organisational propensities of finance capitalism, he argued that in the advanced capitalist states the socialisation of production had proceeded sufficiently far to make 'the introduction of a planned course of social production possible'.[41] He encapsulated what he considered these two inextricably inter-related consequences of imperialism to be: 'The growth of world market connections proceeds apace, tying up various sections of the world economy into one strong knot, bringing ever closer to each other hitherto "nationally" and economically secluded regions, creating an ever larger basis for world production in its new, higher, non-capitalist form.'[42]

Bukharin's analysis of the economics of imperialism also had important political ramifications. Its logic led him, unwillingly, in the direction of Karl Kautsky who had postulated that a federation of the imperialist states, to form a single ultra-imperialist power, was possible.[43] Bukharin admitted that the precondition for the emergence of 'a single world organisation, a universal world trust' was the 'comparative equality of positions in the world market' of the various imperialist states, or 'state-capitalist trusts', as he then termed them.[44] In the absence of such equality, the stronger would resist any agreement since it would hope to use its superior economic power to win out over its rivals. However, if imperialism in fact was producing this 'comparative equality', as his emphasis on its 'levelling' impact suggested, then he was forced to concede that ultra-imperialism, theoretically, was a 'possibility'.[45] 'In the historic process which we are to witness in the near future', he conceded, 'world capitalism will move in the direction of a universal state-capitalist trust by absorbing the weaker formations.'[46] The creation of any such global trust, however, implied, as Charles Barone has remarked recently, that 'imperialism [was] the last *antagonistic* stage of capitalism ... which, by ending competition, would eliminate the "fundamental contradictions of capitalism"'.[47] Bukharin's problem then was to prove that war, which he considered to be an inescapable consequence of imperialism, and necessary, moreover, to goad the workers to rise in revolution by the sufferings that it would entail, was in fact inevitable. He was compelled to adduce 'socio-political' reasons to explain why this was so. The most important of these were the different political and military strengths of the rival imperialist states, which made it advantageous for the finance capitalist oligarchy of the stronger 'to continue the struggle rather than to enter into a compact or to merge with the others', as well as the instability of all international agreements.[48]

While denying Kautsky's vision of a united, ultra-imperialist state, Bukharin did not reject the idea of a United States of Europe. The economic integration engendered by imperialism pointed in this direction. However, he insisted that it was the task of the proletariat to realise this goal through socialist revolution. In February, 1915, in the *Theses on the Tasks and Tactics of the Proletariat* that he presented on behalf of the so-called Baugy group to the conference of Bolshevik émigré sections held in Berne, he declared that 'in reply to the imperialist unification of the countries from above, the proletariat must advance the slogan of socialist unification of countries from below – republican socialist states of Europe – as a political-juridicial form of the socialist overturn'.[49] At the end of his treatise on imperialism he returned to this theme:

> The war severs the last chain that binds the workers to the masters, their slavish submission to the imperialist state . . . In place of the idea of defending or extending the boundaries of the bourgeois state that bind the productive forces of world economy hand and foot, [the international proletariat] advances *the slogan of abolishing state boundaries* and merging all peoples into one socialist family.[50]

For Bukharin, apparently, the growth of an increasingly unified and inter-dependent world economy meant that socialist revolution could no longer be conceived on a narrowly national scale. The revolutionary overthrow of capitalism could not remain confined within the bounds of any national state, now that the whole idea of 'a closed state and economic autarky' was 'absurd'.[51] Socialism, therefore, must conquer on an international scale, which was now feasible given that the economic preconditions for it were present. For the young Bukharin, socialism in one country was simply utopian, for in isolation it would be crushed by the power of capitalism surrounding it.

This belief, that socialist revolution must of necessity take place on an international scale, was common property among the Left, as became clear in their attempts to sketch out the tactics that the Bolsheviks must pursue in the new, imperialist epoch. In particular, this was true of Iurii Piatakov, Bukharin's leading co-thinker in exile during World War I and himself a die-hard Left Communist in 1918. In the theses on the question of national self-determination, sent to the Bolshevik Central Committee by Bukharin, Piatakov and Evgeniia Bosh in November 1915, they argued that the recent development of imperialism demanded changes in the way the party viewed the whole process of revolution. In particular, it would be a reactionary step backwards to support movements for national self-determination, as Lenin continued to insist, since socialist revolution on an international scale had become realisable, since 'now, . . . the question of mobilising the forces of the proletariat on an international scale, of an international struggle to overthrow capitalism, has been raised in a practical manner'.[52] In this new conjuncture, independent nation states were an anachronism, obsolete, appropriate only to the by-gone era of bourgeois-democratic revolutions. In the *Fifteen Point Platform*, written by Piatakov and also forwarded to the CC in November, 1915, the link between the Left's understanding of imperialism and its prognosis of global socialist revolution was explained:

> Finance capital has fully prepared the basis for a social revolution:
> a) By creating such an economic structure as can be consciously organised by the proletariat which has seized power and expropriated the expropriators.
> b) By continually tossing the proletariat into the arena of world struggle, by placing constantly before it questions of world policy in their entire scope, by abolishing thereby the national-state seclusion of the working class and revolutionising the consciousness of the proletariat in an unprecedented manner.
> Socialism, thus, becomes not a theoretical prognosis but

the task of the epoch; social revolution is placed on the agenda for the united action of the proletariat.

... the proletarian struggle must be coordinated internationally on new foundations, which correspond to the new conditions of the struggle.[53]

Later, in August 1916, Piatakov crystallised, succinctly and without equivocation, the vision of socialist revolution to which the Left's analysis of imperialism had led it: 'we picture this process as the united action of proletarians of all countries, who break down the frontiers of the bourgeois state, who remove the frontier posts, who blow up national unity and establish class unity'.[54] The colonial world, of course, was excluded from the immediate orbit of socialist revolution as there capitalism had not yet developed sufficiently to permit the construction of socialism.[55] After the revolution, at the Eighth Party Congress, Bukharin explained further. The imperialist world had to be understood in terms of two sets of social structures, basically those of the advanced capitalist world and those of the colonial world. In the latter, socio-economic development was insufficient to permit socialist revolution, whilst in the former, embracing all the non-colonial world, the preconditions for such a revolution were present. There the immediate task had been to establish the dictatorship of the proletariat, and advance to socialism.[56]

The same schema of socialist revolution, sweeping across Europe and North America, was shared by others on the Left.[57] In June 1915, Karl Radek, then a leading member of the Regional Presidium of the Social Democracy of the Kingdom of Poland and Lithuania (SDKPiL), whose own analysis of imperialism and revolution was remarkably close to that of Bukharin and Piatakov, laid out his own conclusions.[58] In common with all socialist internationalists in the Polish movement, including future Left Communists, such as M. Bronskii, J. Dolecki [Fenigshtein], J. Lenski (Leszczynski) and I. Unshlikht, he claimed that imperialism, and the war that it had caused, meant that '[t]he revolutionary struggle of the proletariat ... must flare up with spontaneous force and on an international and European scale ...'[59] In 1916, developing his thinking in his *Theses on Imperialism and*

*National Oppression*, he affirmed that 'in Central and Western Europe as well as in . . . North America, the time has already come for transforming capitalism into socialism . . .' This revolution, 'for which the economic conditions . . . [were] already ripe', was to be carried out by 'a united struggle' of the proletariat under the slogan 'away with frontiers'.[60] As he later explained, in the integrated world economy created by imperialism socialism in one country, especially a backward country such as Russia, was inconceivable. Indeed, any attempt to introduce socialism there would threaten the interests of world capital so profoundly that it would unite to crush it at birth. If socialism was to survive, therefore, it simply had to expand on an international scale.[61]

Other leading Left Communists had arrived at a similar understanding of the imperialist epoch and its implications for the scale of socialist revolution, as became clear in 1917 itself. In April, Osinskii insisted that the development of an integrated international economy, at least across Europe, made it inevitable that socialist revolution when it came – and he expected 'the final and decisive battle' for socialism would come soon – could only be victorious on an international scale. In a single country it would be crushed by the combined forces of world capitalism.[62] N. Antonov (N. M. Lukin) adopted an almost Piatakovian line, defending the proposition that socialist revolution must occur as 'the simultaneous and agreed actions of proletarians of all countries'.[63] Lomov and D. P. Bogolepov agreed, concurring that 'contemporary capitalism [was] eliminating the peculiarities of capitalism in different countries [and was] driving [us] to work out common methods *and common goals*'. In these circumstances, what was now required was the elaboration of a new 'united international programme for revolutionary social democracy' which would sketch out the measures to be taken to ensure the transition to socialism on a European scale.[64] Aaron Sol'ts and others agreed too. In the present conjuncture, of imminent international revolution, there was no point in having a long-term programme adapted just to Russian conditions.[65] Unsurprisingly, Bukharin himself had come to accept the need for such a programme since in the current situation 'the struggle of the proletariat [for socialism could] not develop other than as an international struggle . . .

the conditions [for which] to a large degree have been made the same by the levelling influence of imperialism and the world war'.[66] Almost as an afterthought, he conceded the need to draw up specific platforms, to take account of any remaining national political peculiarities which might arise in the course of the international revolution.

However, it was not just economic, but also social and political, differences that were being eradicated among the finance-capitalist states.[67] This conclusion also derived logically from their analysis of imperialism. Again following Hilferding, Bukharin had emphasised that the 'organisational process' set in motion by finance capital had quite definite socio-political consequences. It had not 'embraced the economy alone: its significance [was] much more general and profound'.[68] As finance capitalism had developed, it had led to the creation of a united bourgeoisie, although one within which the large financial magnates remained the dominant force.[69] This class had overtly appropriated the apparatus of the state to serve its own ends, that is, to promote its own expansionist objectives abroad and to maintain its position at home. In the highly competitive imperialist world of the early twentieth century, he argued, the state alone had sufficient power to mobilise the resources of the country for the wars that would inevitably occur. Moreover, war itself had compelled the state to intervene to an increasingly greater extent in the economy, to organise it sufficiently to ensure that the necessary levels of military *matériel* were forthcoming. In turn this intervention had resulted in 'an extraordinary reinforcement and intensification of . . . [the] immanent developmental tendencies [of finance capitalism]'.[70] The system produced by this symbiosis of the state and the finance-capitalist clique he termed 'state capitalism'. The expansion of state capitalism itself accelerated the polarisation of society, into a finance-capitalist elite facing an increasingly oppressed and immiserated proletariat. The petty-bourgeoisie, which had formerly allied itself with finance capital was vanishing rapidly as a consequence of the increasing centralisation and concentration of production during the war.[71] Therefore, it could not be considered to be reservoir of support upon which the proletariat could rely in its revolutionary struggle for socialism.[72]

Having followed what was essentially Hilferding's analysis so far Bukharin, however, developed his own ideas on what these developments implied for the political strategy that socialists must pursue. Unlike his mentor, he believed that they ruled out any possibility of a parliamentary road to socialism. For Bukharin, the fusion of the economic and political power of the bourgeoisie that he had sketched out had led to the immense strengthening of all the institutions of the state, coercive – 'police, soldiery' – and ideological – 'the church, the press, the school, etc.' – which were deployed ruthlessly to ensure the continued subjugation and exploitation of the proletariat. The latter, if it sought to achieve any economic or political advances, would find itself in direct confrontation with this new state form, a monolithic 'Leviathan' state with unprecedented power.[73] This fearful comprehension of the monstrous oppressive power of the contemporary imperialist state led him quite naturally to emphasise the anti-statist strand in Marxist thought – he was the first of the Bolsheviks, so Cohen concludes, 'to revive Marx's anti-statism' – and to demand the extirpation of the state as the condition of progress to socialism.[74] He came to deny that even a democratic republic, 'the freest form of bourgeois parliamentary government' imaginable, could be taken over intact by the proletariat and used by it in the construction of socialism.[75] Even in such a state the bureaucracy, the police and the standing army remained nothing but the agents of finance capitalism, employed to suppress the working class. They had to be destroyed, and replaced by totally new, class-based institutions of revolutionary proletarian power. For Bukharin and his fellow thinkers on the Left of the party, such as Vladimir Smirnov and Lomov, there no longer was any viable path to socialism, parliamentary or otherwise, that aspired to use the existing state machine. Any such prospect was simply 'Philistine'.[76]

In 1917 Bukharin applied the conclusions drawn from his general analysis of imperialism specifically to Russia. The significance of this development is that it explains why the Left Communists had come to believe by 1917 that the revolution in Russia would be an integral part of international socialist revolution. Before World War I there is no evidence that they considered socialist revolution to be feasible there. Rather, in common with the overwhelming majority of Russian Marxists, Bolshevik and Menshevik alike, they accepted that in comparison with the West, Russia's retarded development meant that there was no immediate prospect of a socialist revolution within it, as Osinskii frankly admitted.[77] On the contrary, there the bourgeois-democratic revolution awaited completion, although for the Bolsheviks, if not the Mensheviks after 1905, this revolution still had to be led by the proletariat in view of the weakness of the indigenous bourgeoisie.[78] Thereafter, capitalism could develop freely, in turn gradually yet inexorably creating the necessary economic preconditions for socialism.

However, their abandonment of this prospectus and their conversion to the belief in the possibility of socialist revolution in Russia was neither sudden nor without some ambiguity, as the case of Bukharin himself demonstrates. In the *Theses* that he presented at the Berne Conference, he maintained that 'the old fighting slogans of the 1905 revolution' remained correct for Russia.[79] In other words, he still believed that the bourgeois-democratic revolution awaited its completion there. In his tract on imperialism written later (in 1915) his views on the Russian Empire were rather more confused. On the one hand, he did include it within the ranks of the leading imperialist powers, in particular stressing its recent expansion into Central Asia, Persia, Manchuria and Mongolia.[80] On the other hand, he was forced to concede that economically it was much less developed than the modern imperialist states of the West. Russia did not yet belong 'to the category of state capitalist trusts',[81] which according to the logic of his analysis implied that the preconditions for socialism had not developed sufficiently within it.

By 1917, however, Bukharin and his fellow thinkers on the Left of the party no longer harboured any reservations about the feasibility of socialist revolution in Russia.[82] There too, so Bukharin contended, state capitalism, 'the last imaginable form of capitalism',[83] had grown rapidly in response to the demands of war. Its development in Russia had the same economic and socio-political consequences as in the West: there too the centralisation of production in trusts and syndicates, controlled and organised by the banks and, in some instances, directly by the state, had created the economic framework which the proletariat, after it had seized power, could employ as the skeleton for a planned socialist economy;[84] there too the petty-bourgeoisie had allied with the finance-capitalist oligarchy; there too the petty-bourgeoisie was rapidly dwindling; there too the 'iron heel' of state power was repressing the working-class; and there too the final clash between the finance capitalists and the proletariat was imminent.[85]

He conceded, however, that the position of the peasantry in Russia meant that the situation was very different from that in the West. In particular, since the peasants had not yet received the land of the *pomeshchiki* (gentry) they could act together with the proletariat in the first phase of the revolution to overthrow the existing imperialist order. However, once they had been granted land they would become 'satiated' and desert the proletariat and oppose the further advance of the revolution towards socialism. In this latter phase the Russian workers could rely upon only '[rural] proletarian elements and the proletariat of West Europe'.[86] In this new conjuncture, of imminent socialist revolution, the minimum section of the old party programme, designed for the bourgeois-democratic stage of the revolution, of course must be abandoned as obsolete. A new transitional programme, elaborating the practical measures which would lead towards socialism, must replace it.[87]

Other leading theoreticians of the Left had come to the same conclusions. Georgii Safarov explained why this had occurred. He claimed that the demands of World War I had dramatically accelerated economic developments within Russia. Finance capitalism had developed at an unexpectedly rapid pace and beyond any shadow of doubt had come to dominate Russian industry. More than that, the exigencies of war had compelled the bourgeoisie to seek the intervention of the state to centralise and organise production even further in order to guarantee the output of the military equipment on which its survival in the struggle against the might of German imperialism depended. While Safarov himself took his argument to extremes, alleging that the concentration of production in Russia was unsurpassed anywhere, he concluded that the supremacy of finance capitalism within Russian industry indicated that 'the social-democratic regulation . . . of the economy was possible' once the workers, with the poor peasants as allies, had overthrown the capitalists and appropriated the economic apparatus which the latter had built.[88]

The essence of his analysis was repeated by Smirnov, Lukin, and Osinskii, all of whom claimed that finance capitalism had made rapid progress within Russia.[89] Even Lomov concurred, so Antonov-Saratovskii recalled. Before 1917 he had questioned the feasibility of socialist revolution in Russia, conceding, however, that a victorious socialist revolution sweeping from the West might allow the Russian revolution to transcend its bourgeois-democratic limits. He now cast aside his former doubts.[90] He pointed in particular to the massive concentration of production that had occurred, evident in the formation of cartels, syndicates and trusts, particularly in the metallurgical industry but present elsewhere, in the machine-building and cotton sectors. The banking sector had developed similarly, where concentration had been greater than in all other warring imperialist states, with the possible exception of Germany. The regulation of production which had accompanied these processes had been made all the more pervasive and effective by the intervention of the tsarist state in the organisation of the economy during the war and had created the 'objective prerequisites' for the construction of a socialist economy in Russia.[91]

The Left Communists remained aware, however, of the potential problems of applying their conclusions to justify socialist revolution in a Russia that was still, in comparison with the much more advanced West, relatively backward. In 1918, Osinskii confronted this question directly. Proceeding from a fairly abstract level of analysis, he contended that socialist revolution was the product of the combination of certain 'positive prerequisites' created by the development of capitalism, as well as of its 'negative tendencies'.[92] The latter he equated with periodic crises which afflicted capitalism. These crises, historically of over-production, had caused the closure of factories and a fall in production, as well as the ruination of increasing numbers of the petty-bourgeoisie. Consequently, the ranks of the proletariat had become swollen while the means of production had become concentrated ever more in the hands of a declining number of large magnates who alone had the wealth and power to survive such crises. In the three or four decades preceding 1914, he continued more concretely, colonial exploitation and protectionism had enabled the advanced capitalist states to avoid profound crises and to ameliorate the immiseration that would become the material base for the proletariat to rise and overthrow the system that was responsible for its sufferings.[93] World War I, however, had unleashed in full force the destructive tendencies temporarily held in check and would prove to be the final crisis which would impel capitalism 'to devour itself'.[94] He then outlined what he considered the 'positive prerequisites' for socialism to be. He categorically rejected the economic determinist orthodoxy of the Second International in general, and of the Mensheviks in particular, which insisted that 'socialism [could] replace only the most advanced capitalist society and be constructed only by a strong and highly developed proletariat'.[95] Conceding that the centralisation and concentration of production that accompanied capitalist development were increasingly laying the economic foundations for socialism, he hastened to add that no one, not even Marx and Engels, had provided a generally accepted, scientifically-based measure of how far these trends must progress before socialism became objectively possible.[96] The syndicates and trusts created by finance capital, he continued, were 'a new, higher form of the centralisation of capital' which made the planned regulation of production feasible.[97] The final stage in the evolution of finance capital, state capitalism, which he saw as the product of the exigencies of war, itself presaged 'the birth of a system of consciously regulated production, distribution and consumption'.[98] In other words, it had created the framework for the rational organisation of the economy which socialism alone could continue and extend.[99] As far as Russia itself was concerned, by 1917 it had come to possess an advanced industrial sector in which large-scale enterprises were dominant. He referred particularly to the mining, metallurgical, machine-building, transport, chemical and sugar industries which would 'serve as the basis for the organisation of large-scale social production'. Moreover, thanks to the intervention of the banks these industries had become syndicalised or trustified, so generating the framework for the central regulation of industrial production. Furthermore, these syndicates and trusts, together with the regulatory organisations established by the state during the war and the existing consumer and cooperative societies, provided the institutional nexus for the planned distribution and consumption of goods and materials.[100] For Osinskii, apparently, state capitalism had developed *sufficiently* in Russia for socialist revolution to be feasible there. He continued to warn, however, that the complete construction of socialism in Russia remained dependent upon the economic support of the more advanced West. More sanguinely, he concluded that this support would be forthcoming when the revolution conquered internationally, as he believed it inevitably must.[101]

Radek later elaborated more explicitly what remained implicit in Osinskii's defence. He too denied that capitalism must become developed 'fully', somehow defined, before the construction of socialism was possible. Once the main branches of industry and transport had become centralised, he argued, then what could be regarded as the minimum prerequisites for successful socialist revolution would have been established. When that stage of capitalist development was reached, he continued, the proletariat, even if still a minority, could seize power and employ the centralised economic framework already in existence as the foundation on which to construct a socialist economy. For Russia in 1917, therefore, socialism was a legitimate goal, since the key sectors of its economy – the coal, metallurgical, oil, transport and banking industries – had become highly concentrated. In a manner reminiscent of Hilferding, he posited that they would form the first links in a growing chain of socialist production which would eventually embrace the remaining small-scale enterprises and agriculture.[102] Radek warned, however, that the very existence of these minimum prerequisites did not automatically guarantee the victory of socialism. Two other elements were necessary. First, revolution was required, to smash the old order. The proletariat, however, increasingly exploited and immiserated by imperialism and its inevitable wars, he sanguinely concluded, was bound to rise in revolt to remove the cause of its sufferings. And, second, Radek too made the final triumph of socialism contingent upon international revolution, as we have seen.[103]

Hence for the Left Communists, the Russian economy, or, more precisely, the Russian segment of the world economy, had matured sufficiently to permit socialist revolution. The relative backwardness of Russia, however, compared to the West, manifest particularly in the extent of small-scale agriculture in the country, would make the construction of socialism there more difficult.[104] Indeed, as we have just seen, they consistently questioned whether Russia left to its own resources and devices could do so successfully. Nevertheless, any such reservations that they may have held were swept aside by their conviction that socialist revolution would not remain isolated in Russia but would advance to the West which would help, in some ill-explained manner, the beleaguered Russian proletariat to overcome its legacy of backwardness.[105] As Bukharin concluded on the morrow of the October revolution:

> It is impossible right now to consider all the questions of the revolution within the confines of national boundaries . . .
>
> The international revolution means not only the purely political reinforcement of the Russian revolution. *It also means its economic reinforcement.*
>
> . . . The victory of the proletariat in the West makes it possible in planned manner to treat the economic wounds of Russia by applying the highly-developed technology of the West. The economic backwardness of Russia is compensated by the high economic level of Europe, and – with the victory of the proletariat in the West – the Russian economy is drawn into a Pan-European socialist organisation.[106]

However, for the Left Communists this relative backwardness of Russia, whilst making economic reconstruction along socialist lines more difficult, had certain political advantages. In the West, the 'Leviathan' state typical of highly-advanced finance capitalism had grown to such strength that it would prove itself capable of 'tremendous resistance' to revolution. In less developed societies such as Russia, on the other hand, where the fusion of the economic and political power of the bourgeoisie had not advanced as far, much greater opportunities were open to the proletariat to rise and smash the old order. As Bukharin remarked after the revolution, 'the collapse of the capitalist world system began with the weakest systems in terms of political economy, with the least developed state-capitalist systems'.[107]

Lenin's analysis of imperialism, and its implications for the prospects of socialist revolution, both internationally and in Russia, in fact was rather different from that of the Left Communists before 1917. The problem, however, is that in 1917 he appears to have undergone a conversion and come to share in large part the assumptions of the Left. Cohen, for instance, claimed that '[t]he issues that had bitterly divided Bukharin and Lenin in emigration were resolved or rendered inconsequential in 1917 largely because the leader had changed his mind'.[108] Even Harding suggests a similar conversion. Having argued that Lenin unequivocally rejected interpretations of imperialism, such as those of Bukharin and Piatakov, which led to the conclusion that 'socialist revolution would arrive simultaneously on a worldwide scale', nevertheless he also contends that '[t]here can be no doubt whatsoever that he [Lenin] believed that monopoly capitalism had now created the objective conditions, the economic basis, *for an immediate advance to socialism on a world-wide scale*'.[109] Moreover, he continues, '[f]rom the time of his arrival in Russia in April, 1917, Lenin took it as axiomatic that the European revolution against imperialism was on the immediate agenda', one, too, which would embrace Russia.[110] In explaining Lenin's political strategy in 1917, the main thrust of Harding's argument is the proposition that his 'theoretical justification [for socialist revolution in Russia] was spelt out in *Imperialism, the Highest Stage of Capitalism*'.[111] By then, he contends, Lenin had ceased to conceive of Russia as a separate country, but rather had come to see it as just one part of a much broader international finance-capitalist, or imperialist, 'society'.

This society was 'rotten-ripe' for revolution in two senses. First, it possessed all the material prerequisites for the socialist reconstruction of economic and social life. At least, it did 'in all the industrially advanced countries'. Second, war, and the economic destruction and human suffering that it was wreaking, would create the revolutionary crisis which would drive the proletariat to rise and destroy the old order.[112] Russia itself was merely one part of an international finance-capitalist, or imperialist, chain, but also its weakest link. As such, revolution would erupt first, in Russia, and act as the spark to ignite a chain of succeeding revolutions throughout the more advanced West.[113] Thereafter, the advanced West would come to backward Russia's aid materially and so enable the revolutionary regime there to win over the majority, the poor peasantry, by demonstrating the economic superiority of socialism over capitalism.[114] This reading of Lenin's thinking in 1917, of course, elides the major differences that hitherto had distinguished his understanding of imperialism and revolution, in Russia and the world, from that of the Left.

The problem with this line of reasoning, however, as Harding himself admits, is that Lenin's 'very generalised theory of imperialism was never applied at all seriously to the particular case of Russia'. Accordingly, 'the implications of the theory of imperialism [for Russia] were never fully articulated by Lenin'.[115] Harding professes that he was constrained to draw inferences from Lenin's general theory in order to make sense of his ideas on socialist revolution in Russia. In so doing he has constructed a most cogent and compelling model of how he envisages that Lenin's thinking developed between the onset of war in the summer of 1914 and 1917 when he emerged as a protagonist of socialist revolution in Russia.

To assess the validity of such an interpretation, it is necessary to re-examine the evolution of Lenin's thinking on imperialism, and its implications for revolution, within and without Russia. From the early months of the war Lenin on occasion had argued in what can be described as a very Leftist vein. In his lecture, *The Proletariat and the War*, delivered in Lausanne on 14 October, 1914, he postulated that all the countries of Europe had reached 'an equal stage in the development of capitalism . . . [which was] beginning to find its national framework too small for it'. In such circumstances it was 'impossible to go over from capitalism to socialism without breaking up the national framework', an implicit rejection of the possibility of socialist revolution in one country.[116] He repeated the thrust of this argument on several occasions before his return to Russia in April 1917. In the late summer of 1915, for example, he again contended that '[s]ociety's productive forces and the magnitudes of capital have outgrown the narrow limits of the individual national states ... The whole world is merging into a single economic organism ... The objective conditions for socialism have fully matured ...'[117] In these circumstances he denied that the 'individual solution of revolutionary problems [was] possible in any single country'.[118] In this instance, he explained how he envisaged the relationship between revolution in Russia and in the West. If the Russian proletariat, in alliance with the peasantry, rose to carry out its revolution – a revolution, he then hastened to add, which would remain bourgeois-democratic – it could act as the spark 'to kindle the proletarian revolution in the West'. The bourgeois-democratic revolution in Russia, therefore, would be 'not only a prologue to, but an indivisible and integral part of the socialist revolution in the West'.[119]

In early 1917, after the fall of the autocracy, in his *Letters from Afar* and *Farewell Letter to the Swiss Workers*, where he sketched out what he believed Bolshevik strategy now should be, he developed this strand in his thinking. The February Revolution in Russia, he argued, a bourgeois-democratic revolution, could be transformed into a socialist revolution. This possibility could be realised, provided two preconditions were satisfied. First, the Russian proletariat had to mobilise behind itself the majority in the countryside, that is, the mass of rural labourers and peasants, but not the prosperous minority.[120] The second precondition, which alone would guarantee the final victory of socialism, was the expansion of the revolution internationally, an expansion which he increasingly presumed to be all but inevitable.[121] As he wrote to Alexandra Kollontai on 16 March, 'the Russian revolution (first stage) will not be the last, nor will it only be Russian'.[122] Soon after, at the Seventh Party Conference in April, Lenin elaborated his views on international revolution:

From the point of view of Marxism, in discussing imperialism it is absurd to restrict oneself to conditions in one country alone, since all capitalist countries are closely bound together. Now, in time of war, this bond has grown immeasurably stronger. All humanity is thrown into a tangled bloody heap from which no nation can extricate itself on its own. Though there are more and less advanced countries, this war has bound them all together by so many threads that escape from this tangle for any single country acting on its own is inconceivable.[123]

Defending his own resolution on the current situation he repeated that 'it would be wrong to speak only of Russian conditions. The war has bound us together so inseparably that it would be a great mistake on our part to ignore the sum total of international relations'.[124]

Lenin, so it would appear, had come to envisage socialist revolution as an international phenomenon, encompassing all the 'more and less advanced countries', including, as we shall see in detail later, Russia. Indeed, in the preface to *State and Revolution*, written in August 1917, he was quite explicit about the relationship between the Russian and the world revolution. He declared that 'this [the Russian] revolution as a whole can only be understood as a link in a chain of socialist proletarian revolutions being caused by the imperialist war'.[125] In the early autumn he seemed to be confident that international revolution was imminent:

Mass arrests of party leaders in free Italy, and particularly the beginning of *mutinies* in the German army, are indisputable symptoms that a great turning-point is at hand, that we are *on the eve of a world-wide revolution.*

Doubt is out of the question. We are on the threshold of a world proletarian revolution. And since of all the proletarian internationalists in all countries only we Russian Bolsheviks enjoy a measure of freedom . . . to us the saying, 'To whom much has been given, of him much shall be required' in all justice can and must be applied.[126]

That this revolution should have begun in Russia he explained, in a manner akin to that of the Left Communists, by reference to the political weakness and ineptitude of its ruling class, unlike the West where mighty 'Leviathan states' had developed.[127] At first sight, Harding's reconstruction of Lenin's thinking on imperialism and revolution appears to be warranted.

However, such a reconstruction of Lenin's thinking is not as unproblematic or unambiguous as it first appears since, as Tiutiukin aptly remarked, the evolution of his ideas, particularly on the question of international revolution, was equivocal, to say the least.[128] Certainly, both before and after, if not during, 1917 Lenin's vision of international revolution, and of the prospects of socialism in Russia itself, was rather different from the schema outlined above. To understand why this was so, we must focus on what fundamentally distinguished his analysis from that of his allies on the Left, that is, on his whole conception of the uneven development of capitalism, even in its imperialist phase, and of its implications for the pattern of socialist revolution.

Although Lenin himself categorised the current epoch as imperialist, he also hastened to stress that it, as earlier epochs, was in no sense purely imperialist.[129] While finance capitalism was its dominant and determining feature, it had not spread its tentacles evenly throughout the world and entirely eliminated earlier social structures. Unlike the Left, which emphasised the increasing homogeneity of imperialist societies, Lenin insisted on a continuing heterogeneity in the imperialist world. Extensive vestiges of pre-imperialist formations continued to exist, most evidently in the colonial world, *but also* in East Europe where the absence of thorough-going bourgeois-democratic revolutions meant that feudal and pre-monopoly capitalist features of economic, political and social life had survived and in places were quite pervasive.

For Lenin, this intertwining of finance capitalism with socio-economic and political structures of a lower order meant that it was impossible to anticipate any 'pure' social, or socialist, revolution. It would not occur as a simple struggle between the proletariat and the bourgeoisie, but rather would be a very complex phenomenon, 'not a single act, . . . not one battle on one front, but a whole epoch of acute class conflicts on all fronts, i.e. on all questions of economics and politics, battles that can only end in the expropriation of the bourgeoisie'.[130] He continued to stress, ever more explicitly, that '[t]he social revolution can only come in the form of an epoch in which are combined civil war by the proletariat against the bourgeoisie in the advanced countries and a whole series of democratic and revolutionary movements, including the national liberation movement, in undeveloped, backward and oppressed nations'.[131]

More than that, however, his conviction that capitalism, even in its imperialist phase, continued to develop unevenly, led him to picture the very process of international revolution rather differently from the Left. Attacking Kautsky in particular, but an attack that equally could be directed against the Left, he contended that uneven development, 'an absolute law of capitalism', totally precluded the peaceful emergence of any 'ultra-imperialist' confederation, since the faster growing states would seek to use their increasing strength to carve out greater spheres of influence for themselves.[132] Equally, it inevitably meant that the prerequisites for socialism would not mature simultaneously in all capitalist countries, making it inconceivable that 'the various sources of rebellion [could] immediately merge of their own accord, without reverses and defeats'.[133] Repeatedly, he hammered home this conclusion, that socialist revolution would *not* sweep across the world in one mighty, unconquerable wave, but rather would advance in a more protracted and complex manner. On the contrary, as a consequence of uneven development 'it follow[ed] irrefutably that socialism [could] not achieve victory simultaneously *in all* countries', that 'the victory of socialism is possible first in several or even in one capitalist country alone', that it would 'achieve victory first in one or several countries while the others *for some time* remain bourgeois or pre-bourgeois'[134] – which implied, of course, that the country, or countries, where it first was victorious might be forced to wage revolutionary war against the surviving imperialist powers. In a savage critique of Piatakov, 'quite a little pig . . . [without] a drop of brains',[135] Lenin unequivocally rejected the Left's conception of socialist revolution as brought about by 'the united action of the proletarians of all countries . . .':

The social revolution cannot be the united action of the proletarians of all countries for the simple reason that most of the countries and the majority of the world's population have not even reached, or have only just reached, the capitalist stage of development . . .

Socialism will be achieved by the united action of the proletarians, not of all, but of a minority of countries, those that have reached the *advanced* capitalist stage of development . . .

The undeveloped countries are a different matter. They embrace the whole of Eastern Europe and all the colonies and semi-colonies.[136]

Even after the February Revolution, as his expectation of international revolution grew, he still harboured fleeting doubts about the likelihood of united action on the part of the international proletariat.[137] Shortly before the October Revolution he again expressed some reservations about the imminence of international revolution, insisting that it remained impossible to 'know how soon after our victory revolution will sweep the West . . . whether or not victory will be followed by temporary periods of reaction and the victory of the counter-revolution – *there is nothing impossible in that* . . .'.[138]

This concept of the uneven development of capitalism was also the foundation of his supposition that it was analytically essential to classify the countries of the imperialist world into three distinct categories. In the first category he included 'the advanced capitalist countries of West Europe and the United States'. There the prerequisites for socialism undoubtedly had matured and this was what the proletariat must fight for. To the second category he assigned 'East Europe: Austria, the Balkans and *particularly Russia*'. There bourgeois-democratic revolutions had not yet been completed. In fact, the early twentieth century had witnessed the rapid development and intensification of democratic and national movements in this part of the world. There the proletariat must assist in the completion of bourgeois-democratic revolution which would clear the way for the free and unfettered development of capitalism and, subsequently, the transition to socialism. '[T]he semi-colonial countries . . . and all the colonies' were in his final category, where 'bourgeois-democratic movements either have hardly begun, or still have a long way to go'.[139]

Such a three-fold categorisation contrasts markedly with the dualistic view of the world held by the Left. But what is equally striking about Lenin's analysis was his clear conviction that socialist revolution was not immediately on the agenda for Russia, a conviction which he had defended with remarkable consistency from the outbreak of World War I until the fall of the autocracy.

At the beginning of the war, in September 1914, Lenin had declared his position in no uncertain terms. Since Russia was among the most backward of the European states and had 'not yet completed its bourgeois revolution', then the duty of revolutionary socialists was to strive for the completion of this revolution. He distinguished Russia from 'all the advanced countries' where socialist revolution was immediately realisable.[140] Throughout 1915 and 1916, he returned frequently to this theme. While 'the objective conditions in Western Europe [were] ripe for socialism', for Russia 'immediate socialist revolution [was] impossible'. Although 'capitalist imperialism of the latest type' had developed in Russia, he contended that 'in general military and feudal imperialism [was] predominant . . .' within it. Therefore, the task remaining there was to consummate the bourgeois-democratic revolution, by destroying the autocracy and the surviving vestiges of feudalism. This could be achieved, he believed, only by the proletariat allying with the peasantry and fighting to establish a democratic republic which then must confiscate the lands of the *pomeshchiki*.[141]

Even in his famous study, *Imperialism, the Highest Stage of Capitalism*, completed in the first half of 1916, he did not alter this schema fundamentally. In the most general of terms he conceded that 'imperialism is the eve of the social revolution of the proletariat'.[142] Following Hilferding, he too subscribed to the belief that the 'comprehensive socialisation of production' caused by the growth of finance capitalism had made the transition to socialism economically feasible.[143] Admittedly, he did lay more emphasis on the fact that finance capitalism, typified by the formation of monopolies and the merger of banking and industrial capital, had 'made enormous strides in Russia'.[144] Yet the Russian Empire, he continued, still remained economically backward, a country 'where modern capitalist imperialism is enmeshed, so to speak, in a particularly close network of pre-capitalist relations'.[145] For Lenin, Russian imperialism remained primarily of the 'military-feudal' sort which first had to be extirpated by a bourgeois-democratic revolution before there could be any thought of socialist revolution.[146]

In the autumn of 1916 he reiterated, quite unequivocally, that '[o]nly the advanced countries of Western Europe and North America' possessed the preconditions which would permit the immediate transition to socialism. In East Europe, and elsewhere in the world, democratic revolution remained the immediate task.[147] The victory of the democratic revolution there, he explained in a letter of 25 November to Inessa Armand, would clear the way for the development of capitalism, the essential prerequisite for the progress of 'our movement', that is, for socialism. [148] Indeed, he appears to have clung to this appraisal of the forthcoming revolution in Russia right up until the fall of the autocracy, when again, in January 1917, he clearly distinguished it from the advanced West.[149]

Yet within days of the February Revolution Lenin's thinking changed profoundly, as we have seen. In the final weeks of his exile in Switzerland, in his *Draft Theses* and his *Letters from Afar*, he repeatedly argued that the revolution in Russia had not ended with the fall of the autocracy. The Russian proletariat, in alliance with the proletarianised and poor peasants, and with the proletariat of the West, must struggle to advance the revolution from its bourgeois-democratic to its socialist stage. He concluded the first of his *Letters from Afar* thus:

> With these two allies, the proletariat, utilising the peculiarities of the present situation, can and will proceed, first, to the achievement of a democratic republic and complete victory over the landlords, instead of the Guchkov-Miliukov semi-monarchy, and then to socialism, which alone can give the war-weary people peace, bread and freedom.[150]

In the last of these *Letters* Lenin outlined the measures necessary to guarantee the continued progress of the revolution. First, and foremost, he now conceded to Bukharin that the workers and their peasant allies must smash the old state, and its organs of coercion – the army, the police and the bureaucracy – and make the soviets, not the Provisional Government, the new organs of political power. The success of this first step demanded that the proletariat secure the support of the entire peasantry, then solely interested in the confiscation and division of the land. Thereafter, the workers, allied only with the poor peasants, must proceed to 'control ... production and distribution of basic products and establish "universal labour service"'. He added the *caveat* that such policies in themselves would not signify the victory of socialism in Russia, but only 'the transition to socialism which cannot be achieved in Russia directly, at one stroke, without transitional measures, but is quite achievable and urgently necessary as the result of such transitional measures'.[151]

Lenin's triumphant return to Russia in April, 1917, produced immediate confusion in socialist ranks. To the astonishment of the Mensheviks, and the consternation of most leading Bolsheviks, who assumed that the new, bourgeois-democratic, regime must exist for a lengthy period, during which time the prerequisites for socialism would mature, Lenin defended his call for the transformation of the revolution into one for socialism.[152] 'The specific feature of the present situation...', he repeated, 'is that the country is passing from the first stage of the revolution ... to its second stage, which must place power in the hands of the proletariat and the poorest sections of the peasantry'.[153] His critics within and without the party were quick to pounce upon what they perceived to be the weak and contradictory points in his strategy. Its major defect, as the Menshevik-Internationalist, N. Sukhanov, remarked was that

It had no analysis of 'objective premises', no analysis of the socio-economic conditions for Socialism in Russia. No economic programme was even referred to. There was the embryo of what Lenin repeated many times later: namely, that the backwardness of our country, the weakness of its productive forces, did not allow it to sustain the desperate tension of the whole organism demanded by the war; this was why Russia had been the first to produce a revolution. But of how this backwardness, this petty-bourgeois, peasant structure, this extreme exhaustion and chaos could be reconciled with a Socialist reorganisation independently of the West, before the worldwide Socialist revolution – not a word was said.[154]

The April Theses, Sukhanov continued, were no better, equally lacking 'an economic programme and a Marxist analysis of the objective conditions of our revolution'.[155] Essentially, Sukhanov was arguing that Lenin's first statements of policy after the February Revolution were not underpinned by any reference to his theoretical investigations of imperialism, either in general or with respect to Russia in particular. As the preceding examination of Lenin's analysis of imperialism has sought to establish, there was indeed such a *lacuna* in his thinking. From 1914 until the morrow of February he failed to provide any convincing rationale for advocating *socialist* revolution in Russia, either in terms of the indigenous maturation of its material prerequisites or in terms of weak links in supposed imperialist chains.

In response to similar criticisms – the Menshevik B. O. Bogdanov apparently derided his promulgation of socialist revolution in such a poorly developed capitalist and predominantly peasant country as Russia as 'the raving of a madman', while at the Seventh Party Conference in April Aleksei Rykov deemed it unthinkable in 'the most petty-bourgeois country in Europe', where 'the objective conditions for it did not exist'[156] – Lenin was to pay increasing attention to providing an explicit theoretical justification for his new revolutionary strategy with respect to Russia. In April and May, particularly in his writings on the proposed revisions to the Party programme, he began to lay more stress on the development of finance capitalism within Russia, in banking and key sectors of the industrial economy, though still conceding that 'there [were] no few fields and branches of labour that are still in a state of transition from natural or semi-natural economy to capitalism'.[157] During the summer he came to assert more categorically that state capitalism, the most advanced form of finance capitalism, did exist in Russia[158] and argued, in a manner analogous to Hilferding and the Left, that despite the continuing wide-spread existence of a small-scale economy 'big [finance] capital rule[d] the country, primarily through banks and syndicates'.[159]

By September, in *The Impending Catastrophe and How to Combat It*, Lenin had become quite unequivocal. Imperialism, which 'is merely monopoly capitalism', existed in Russia – he cited the examples of *Produgol*, *Prodamet* and the Sugar Syndicate to prove his point. During the war, he continued, the capitalists had converted their monopolies into state monopolies, in order to use the powers of the state to subjugate the working class and protect their profits. This development had made the transition towards socialism objectively possible, since 'socialism is merely the next step forward from state-capitalist monopoly'.[160] He concluded:

> Imperialist war is the eve of socialist revolution. And this not only because the horrors of the war give rise to proletarian revolt – no revolt can bring socialism unless the economic conditions for socialism are ripe – but because state-monopoly capitalism is a complete material prepara-tion for socialism, the threshold of socialism, a rung on the ladder of history between which and the rung called socialism there are no intermediate rungs.[161]

In *Can the Bolsheviks Retain State Power?* he rammed this message home. Here he stressed the high levels of centralisa-tion and organisation already reached in banking and other major industries in Russia. The revolutionary state must take over these sectors of the economy intact and use the institu-tions created for controlling production within them as the skeleton of the planned socialist economy of the future. Without these prerequisites there would have been no pros-pect 'of taking immediate steps towards socialism'.[162] He continued:

> In addition to the chiefly 'oppressive' apparatus – the standing army, the police and the bureaucracy – the modern state possesses an apparatus which has extremely close connections with the banks and syndicates, an appar-atus which performs an enormous amount of accounting

and registration work ... This apparatus must not ... be smashed. It must be wrested from the control of the capitalists ... it must be *subordinated* to the proletarian Soviets; it must be expanded, made more comprehensive, and nation-wide. And this can be done by utilising the achievements already made by large-scale capitalism. ...

Capitalism has created an accounting *apparatus* in the shape of the banks, syndicates, postal service, consumers' societies and office employees' unions. *Without big banks socialism would be impossible.*

The big banks are the 'state apparatus' which we *need* to bring about socialism, and which we take *ready-made* from capitalism ...[163]

The criticism of Sukhanov, and others, had apparently been answered. Lenin had provided a justification of his promotion of socialist revolution in Russia, both in terms of the presence of sufficient prerequisites within Russia itself, but also, as we have seen, as the first in an inevitable chain of revolutions which would sweep across the advanced West.[164]

The failure of the October Revolution, however, to ignite proletarian revolution in Europe, upon which socialist Russia's fate ultimately was to rest, thrust on Lenin the growing awareness that his expectation in 1917 of rapid international revolution in fact had been exaggerated. Moreover, in this new conjuncture of the continuing isolation of the revolution, he was also compelled to reappraise his assessment of the ripeness of conditions in Russia for socialism. Then, as Harding has remarked, rather ironically much of the analysis that he had elaborated before 1917 emerged to the fore again.[165] In March, 1918, shortly after the conclusion of the peace of Brest-Litovsk, which Lenin deemed to be vital if the revolution was not to succumb to the military steam-roller of German imperialism, he began to call in question just how far state capitalism had developed in Russia. It was the Germans, he now argued, who possessed 'discipline, organisation, harmonious cooperation on the basis of modern machine industry, and strict accounting and control'. He continued: 'And that is just what we are lacking'.[166] He was even more unequivocal in his most sustained and trenchant polemic against the Left Communists, *'Left-Wing' Childishness and the Petty-Bourgeois Mentality*, where he repeatedly maintained that state capitalism would be progressive, 'a *step forward*', 'a gigantic step forward' for Soviet Russia.[167] He retreated even further, candidly admitting his doubts whether Russia possessed the prerequisites for the construction of socialism:

> Is it not clear that from the *material*, economic and productive point of view, we are not yet on 'the threshold' of socialism? Is it not clear that we cannot pass through the door of socialism without crossing 'the threshold' we have not yet reached?[168]

His optimism regarding the prospects for an immediate international revolution also declined markedly after October. Admittedly, at the Third All-Russian Congress of Soviets in January 1918, he still claimed that 'socialist revolution is maturing by the hour in all countries of the world' and continued to link '[t]he final victory of socialism' in Russia to the triumph of revolution on an international scale.[169] Indeed, in his final speech at the Congress he reaffirmed his faith in 'the mounting world revolution', concluding that 'the time is not far off when the working people of all countries will unite into a single world-wide state and join in a common effort to build a new socialist edifice'.[170] Yet even then his doubts were evidently growing. At the Extraordinary All-Russian Congress of Railwaymen, which met concurrently with the Congress of Soviets, he was markedly more cautious in his prognosis. Echoing earlier warnings, he reminded his audience that it remained impossible to predict when revolution in the West would 'break out', that it '[might] take a long time', and that it could not be made to order.[171] Such pessimism was increasingly to colour Lenin's thinking in the winter and spring of 1918. By May, his vision of international revolution had also reverted to that which he had outlined before 1917. Conceding that revolution might come 'even later than we desire or expect', 'at an immeasurably slower pace than we expect or wish',[172] he once again rejected the premise that socialist revolution would take place synchronously on an international scale:

> I know that there are . . . wiseacres . . . calling themselves

socialists, who assert that power should not have been taken until the revolution broke out in all countries. They do not realise that in saying this they are deserting the revolution and going over to the side of the bourgeoisie. To wait until the working classes carry out a revolution on an international scale means that everyone will remain suspended in mid-air. This is senseless. Everyone knows the difficulties of a revolution. It may begin with brilliant success in one country and then go through agonising periods, since final victory is only possible on a world scale, and only by the joint efforts of the workers of all countries . . .[173]

Before proceeding to investigate the precise areas of conflict that brought Lenin and the Left Communists to loggerheads in the first six months of 1918, some attempt to explain Lenin's shifts in strategy is unavoidable. The supposition, proposed by Robert Daniels among others, that Lenin simply 'sacrificed the [Marxist] philosophy of history' in response to the pressure of 'revolutionary fervor' in Russia since he was 'determined to have his revolution whatever the circumstances' has been shown to be too one-sided.[174] Harding has restored the other side of Lenin, emphasising that he was 'an extraordinarily doctrinaire politician ... [who] altered his political course only after thorough theoretical work had convinced him of the need to do so'.[175] Yet Harding himself tends to glide over the problem that Lenin called for socialist revolution in Russia before, so it would appear, he had seriously applied his theoretical conclusions to his country. Another possible answer suggests itself. Clearly, Lenin's study of finance capitalism, of imperialism, had raised his expectations of socialist revolution in general. Moreover, he had also come to the conclusion that finance capitalism had made substantial advances within Russia itself. Caught up by the euphoria surrounding the collapse of the autocracy, he appears to have exaggerated the feasibility of propelling the revolution forward, to socialism. Certainly, he quickly justified this strategy by reference, first, to the evident growth of finance capitalism within Russia and, second, to the fact that 1917 more generally had witnessed strong signs of unrest in the more advanced countries of the

West, if not against capitalism, then certainly against the war. Arguably, Lenin saw this unrest as the harbinger of socialist revolution which he thought would unfold rapidly across Europe once Russia had given the lead. However, a certain intoxication at the prospect of realising the goal to which he had devoted his life led him to over-estimate the prospects for international revolution. At the same time, he also appears to have been induced to overstate, so Remington concludes, the extent to which state capitalism had developed within Russia, reminiscent of his overstatement more than a decade previously, as Service has pointed out, of the level to which capitalism *per se* had developed in Russia, especially in the countryside.[176]

However, the primary purpose of this investigation has not been to offer yet another interpretation of Lenin's political thought. Instead, its main task has been to establish that Bukharin's own rather cryptic contention, that the conflict between Lenin and the Left Communists in early 1918 was rooted in differing assessments of the prospects for socialism both internationally and within Russia, and not simply reducible to the level of emotions, to a clash of generations, of 'sons against fathers', merits serious consideration.[177] In fact, with the temporary exception of 1917 itself, when their views in large part came to coincide, they do appear to have subscribed to distinct analyses of imperialism and, henceforth, to divergent prognoses of the course of socialist revolution. Lenin's own understanding of the imperialist world as a very heterogeneous entity led him, before and after the heady days of 1917, to reject the notion that socialist revolution would unfold as the unilinear international phenomenon that Bukharin and others on the Left deduced it would be.[178] Moreover, his own re-emerging doubts about the stage to which capitalism in Russia itself had developed were to influence his domestic policies in the spring of 1918, especially for the organisation of industry but also concerning the shape of the revolutionary state, where he again came into conflict with the Left.[179] It is to an examination of the particular instances of the intra-party struggle in the first half of 1918 that the following chapters are devoted.

# 3 Brest-Litovsk

While Brest-Litovsk may have remained, in John Wheeler-Bennett's memorable phrase, 'the forgotten peace' of World War I, the same has not been true of its place in histories of the Russian Revolution and the Bolshevik Party. As one biographer of Alexandra Kollontai recently remarked, '[H]istorians have analysed many times the bitter conflict among Party leaders' that the question of a separate peace with Germany provoked, so much so that 'we need not concern ourselves ... with the intricacies of the struggle.'[1] The implication of this conclusion, that there is little more to be said on this question, is quite unwarranted. On the contrary: the sources of the conflict within the party inflamed by Lenin's preparedness to accept peace with Imperial Germany have not as yet been explained fully.

For decades, in fact, little new has been added to our understanding of this episode in Bolshevik history. For example, in his classic account of the revolution W. H. Chamberlin devotes one chapter to Brest-Litovsk, yet pays little attention to the reasons why it led the Bolshevik party to the verge of a split. His explanation of the Left Communists' opposition to peace does little more than echo that of Lenin himself. Unlike the latter, 'whose hard realistic mind was not intoxicated by the success of the Revolution ...', Chamberlin suggests that the Left Communists, supported for a time by a majority of the party, were so seduced by the ease of the October Revolution, and by the subsequent rapid and triumphal march of Soviet power, that they found any 'retreat psychologically very difficult'.[2] Hence they refused to compromise with German imperialism and accept an annexationist peace, and instead called for revolutionary war.[3] A contemporary of Chamberlin, but one of a considerably more radical disposition, Victor Serge, also accounted for the Left Communists' opposition to peace by reference to their psychology, attributing it in particular to an unrealistic revolutionary romanticism.[4] More recent scholarship too has tended to follow suit. For Leonard Schapiro, the Left Communists' 'outlook was emotional rather than rational', a rejection of anything smacking of expediency in defence 'of the purity of Bolshevism . . .' Similarly, Robert Daniels attributed much of their intransigence on the question of peace to 'emotional impulse'.[5] Stephen Cohen also has stressed the Left Communists' 'emotional commitment to cherished ideals', attributing their opposition in large part to a 'youthful righteousness . . .', as Lenin himself had on occasion.[6]

No doubt passions and questions of principle were stirred up by Lenin's readiness to accept a separate, and punishing, peace with Germany. Certainly, the Left Communist leadership itself was not immune to the power of its emotions. Mikhail Pokrovskii, for instance, is reported to have been reduced to tears when Major-General Max Hoffman communicated Germany's initial conditions for peace to the Soviet delegation at Brest, sobbing: 'How can you talk of peace without annexation when nearly eighteen provinces are torn from Russia?'[7] Later, after the CC had voted on 22 February to accept Allied aid to help Soviet Russia resist the German advance – a policy 'of taking potatoes and weapons from the Anglo-French imperialist robbers', as Lenin caustically yet approvingly dubbed it – Bukharin is alleged to have cried in despair that '[w]e are turning the party into a dung heap'.[8] Moreover, similarly strong passions were evident at the grass-roots. While it remains difficult to establish with complete certainty what impelled the rank-and-file to oppose separate peace with Germany one reason, according to William Rosenberg, appears to have been a reluctance to betray 'the international proletarian movement', an attitude no doubt encouraged by the vociferous denunciations launched by Polish and Baltic revolutionaries then in Soviet Russia. At the same time, many ordinary workers appear to have feared that peace or no peace, German imperialism would not stop short of destroying all the gains achieved by them in the course of the revolution. Perhaps, too, a naive optimism about easy victory over the Germans, fuelled by expectations of the imminent spread of revolution across Europe, survived, at least until military realities dictated differently.[9]

For the most part, however, the Left Communist leadership strenuously denied that their advocacy of revolutionary war was simply or primarily the product of emotion, youthful or otherwise. Quite the contrary, it saw its opposition to peace to be based on 'cold calculation', as Cohen has remarked.[10] At the heart of this calculation was a vision of the course of proletarian revolution which differed from that of Lenin, as we saw in the previous chapter, as well as a mortal fear for the fate of socialism, in Russia and beyond, should peace be signed on German terms. As even Schapiro remarked, unfortunately with but little explanation, while 'emotional dissent' may have motivated much of the opposition within the party, for some Left Communist leaders, in particular, Bukharin and certain of his allies within the Moscow organisation, theoretical differences with Lenin, rooted in subtly divergent analyses of imperialism and of the international development of socialist revolution, also determined their rejection of peace.[11]

But before proceeding to reconstruct the debate within the party on peace in all its 'intricacies', and the more coldly calculated reasons for opposing it elaborated by the Left Communists, a brief digression is necessary in order to elucidate precisely what it involved. Typically, it has been seen as the product of Lenin's *volte-face*, from support of revolutionary war to acceptance of a separate, and annexationist, peace on German terms.[12] To the Left this appeared to be the abnegation of an established party principle of which Lenin himself had been the chief architect. In October, 1915, for example, in his *Several Theses*, Lenin had been quite unequivocal about what the Bolsheviks must do should they come to power in Russia:

> We would propose peace to all the belligerents on the condition that freedom is given to the colonies and all peoples that are dependent, oppressed and deprived of rights. *Under the present governments, neither Germany, nor Britain and France would accept this condition. In that case, we would have to prepare for and wage a revolutionary war* . . . first and foremost, we would raise up the socialist proletariat of Europe for an insurrection against their governments.[13]

A year later, he reiterated that revolutionary war was unavoidable, a conclusion derived quite logically from his analysis of imperialism, which posited that socialist revolution would not triumph immediately on an international scale. Since socialism will conquer 'first in one or several countries . . . [t]his is bound to create not only friction, but a direct attempt on the part of the bourgeoisie of other countries to crush the socialist state's victorious proletariat. In such cases a war on our part would be a legitimate and just war'.[14] In March, 1917, he once again emphasised the inevitability of such a war and his preparedness in fact to wage it.[15] *Prima facie*, the Left Communists' critique of Lenin seems to be perfectly justified.

Yet the truth in fact is rather more complex, as soon after his return to Russia Lenin's enthusiasm for revolutionary war began to wane.[16] Speaking at the Petrograd City Conference in mid-April, he re-affirmed that in power 'we ourselves would start a revolutionary war', *but* only if the warring imperialist states rejected the Bolshevik appeal to conclude a general, democratic peace.[17] Days later, at the April Conference, he backtracked a little further. Of course, he argued, '[w]e are not pacifists, and we cannot repudiate a revolutionary war'. Again confirming that the Bolsheviks would honour their commitment to come to the aid of socialist revolution when it spread beyond Russia, he rather tamely concluded that '[w]e shall help it along, but in what manner, we do not know'.[18] His adherence to revolutionary war, to stimulate 'insurrection' in Europe, already had become much diluted. Thereafter, until October, Lenin made but few references to revolutionary war. Moreover, his thinking on the question had changed in another respect. Categorically rejecting the prospect of an offensive to carry the revolution abroad, he increasingly saw revolutionary war as one of defence, thrust upon Russia by the imperialist powers of the West, which would most probably ignore Bolshevik appeals to negotiate an immediate democratic peace.[19] However, he continued to reject, repeatedly and unequivocally, the idea that a Soviet government would conclude a separate peace with Germany, or any other imperialist power.[20] At least, he did so until 10 November, when he first admitted that an 'independent peace' might be acceptable.[21]

The reasons for Lenin's rapidly waning enthusiasm for revolutionary war remain uncertain and are undoubtedly complex. A number of reasons suggest themselves. Most important, perhaps, soon after his return to Russia he calculated it was 'simply impracticable', or 'a political liability for the party while it struggled for votes in the soviets', as Robert Service has argued.[22] Certainly, even before October he had come to doubt the Russian army's will to fight any longer, and, as we shall see, shortly after the revolution he admitted that the overwhelming majority of the people just sought an end to the war.[23] Perhaps, too, he simply came to believe that the prospect of any revolutionary war was unlikely, because of his growing optimism during 1917 that revolution in Russia quickly would spark off a chain of revolutions elsewhere. More soberly, he may have reckoned that the war continuing in the West would preclude the 'practical likelihood' of revolutionary war since the rival imperialist camps would be 'unable to "come to terms" against revolutionary Russia',[24] or because rejection of the democratic peace proposed by a revolutionary government in Russia would make it more difficult for the capitalist powers to stem the rising tide of revolution, in large part swollen by anti-war sentiments.[25]

Lenin was not alone, however. During 1917 other leading Bolsheviks came to temper their commitment to revolutionary war, certainly as conceived as a holy crusade to carry socialism abroad. On the right of the party, for example, Lev Kamenev and Grigorii Zinoviev displayed a distinct lack of enthusiasm for it. More significantly, some on the left too were less militant than has been believed. Bukharin, for one, evinced a marked caution on the question at the Sixth Party Congress. The original draft of his resolution on the current situation and the war, he admitted, had made no reference to revolutionary war. At the insistence of the Congress, he had inserted a commitment to such a war should the proletariat come to power first in Russia. Yet at the editorial stage, he continued, his resolution had been watered down when doubts emerged whether the forces required to wage war would exist. Bukharin himself appeared to reckon then that the most that could be hoped for, given Russia's shattered economy, was a defensive revolutionary war – one, nevertheless, which he hoped would still ignite the flames of world revolution. Unlike Bukharin, however, Preobrazhenskii remained adamantly opposed to any equivocation, but his amendment advocating the uncompromising prosecution of revolutionary war was defeated.[26]

There is some reason to doubt whether these retreats from unequivocal support for revolutionary war were clear to all Bolsheviks. For instance, in the summer and autumn of 1917 a number of Bolshevik organisations, ranging from Petrograd itself to Perm' in the east, to Khar'kov and Tiflis in the south, to the south-west and to Latvia in the west, continued to defend revolutionary war as one of the immediate and vital tasks that would stand before the victorious Russian proletariat.[27] And many Left Communists appear not to have grasped just how far Lenin was prepared to go to secure peace. In the winter of 1917–18 they continued to claim that revolutionary war was a fundamental tenet of Bolshevism, in accord with what they perceived the decisions of the April Conference and the Sixth Party Congress to have been.[28] Moreover, however compromised and ambiguous the Bolsheviks' commitment to launch an offensive against world imperialism may have become before October, the very idea of separate peace with Germany was anathema to them all, including Lenin.[29] It was Lenin's apostasy on precisely this issue, that is, his willingness to accept such a peace on German terms to buy a 'breathing-space' for the revolution, that precipitated the formation of the Left Communist movement in late 1917, as we saw in Chapter 1.

At the beginning of the debate the Left Communists appear to have taken an intransigent line, demanding that the Soviet government break off negotiations with Germany and cease seeking to conclude a general democratic peace embracing all the other imperialist powers. For instance, on 28 December the Left-dominated Moscow Regional Bureau insisted on the need '[t]o form a volunteer revolutionary army and fight ruthlessly against the whole world's bourgeoisie for the idea of international socialism', a point of view supported by the Petersburg Committee in a resolution issued the same day.[30] Then, on 8 January 1918, a meeting of the CC with party leaders from Petrograd, Moscow, the Urals, the Ukraine and the Volga, in the capital for the forthcoming Third All-Russian Congress of Soviets, witnessed the triumph of this policy. Of the sixty-three present, thirty-two supported unequivocally the call made by Osinskii and Preobrazhenskii for revolutionary war; fifteen were for immediate peace on German terms; while sixteen favoured Trotsky's position, of declaring the war to be at end, but not signing an annexationist peace with Germany.[31] Never again was there to be a clear majority for revolutionary war at the highest levels of the party. In fact, as the struggle over peace or war dragged on in the first months of 1918, it soon became clear that of the Left Communists Bukharin was far from alone in harbouring reservations about the feasibility of a *jihad* to carry the revolution abroad. Indecision and a lack of clarity on precisely what was to be done were to plague them during the rest of the Brest debate.

Within just three days of their victory, divisions emerged among the leading Left Communists, the majority of whom became considerably less resolute in their advocacy of revolutionary war. At a meeting of the CC on 11 January, of those Left Communists present only Lomov and Krestinskii ultimately voted in favour of revolutionary war. Yet even they had raised doubts about it during the debate which preceded the vote. Lomov had suggested adopting Trotsky's position, at the same time 'combin[ing] it with maximum activity in preparing for a revolutionary war', while Krestinskii conceded revolutionary war would be possible only when a new army had been created. Of the others, Bukharin now concurred that 'comrade Trotsky's position is the most correct' and again raised the question of 'defining what we consider to be a revolutionary war: an attack or staying where we are?' Uritskii admitted that '[o]f course, we cannot wage a revolutionary war – cannot because the moment we begin it, we will lose our army, the soldiers; and the bourgeoisie will immediately conclude a peace'. Summing up, Bubnov concluded that now 'no one is advocating the point of view of the revolutionary war'. Having rejected revolutionary war by a vote of eleven to two, the CC resolved by a vote of twelve to one to prolong negotiations with Germany for as long as possible, in the hope that revolution in Germany would erupt in the meantime, while Trotsky's policy of 'no war, no peace' also won a majority of nine to seven. The entire Bolshevik leadership indeed was in a state of flux, and no little confusion.[32]

With increasing candour, the Left Communists denied that they sought a crusade to carry revolution abroad at the point of Red bayonets. On 11 January the Left-dominated Moscow Committee defined 'a holy war for socialism' as one fought 'within the country and against any outside encroachment on the conquests of [the] revolution'. On 18 January the Petersburg Committee declared that its conception of revolutionary war had 'no necessary connection with an offensive of any kind'.[33] Evidently they were moving their ground to support of a defensive revolutionary war, as Bukharin had suggested the previous summer. At the same time it also became ever clearer that they did not have a conventional war in mind. The disintegration of the old army made such a war inconceivable. More than that, they did not aspire to re-create a conventional army to fight the Germans, since they saw such an institution as totally alien to the new socialist order in the making.[34] Defending a strategy uncannily similar to that of the *SR*s, they advocated partisan war, to be fought by a workers' and peasants' militia. Armed detachments of workers and peasants, they anticipated, would arise spontaneously to resist any German advance which would inevitably threaten the gains that they had made in the revolution.[35]

The Left Communists, however, retreated no further. For them, revolutionary war, even of a defensive, partisan nature, remained vital for the salvation of the revolution in Russia. Separate peace with Germany, they were convinced, would simply retard the development of international revolution. More ominously, any such delay would be fatal for socialism in Russia, which would find itself suffocated at birth, a fear which Bukharin stressed again at the Seventh Congress, arguing that '[i]n the final analysis international revolution – *and it alone* – is our salvation'.[36] Their vision of international revolution and their fears for the future of an isolated Soviet Russia were not just emotional responses, but were underpinned by a quite rational and coherent set of arguments which deserve to be taken seriously, if their opposition to peace is to be understood fully.

At the highest theoretical level, the preceding chapter has focused on the respective analyses of imperialism developed by the Left Communists and Lenin, and their implications for the pattern of socialist revolution. As we have seen, their analyses differed in certain crucial respects which help explain their divergent responses to the prospect of separate peace with Germany in early 1918. In the case of Lenin, for example, it was not, as one commentator has alleged recently, simply 'hard-headed pragmatism [which] led him to accept, much more easily than most of his comrades, a *Diktatfrieden* which would deprive Soviet Russia of much of its most valuable resources and seriously weaken its ability to promote international revolution . . .'.[37] More than that, his understanding of how world revolution would develop had alerted him to the possibility that the revolution could remain confined to Russia for some time. Arguably, this awareness helps to explain why he, as E. H. Carr has suggested, 'was perhaps better prepared than most of his followers to take a realistic view of the resulting situation' when Soviet Russia did find itself alone and, consequently, to take whatever course of action was required to preserve it until socialist revolution was able to advance internationally.[38] In early 1918, as we also saw, Lenin still linked the *ultimate* victory of socialism in Russia to world revolution. But he repeatedly warned his comrades that world revolution itself would embrace an entire epoch of advances and retreats, just as he had before the heady days of 1917. Claiming that it remained impossible to predict with any certainty precisely when it would begin, at the enlarged session of the CC which met on 8 January he dismissed out of hand the idea that there could be any guarantee that 'the European, and especially the German, socialist revolution [would] take place in the next six months (or some such brief period)'.[39] In these highly uncertain circumstances, any strategy which assumed the impending triumph of world revolution was to him totally misguided, and in all probability would prove to be fatal for the survival of the revolution in Russia itself.

For their part, the Left Communists rejected Lenin's cautious evaluation of the international situation. Their own theorisation of the imperialist world had convinced them that socialist revolution, when it broke out, must develop of its own inexorable logic on an international scale. But it would be foolish to imagine that it was just abstract theorising that led them to believe so. The situation in Europe at the beginning of 1918 was taken as confirmation of their theoretical prognosis, that socialist revolution in reality would advance in a more or less unilinear wave across the world. Bukharin and Radek argued that the strikes then gripping Austria-Hungary and Germany left no doubt that the proletariat there had 'at last awoken'.[40] In fact, as one observer recalled, giant strikes in Berlin at the end of January, combined with the establishment of Soviet power in the Ukraine and Finland, had convinced many Bolsheviks 'that the world revolution was indeed on the point of breaking out'.[41] Nascent anxieties notwithstanding, the Left Communists, unlike Lenin and his faction, persisted in claiming throughout the winter of 1918 that revolution in the West was imminent.[42] Overwhelming evidence to the contrary – the ebb of the strike movement in Germany; and the collapse of Soviet power in the Ukraine in face of the still awesomely powerful German military machine – did not shake their confidence. Despite all this, at the Seventh Congress Bubnov still declared that 'the revolutionary crisis already has matured in West Europe . . . international revolution is on the verge of erupting in the form of a very acute and extensive civil war . . .', while V. F. Stozhok, the delegate of the Left-dominated Gorlovo-Shcherbinsk organisation in the Donbass, went as far as claiming that revolution was already underway in Germany.[43]

In these circumstances separate peace with Germany would be, at best, superfluous and, at worst, harmful. It would be superfluous, they repeatedly argued, since the growing revolutionary crisis within the Central Powers would make it impossible for them to mount any full-scale, sustained offensive against Russia.[44] Convinced that the imminence of revolution would scupper the ultimate designs of the German imperialists to crush the revolution, they did not deny, however, that the latter would be able to begin to advance against Soviet Russia. Yet they regarded even this prospect with a surprising degree of sanguinity. Conceding that the old army would not fight, they admitted that in the first stages of war retreats were inevitable. However, such retreats would have their advantages, as they would draw German troops ever further into the depths of Russia where they would find themselves over-extended and hence vulnerable to counter-attack by partisan detachments. In this military conjuncture, and with the war continuing in the West, they continued, it was in all likelihood probable that the Germans would have insufficient forces to consolidate their initial victories. In the meantime, any defeats suffered by Russia would prove to be temporary and, more than that, well worth the price.[45] The renewal of the war against the workers' government in Russia, combined of course with fraternisation at the front, would lead to the contamination of the German army by revolutionary socialist ideas and thus to its demoralisation and disintegration. The prolongation of revolutionary war, Bukharin optimistically claimed, would accelerate this process of disintegration.[46] Despite clear evidence of the continuing discipline of the German forces, at the Seventh Party Congress Uritskii continued to hold to this optimistic prognosis. Early defeats, he again repeated, were inevitable, but even defeats would contribute to the crisis in Europe and do 'much more to bring the revolution to a head ... than that obscene peace which we are now asked to ratify'.[47]

If Lenin's policy of peace were pursued, they continued, then it would strike a devastating blow to the prospects of socialist revolution in Germany. Opposition to the war had been one of the most important issues behind the recent militancy of many German workers. Should Soviet Russia now bow to German demands and sign the Brest peace, so Bukharin argued, this action would cut the ground from under the feet of the growing revolutionary movement there.[48] The German government would then presumably be able to sow the seeds of confusion amongst its own workers by claiming that military strength and intransigence alone could provide peace. At the same time, it could exploit the territories that would effectively fall under its control, especially the Ukraine, to ease its domestic food crisis and so appease civilian unrest at home. In view of this prospect, Soviet Russia must do its revolutionary duty and fight as best it could, since any prolongation of the war would exacerbate the tensions within Germany and so hasten the victory of socialism there.[49]

Yet the Left Communists' obdurate defence of revolutionary war was motivated not just by their optimism regarding the imminence of world revolution, nor by a sense of duty. They remained deeply pessimistic about the consequences of a separate peace, not just for the prospects of revolution in Germany but also for the very survival of Soviet Russia itself. It would provide a breathing-space, but not for Russia. On the contrary, it would simply provide a respite for the warring imperialist camps. They would avail themselves of this opportunity to reconcile their own differences and unite to crush the common danger posed to them by the Russian Revolution, a fear which Bukharin had expressed at the Sixth Party Congress the previous summer.[50] Regardless of how moderately it attempted to act, the very existence of a socialist regime in Russia would be perceived by international capitalism as a threat to its own existence. And, unlike Lenin who was certain that any 'ultra-imperialist' coalition was unrealisable, their own analysis of the imperialist world did not preclude such a possibility. In fact, they frequently claimed that this possibility was becoming a reality. Early in January, Preobrazhenskii argued that soon Russia would find itself facing a united imperialist front, embracing the Kaiser's Germany and Lloyd George's Britain.[51]

This fear of imperialist union persisted amongst the Left Communists in the winter of 1918, perhaps fuelled by rumours, as Carr has pointed out, 'that Germany and the allies would come to terms at the expense of Russia...'.[52] During the first session of the CC on 18 February Bukharin raised these fears again, admitting, however, that the prospects for an imperialist alliance were not yet clear. Just two and a half weeks later, at the Seventh Party Congress, he was quite certain. Imperialist unity, so he claimed, had become a reality: 'many facts indicate that this agreement between the two hostile coalitions already has taken place'.[53] A week later, at the Fourth Congress of Soviets, the Left Communists were rather less sure. Conceding that no formal alliance between the rival imperialist camps had yet emerged, nevertheless in their declaration protesting against the ratification of the Brest-Litovsk treaty they still insisted that the commonality of interests existing between them would lead them to unite, probably sooner rather than later, in order to crush the revolution in Russia.[54] The whole notion, therefore, of attempting to preserve socialism in Russia by means of a separate peace with Germany was illusory, since it would do nothing to prevent a general imperialist assault that would prove to be fatal for the revolution.

But even in the unlikely circumstance that the imperialist powers did not coalesce rapidly to crush the revolution, a possibility they grudgingly conceded in the spring, its prospects of survival were equally bleak.[55] Imperialist coalition or not, Russia would still not be given any lengthy respite in which to restore its war-ravaged economy and rebuild its military strength. Whether it signed a separate peace or not, Imperial Germany would remain the most immediate threat. Politically, it would be compelled to destroy the Soviet republic lest its continued existence act as a source of domestic ferment, undermining its ability to continue its war on the western front.[56] Economically, the outlook was equally grim. They calculated, and did so with a considerable degree of accuracy, that Germany would be forced to plunder the East, both to feed its own populace and so reduce growing revolutionary tensions, and to gain the resources with which to continue its war in the West. In particular, the separation of the Ukraine, a vital source of grain, and its exploitation by Germany, would threaten Soviet Russia with what G. A. Usievich, sardonically borrowing from Riabushinskii, termed 'the bony hand of hunger'. Similarly, the inevitable loss of the Donets basin and the Caucasus would cripple its economy by depriving it of equally vital supplies of coal, iron ore and oil. Consequently, the decline of Russian industry would accelerate dramatically, with the Petrograd region becoming an industrial desert and Moscow suffering to a lesser, but still significant, extent. In turn, the socio-political base of the regime, already decimated by the loss of proletarian bastions in the west and south of the country, especially Riga and the Donets Basin, would disintegrate even more rapidly than it had hitherto, if not be destroyed entirely.[57]

Given these losses, it remained irrelevant to the Left Communists whether the rump of Soviet Russia secured a protracted breathing-space or not, for its situation would still be hopeless. Brest-Litovsk, according to Lomov, had cost Russia one-third of its grain-producing area, including, more

significantly, the sources of three-quarters of its grain surplus; two-fifths of its industry and industrial work-force;
nine-tenths of its easily exploitable coal reserves; and three-
quarters of its iron production.[58] Despite these swingeing
losses and further German advances in the south after the
peace had been signed, Lomov himself for a time, and
subsequently Radek and S. V. Kossior, optimistically claimed
that progress towards the construction of socialism in Russia
was not totally excluded in the interim, until international
revolution came to their rescue, as it soon must. In particular, Lomov singled out the Urals and West Siberia as regions
of potentially significant development.[59] However, the remainder of their comrades appear to have remained much
more realistic – and pessimistic! By the time that the First
Congress of Economic Councils convened in late May,
Lomov had revised his assessment of the economic situation.
Now he rebutted Radek's argument that Soviet Russia would
be able to restore economic links with the territories stripped
from it and on this basis rebuild its industry.[60] Osinskii, too,
maintained that the losses of food, fuel and raw materials,
especially from the Ukraine, suffered by Russia precluded
the restoration, let alone any further development, of its
industry. Any recovery would require aid from abroad.
However, Soviet Russia could not accept assistance from the
advanced imperialist powers, should they be willing to provide it, lest it be used to convert Russia into something
approaching a semi-colonial dependency. Only revolutionary war, initially to regain the south, and ultimately to spark
off international revolution, offered any hope for the survival of socialism in Russia.[61] For the majority of the Left
Communists, the idea that peace would preserve Russia as a
bastion of socialism, with the resources and cadres later to
come to the aid of revolution elsewhere, was the triumph of
hope over reason.[62]

For the Left Communists, therefore, the ultimate outcome
of a separate peace could only be the degeneration of the
revolution. Economically emasculated, and hence vulnerable, Soviet Russia would rapidly become transformed into a
virtual satellite of Germany. The latter had protected its own
property interests, in industry, finance and the land, by
demanding at the very least compensation for any damage

done to them or for their nationalisation. Since Soviet Russia simply did not possess the means with which to pay such compensation, then it would be compelled to cease the nationalisation of German-owned industry and return to German hands that already expropriated. Substantial capitalist enclaves, therefore, especially in the electrical and chemical industries but also in mining, would continue to exist, and the party's policy of socialising the economy root and branch would be subverted.[63] However, financial compensation was not the ultimate objective of the Germans. Rather, as payment for damages to German property incurred in the war, as well as for the maintenance of Russian prisoners-of-war, they sought food, raw materials and industrial products to fuel the continuing war in the West. To ensure the flow of these goods in face of resistance to such exploitation from the workers and peasants, they would be forced to intervene directly in the management of industry and agriculture. In consequence, in the near future capitalism would be restored, with German imperialists brutally coercing the Russian workers and peasants. In these circumstances, there was no prospect of beginning the construction of socialism.[64]

There was another possibility, or, more accurately, another path to the same sad end. Isolated in Russia, the revolutionary government would be forced to retreat in its domestic policy too, to reach some *modus vivendi* with the surviving native capitalists. Lenin's ideas of collaboration with these capitalists to facilitate economic recovery were simply the first, pernicious, fruits of this consequence of separate peace. The next retreat, they feared, in all probability would be the return of the newly nationalised banks into hands of the capitalists too, and of their German patrons. The final outcome of such a policy would be the surrender of all socialist positions and policies, the restoration of capitalism and subordination to German imperialism, if by a more circuitous route.[65]

For the Left Communists, therefore, there was absolutely nothing to be gained from a separate peace with Germany. Even should Soviet Russia gain a breathing-space from immediate imperialist attack, the economic losses and other conditions that would flow from the Brest-Litovsk treaty precluded any advance towards socialist reconstruction internally. In the final analysis, peace would not save the revolution, but simply prolong its death agonies. As they saw it, the only real choice was that between an ignominous death by slow strangulation or the prosecution of a revolutionary war while they still had the strength to do so, in the hope of igniting the European revolution that alone could save them. If it failed, at least then the revolution would perish with honour, and not tarnish the cause of international socialism for the sake of an obscene, and in the final analysis, unworkable peace with German imperialism. Vardin-Mgeladze captured their mood:

> We must fight. And if our hopes for world revolution are not destined to be fulfilled today, then it is of no account, for our death cannot be avoided. But it is better to die in battle than to surrender all the positions of the revolution without a struggle.[66]

The case that the Left Communists presented against a separate peace with Germany was, arguably, not without its logic, as well as its passion. While it is impossible to say with certainty what the fate of Soviet Russia would have been had not the war in the West turned against the Central Powers in the summer of 1918, it remains probable that sooner or later Germany would have extirpated all vestiges of socialism there, as the Left feared.[67] But however well-founded their apprehensions were, however rational a case for their opposition to a separate peace can be presented, ultimately their plea that it was better to die with honour defending the revolution than to suffer its more gradual yet inevitable degeneration foundered, ultimately, on the unwillingness of the majority of workers and peasants to fight. Admittedly, the picture was not all black. As we saw in Chapter 1, in late February the threat posed by the renewed German advance provoked no mean degree of militancy in Petrograd, as thousands of workers volunteered to conduct a revolutionary war. But Petrograd was not alone. In Moscow too, rousing declarations in support of revolutionary war prevailed, and young workers from the city appear to have taken up arms. And at the front, and later in the south, in the areas which suffered directly from the rapacious economic policies implemented by the Germans, there were instances, so Ionov reported, of the peasants spontaneously mobilising to carry out guerrilla war.[68]

Yet it would be unwise to exaggerate the extent to which ordinary Russians, in the final analysis, were ready to fight. For example, in Moscow rhetoric appears not to have been matched by deed, and the number of actual recruits, less than 3000, ready to go to the front proved to be disappointing.[69] Moreover, despite continuing protests against a separate peace, from the beginning of March there appears to have been a general and noticeable decline in the preparedness of much of the rank-and-file in practice to engage in revolutionary war – with the exception, of course, of the regions directly under the German jackboot. As Zinoviev caustically remarked at the City Conference of the Moscow party on 4 March, declarations of militancy were all very well, but experience in Moscow had shown that very often they were not translated into action.[70] Petrograd too was not free from similar contradictions. For instance, at the Seventh Party Congress, K. I. Shelavin recounted that of the 7000-strong work force of the Trubochnyi plant which had overwhelmingly voted in favour of revolutionary war, only fifteen had in fact volunteered to fight! Similarly, of the 300 workers still employed in the Nobel plant, only ten had volunteered, while the others simply sought to get paid and to leave the city as quickly as possible. As an observer recalled several years later, in Petrograd many conscious workers 'declined to take on a hopeless fight against the well-equipped and disciplined German armies without the support of the peasants, who had been the backbone of the old army'.[71] In face of a German army that remained a disciplined and powerful fighting force, in the main invulnerable to revolutionary propaganda, an erosion of the will to fight soon occurred, to be replaced by a mood of despondency. Lack of equipment and training, war-weariness, and rising unemployment and hunger all too quickly led to the disintegration of effective resistance.[72] The Left Communists grudgingly accepted that this was the case, but they repeatedly argued that the fighting spirit of the workers in particular was being undermined by Lenin and his faction dangling the prospect of a speedy peace before them.[73]

The weight of evidence, *pace* Left Communist claims, suggests that in the final analysis their hopes for waging a successful revolutionary war in the winter of 1918 were much exaggerated. Revolutionary rhetoric, without an equipped and disciplined army, was insufficient to halt the German advance. Certainly, Lenin himself was convinced that this was the case. His analysis of the economic and socio-political condition of Soviet Russia in early 1918 led him to conclude that there was no possibility of organising such an army in time to combat the German military machine and so prevent the complete and utter defeat of the revolution. The old, largely peasant army was in the throes of rapid disintegration, caused by war-weariness, the desire to return home to share in the division of the land, and by the very success of the Bolsheviks' anti-war propaganda. Even the Left-dominated Moscow Regional Bureau tacitly conceded in late September 1917 that the Bolsheviks had become identified as the party of peace.[74] In these circumstances there had been scant choice but to demobilise it, and to proceed with the building of a new socialist army, a task which would require months, not days or even weeks. At the critical session of the CEC on 24 February which voted to accept peace on German terms, Lenin bluntly argued that

> after three years of war our army is altogether unable and unwilling to fight. That is *the basic cause*, simple, obvious and ... bitter and painful, but absolutely clear why, living side by side with an imperialist plunderer, we are compelled to sign peace terms when he puts his knee on our chest.[75]

Certain that the overwhelming majority of the peasantry, and most workers too, were as yet unprepared to take up the call to arms, he calculated that any attempt to compel them to continue the war, revolutionary or otherwise, would have one, and only one, outcome – the overthrow of the Bolsheviks. A speedy peace alone would consolidate the alliance, the *smychka*, between the proletariat and the peasantry, the essential basis of Soviet power in Russia.[76] To preserve it he was determined to resist all efforts to wage a revolutionary war of any sort and to accept a separate if heinous peace, a 'Tilsit peace', as he frequently termed it.[77] Such a course of action was 'shameful', signifying 'a turn to the right and . . . rub[bing] our noses in the dirt; but it has to be done'. Only by leading the revolution through 'a very dirty stable' would it be possible to secure for Russia the breathing-space that he believed it must have in which to restore its economic and military strength. Only then would it be able to defend itself if need be, or, more optimistically, to come to the aid of revolution in Europe when it finally broke out.[78]

This conviction, that the army could not, and the majority of the populace would not fight, arguably was the most important determinant of Lenin's implacable pursuit of peace, at virtually any price, with Imperial Germany. Yet this was not his only reason. His growing doubts concerning the imminence of revolution in Europe, especially in Germany, meant that he harboured no illusions about the impossibility of a renewed German attack. He scornfully dismissed the argument propounded by the Left Communists that revolutionary war, even if it was feasible, would precipitate revolution in Germany, to give it 'a push', and so stymie any advance. Not only was this whole idea ill-founded but also profoundly un-Marxist, since it failed to consider whether 'the class antagonisms that engender revolution' had matured fully within Germany itself.[79] Revolution in the West, he reminded them, would face far greater obstacles than it had in Russia where state power had all but disintegrated in 1917 and the forces of reaction were 'miserable, despicable . . ., an idiot called Romanov, Kerensky the boaster, gangs of officer cadets and bourgeois'. Elsewhere in Europe the bourgeoisie remained strong and organised and the state powerful. There socialist revolution could not triumph as easily or as quickly as it had in Russia.[80]

In the meantime Soviet Russia must agree to a separate peace lest it be crushed by the power of German imperialism. By so doing it would buy for itself a breathing-space. The uneven development of capitalism, he reiterated, and the persistent and irreconcilable rivalries that it created amongst the imperialist powers, precluded the formation of any ultra-imperialist combination intent solely on extinguishing the revolution, as the Left Communists feared. These rivalries, particularly Germany's desire to redivide the world to take account of its own dynamically growing strength, had caused the world war. Any apprehension that the imperialists now would be able to settle their differences amicably was exaggerated: 'an alliance of the great imperialist powers against the Soviet Republic', he repeated, was 'well-nigh impossible'.[81] The basis for such an agreement simply did not exist. Germany would resist surrendering the effective expansion of its power in East Europe, especially since it required the economic resources of the area to pay for the war without inflicting intolerable burdens on its own people. Equally, the *Entente* could not concur with what it had gone to war to oppose in 1914, the establishment of German hegemony in Europe. Consequently, the imperialist war would continue until one side was victorious. This bitter, draining struggle in the West would rule out, for the time being at least, any concerted imperialist action to destroy Soviet Russia root and branch. Moreover, any independent assault was also out of the question. For Germany, in particular, its preoccupation with winning a final and decisive victory in the West would prevent it releasing sufficient forces to achieve its ultimate objective in the East, the conversion of Russia into a satellite of itself.[82] 'Under these circumstances,' he concluded, 'the only real, not paper, guarantee of peace we have is the antagonism among the imperialist powers'.[83]

Without peace, however, Lenin was certain that Germany would take advantage of Russia's present weakness and vulnerability and seek, by force if necessary, to end its war in the East. In the process, it would inflict a fatal defeat on the revolution. For him, peace was the only means to avoid this fate. The costs, he conceded, were punitive, but not crippling. The time won was to be used to rebuild Russia's military strength, to make 'a lengthy preparation' for future war.[84] He dismissed, perhaps too abruptly, the efficacy of partisan war as a viable strategy against any regular imperialist army, insisting instead that only a new, disciplined and adequately supplied Red Army would be able to rebuff any future assault by world imperialism. The construction of such an army, he continued, presupposed an end to the economic chaos and disorder gripping Russia: the food crisis threatening the cities with famine must be solved; its devastated transport system, especially the railways, repaired; and

industrial production revived. Despite the territorial losses
that would be inflicted by a German-dictated peace, sufficient, but only just sufficient resources, he added, would be
left to realise his projected programme of economic and
military reconstruction, provided they were mobilised effectively. If the realisation of these goals required the collaboration of the remaining native capitalists, then Lenin, as it soon
became clear, was prepared to come to some compromise
with them in the short term for what he believed would
advance the prospects for socialism in the long term. If it
required the reintroduction of one-person management and
of strict, hierarchical forms of labour and military discipline,
again he was willing to abandon the commitments he had
made in 1917.[85]

While remaining at loggerheads over the necessity of a
separate peace, and its likely consequences, rather ironically
Lenin and the Left Communists agreed on what had brought
it about. Speaking to delegates of the Petrograd garrison
days after the revolution Lenin conceded that peace was 'not
a Bolshevik policy', but rather what '[t]he vast majority of
workers, soldiers and peasants want....'.[86] In other words,
pressure, largely from the peasantry, but supported by what
the Left Communists considered to be backward and 'declassed' elements within the working class, had compelled the
Soviet government to abandon all thoughts of revolutionary
war and accept peace on terms dictated by the Germans. On
this issue, as on that of land, Lenin was prepared to retreat,
to appease the vast majority of the population. At the
Seventh Party Congress he candidly admitted that he was
ready to 'argue from the point of view of the peasant' who
sought peace at virtually any cost if that was the price of
securing peasant support for Bolshevik power.[87]

From the Left Communists' point of view this was all too
true. In the CC on 8 January Osinskii and Lomov condemned separate peace with Germany as a 'peasant, petty-
bourgeois peace', a *'muzhik* peace', while on the very eve of its
signature, at an enlarged session of the Moscow Regional
Bureau, Stukov again sardonically dubbed it a *'muzhik*
peace'.[88] Rather paradoxically, however, having dismissed
the peasants as the main force compelling the government to
accept peace, at the same time some Left Communists looked
to them to provide the mass base for revolutionary war. At

the meeting of the CC held on the evening of 18 February Bukharin, defending the possibility of revolutionary war, claimed that '[w]e can also set the *muzhiks* on the Germans'. Later, at the Seventh Party Congress, Bubnov continued to count on the peasants being drawn into a partisan war, explaining that German expropriation of the land would impel them in this direction.[89]

Such confusions and contradictions notwithstanding, the Left Communists disagreed with Lenin on what the costs of accommodating peasant aspirations for peace would mean for socialist revolution in Russia. Isolated in Russia, the revolutionary government would be compelled to bow to the wishes of the numerically predominant peasantry and abandon all efforts to refashion Russia along socialist lines. For Lomov, the outcome of the revolution would then be a dictatorship of the peasantry, not of the proletariat.[90] They expanded on this gloomy prospect in their *Theses on the Current Situation*:

as a result of the immediate, direct consequences of the peace ... there arises the strong possibility of a tendency towards deviation on the part of the majority of the Communist Party and the Soviet government led by it into the channel of petty-bourgeois politics of a new type.

In the event that such a tendency should materialise, the working class will cease to be the leader and guide of the socialist revolution inspiring the poor peasantry to destroy the rule of finance capital and the landowners. It will become a force which is dissipated in the ranks of the semi-proletarian, petty-bourgeois masses, which see as their task not proletarian struggle in alliance with the West European proletariat for the overthrow of the imperialist system, but the defence of the petty-proprietor fatherland from the pressure of imperialism. This aim is also attainable through compromise with the latter. In the event of a rejection of active proletarian politics, the conquests of the workers' and peasants' revolution will start to coagulate into a system of state capitalism and petty-bourgeois economic relations. 'The defence of the socialist fatherland' will then prove in actual fact to be defence of a petty bourgeois motherland subject to the influence of international capital.[91]

At this juncture we can appropriately turn to consider in more detail the Left Communists' fears of, and hostility towards, the peasantry, and, more generally, their vision of how the socialist transformation of the countryside was to be achieved.

# 4 The Agrarian Question

Just as Lenin's *volte-face* on foreign policy, or more precisely, his preparedness to accept a separate peace with Imperial Germany, had brought him into conflict with the Left Communists, so too his abandonment of apparently agreed measures for the construction of socialism within Russia intensified and prolonged the clash. While the principal focus of this controversy was to be, as Robert Daniels has indicated, 'the general question of authority and discipline in the revolutionary society, particularly as applied to the organisation of industry',[1] it was not confined to that issue. In fact, the first major instance of intra-party opposition to Lenin on an issue of domestic policy centred on the question of agriculture, a question much neglected, certainly in Western studies. In January 1918, the Left Communists began to attack Lenin bitterly for what they saw to be his abject surrender to the petty-bourgeois aspirations of the peasantry. This surrender was manifest in his readiness to carry out land reform largely along the lines traditionally advocated by the SRs. Their programme of land socialisation had for long been rejected by Russian Marxists of all persuasions – including Lenin – as fundamentally reactionary, inimical to any progress towards socialism in the countryside.[2] Given this shared legacy of antipathy to land socialisation, it is little wonder that the Left Communists perceived themselves to be defending orthodox socialist principles, and principles, moreover, which they believed had been incorporated in the agrarian programme adopted by the party in 1917. Hence to locate the origins of this particular conflict it is logical to examine how the thinking of the Left Communists, and of Lenin too, evolved on the question of agriculture during 1917.

On the few occasions, however, that the Left Communists had addressed themselves to this issue in 1917 they had displayed some hesitancy. On the morrow of the October Revolution, Bukharin, for one, conceded that the transformation of the countryside along socialist lines could not be achieved quickly. In general, agriculture was unlike industry,

83

where the evolution of state capitalism had created a highly developed framework for the socialist organisation of production. In Russia in particular, agriculture had not remotely approached the same level of capitalist development and concentration as industry had. This limited growth of capitalism was manifest in the continued predominance of small-scale peasant farming and the relative paucity of large capitalist estates. Consequently, the basis for the extensive introduction of socialist methods of farming, which in common with most Marxists of their time they equated with large-scale collective agriculture, had not yet been laid.[3]

Yet at the same time they did contend that significant changes had taken place in the countryside since 1906, when the party had last revised its agrarian programme. First, the erosion of the old feudal estates of the gentry had been accelerated, partly as a consequence of the Stolypin reforms. Similarly, the *obshchina* had been stripped of land in order to satisfy the demands of an emergent peasant bourgeoisie for large, individual farms. Finally, the recent rise in grain prices, after decades of decline, had provided a marked stimulus to capitalist agriculture in Russia. While not amounting to a total economic transformation of the countryside, these developments meant that capitalism had made considerable advances there, particularly evident in the growing number of large *pomeshchik* estates run on capitalist lines.[4]

But more than that, they also emphasised that the essential character of the revolution in 1917 was quite different to what it had been in 1905–6. Then, in the course of what was still a bourgeois-democratic revolution against feudal absolutism, division of the large landed estates had been the appropriate policy to pursue. Land division then, according to Ivan Skvortsov-Stepanov, would have caused 'the destruction of *pomeshchik* landownership, the prop of the old [autocratic] political order'. Equally, by destroying the estates of the gentry which remained feudal it would have removed the obstacles to 'the rapid development of agriculture through capitalism to socialism'.[5] However, in 1917 bourgeois-democratic revolution had given way to socialist revolution. This change too had to be taken into account in framing agrarian policy, as Skvortsov-Stepanov intimated in April

1917 at the Second City Party Conference in Moscow. Land division was no longer a suitable course of action. Rather than facilitate the transformation of the countryside along socialist lines it would do nothing but destroy what progress had been made and surrender 'agriculture into the power of petty-bourgeois illusions'.[6]

In these circumstances, they insisted that nationalisation of the land, encompassing the confiscation of *pomeshchik* and church estates, was essential to destroy the economic power of counter-revolutionary forces in the countryside. It was even more vital, however, to ensure that those farms which had become capitalist, in particular the large estates, were preserved intact. They would form the initial links in a slowly growing chain of large-scale, collective socialist agriculture. At the same time, the poor peasants were to be encouraged to unite and set up their own collectives, presumably to be provided with the needed equipment and seed stocks by the revolutionary state.[7] No other policy would establish the foundations for the future development of socialism in agriculture. Land division must be avoided at all costs, as Bukharin had stressed at the Sixth Party Congress in the summer of 1917, in particular lest it produce a large class of 'satiated' peasant proprietors who would desert the revolution to defend their newly-won property.[8] Moreover, land division would reverse the stratification that he believed had intensified recently in the countryside, the division of the peasantry into a bourgeois minority and a pauperised majority. The latter, itself becoming increasingly proletarianised according to Innokentii Stukov, was alone considered to be a reliable ally of the proletariat and was to be encouraged to conduct a class war against the landlords and their richer capitalist neighbours in the interests of consolidating the revolution.[9]

For all Lenin's 'awareness (uncommon among Russian Marxists of his time) that Russian revolutionaries could not very well ignore the peasant majority of the population',[10] for much of 1917 he gave no clear indication of the compromises that he would become prepared to make to secure the support of the peasants for – or at the very least 'neutralise' their opposition to[11] – a seizure of power by the Bolsheviks. On his return to Russia in April, 1917, in *The*

*April Theses,* he baldly outlined the agrarian programme that he believed the party now must adopt:

The weight of the emphasis in the agrarian programme to be shifted to the Soviets of Agricultural Labourers' Deputies.
Confiscation of all landed estates.
Nationalisation of *all* lands in the country, the land to be disposed of by the local Soviets of Agricultural Labourers' and Peasants' Deputies. The organisation of separate Soviets of Deputies of Poor Peasants. The setting up of a model farm on each of the large estates (ranging in size from 100 to 300 dessiatines, according to local and other conditions, and to the decisions of the local bodies) under the control of the Soviets of Agricultural Labourers' Deputies and for the public account.[12]

Lenin frankly admitted that nationalisation of the land *per se* did not amount to socialism. During the April Conference he conceded that far from being incompatible with capitalism land nationalisation was 'a grand bourgeois project'. But while not socialist in itself, nevertheless it remained progressive. Not only would nationalisation 'representing as it does the abolition of private ownership of the land . . . deal such a powerful blow to private ownership of all the means of production in general', it would also destroy 'feudalistic big landownership and all the feudal fetters of the entire system of landownership and land tenure'.[13] The destruction of feudalism would hasten the process of class polarisation in the countryside, already much accelerated by the Stolypin reforms. The peasantry would become stratified ever more clearly into, on the one hand, a small minority of wealthy proprietors (a peasant bourgeoisie) and, on the other hand, a large majority of poor, semi-proletarian peasants and agricultural labourers. The latter, Lenin insisted, were to be organised in separate soviets and won over to the side of the urban proletariat, to advance the revolution towards socialism.[14]

At the same time he warned the party against harbouring any illusions about the prospects for the immediate introduction of socialism in Russia, especially in the countryside. Again at the April Conference he scathingly dismissed any such thinking as 'the height of absurdity' in a country where '[t]he majority of the population are peasants, small farmers who can have no idea of socialism'.[15] Yet he also had no illusions about the future of small-scale peasant farming. He too, as the majority of Marxists of his time, was convinced that peasant farming was doomed to extinction in face of competition from large-scale, mechanised agriculture, just as small-scale manufacturing had increasingly been displaced by large-scale industrial production. He reiterated what he had argued repeatedly before 1917, that 'small-scale farming under commodity production [could] not save mankind from poverty and oppression'.[16] In Russia in particular, land division was no solution to the impoverishment of the countryside. In the first place there was insufficient land to provide all the rural poor with an adequate plot, and in the second place it would prove impossible to supply them with the livestock, equipment and seed reserves required for proper cultivation.[17]

For Lenin the only solution to this problem, and the only basis for the eventual socialist restructuring of the countryside, remained the development of large-scale collective agriculture. At the caucus of Bolshevik delegates to the All-Russian Conference of Soviets in April 4; at the April Conference; even in the face of peasant scepticism at the First Congress of Peasant Deputies in May, he insisted on the preservation of the existing large estates intact for common cultivation – and, in fact, not so large estates, as 100 dessiatines was, according to E. H. Carr, 'a low limit for [that] category'.[18] They were to become the foundations of the socialist agriculture of the future. He hastened to emphasise, however, that collective cultivation, while 'a difficult business', could not be imposed upon the peasants by *fiat*. He anticipated that the superiority of large-scale mechanised farming would induce the peasants '*by force of example*' to embrace such a system voluntarily.[19] Quite logically he was then able to reassure the small and middle peasants that the continuation of the revolution towards socialism would not necessitate the forcible expropriation of their property.[20]

The prescriptions outlined by Lenin in his *April Theses* in all their essentials were adopted as policy by the party at its April Conference, although not without some dissent. A. I.

Rykov for one questioned, 'with paralyzing ideological consistency' as Esther Kingston-Mann has wrily remarked,
whether it was at all realistic to contemplate winning the
peasantry, petty-bourgeois proprietors all, over to the cause
of socialist revolution. N. S. Angarskii too cast doubts on
Lenin's understanding of peasant aspirations, suggesting
that what the peasants sought was not nationalisation but the
transfer of the land into their own possession.[21] And later, at
the Sixth Party Congress, Evgenii Preobrazhenskii expressed
additional reservations from the Left. He asked what a policy
designed to foster an alliance between the proletariat and the
poorest peasants in fact meant, as no one yet had defined
precisely who the poorest peasants were or how an alliance
with them was to be made effective.[22] Such concerns notwithstanding, there did not seem to be any serious basis for a
major split between Lenin and the Left of the party on the
question of agriculture. They appeared to be in agreement
on the broad, if at times nebulous, lines of what the party's
agrarian policy should be.

From the late summer, however, Lenin began to espouse
increasingly 'heretical' views on agriculture. In all probability, news of an escalation in seizures of gentry estates land by
the peasants led him to reflect anew on what their aspirations
were. His reappraisal was self-confessedly shaped by the
model mandate, *The Peasant Mandate on the Land*, published
in *Izvestiia Vserossiiskago Soveta Krest'ianskikh Deputatov* on 19
August, based on the 242 resolutions which various peasant
organisations had submitted to the First Congress of Peasant
Deputies indicating the changes that they sought in the
countryside. On 29 August he signalled his willingness to
bow to this expression of peasant demands to win their
support. In *From a Publicist's Diary. Peasants and Workers*, he
conceded that '[w]e [the Bolsheviks] . . . can and will give you
what the peasant poor want and are searching for. . .'.[23] In
essence, he was now prepared to accept land socialisation,
including 'equalised distribution of land among the working
people', which hitherto he had categorically resisted. Still
clinging to his belief in the superiority of large-scale agriculture he thus added that 'the highly efficient farms must not
be "divided up"', presumably in the hope of preserving them
as the oases of collective agriculture in a desert of petty

peasant farms.[24] He justified his continued defence of model farms by reference to the third and fourth points of *The Peasant Mandate*, where demands for the preservation of the advanced, specialist estates were expressed.[25]

Yet soon he was to downplay, publicly at least, any emphasis on collective agriculture. His work *The Tasks of the Revolution*, for instance, written in September, contained no reference to the preservation of model estates.[26] As he openly admitted shortly after the Bolsheviks came to power, he had shifted his ground on the question of agrarian policy. Just as peace was 'not a Bolshevik policy' but that of the majority of the population, so too was the decree on land which had been 'taken bodily from peasant mandates'.[27] With characteristic vigour he justified his change of tack. The victory of the revolution, he argued, demanded that the party yield to peasant aspirations. But, he hastily and rather sanguinely continued, the party could do so certain in the knowledge that land division was not fundamentally inimical to the eventual transition to socialism in the countryside, especially in a country such as Russia where large-scale farming remained far from predominant. Provided power remained 'in the hands of a workers' and peasants' government, if workers' control has been introduced, the banks nationalised, a ... supreme economic body set up to direct (regulate) the *entire* economic life of the country', then the future for socialism would be secure.[28] At this stage in the revolution he had apparently neglected to consider fully what obstacles the creation of a 'satiated', and a less stratified, peasantry might pose for the construction of socialism in Russia, as well as the immediate impact of land division on agrarian productivity.

Despite this retreat, and the absence of overt references to 'model estates', Lenin had not abandoned his ultimate commitment to large-scale collective agriculture. The land socialisation law of February, 1918, was not quite a total surrender. While sanctioning 'distribution of the land among the toilers ... on an equal basis' it also sought 'to encourage the collective system of agriculture at the expense of individual farming, the former being more economical and leading to socialistic economy', and to establish 'model farms and experiment stations'.[29] At the Seventh Party Congress in

March he again insisted that the Soviet government, despite its agreement to land division, would continue to 'give preference to communes and big labour co-operatives'.[30] In the first months after the revolution, however, these commitments remained largely statements of intent and in practice, as Wesson has pointed out, little was done to foster the development of collective agriculture.[31]

The Left Communists had no doubt that Lenin had compromised party policy. Unconvinced by his defence of his *volte-face*, in the first months of 1918 they openly assailed him for his acceptance of what was essentially the agrarian programme of the SRs, for what in their minds was an abrogation of socialist principles. One of their opponents encapsulated, with commendable brevity and accuracy, the essence of their critique:

> The new land law is characterised by the majority of its critics as a reactionary act. Its reactionary character is seen chiefly in that it opens the way to small-scale farming, that it creates and increases the number of 'petty farms', that it produces an inevitable shift of all agriculture towards a natural economy, which inevitably entails a fall in its productivity.[32]

Such objections were articulated most cogently and forcefully by Preobrazhenskii. He contended that 'the chief task' facing the new Soviet government in the countryside, 'after the liquidation of *pomeshchik* landownership', was 'the reconstruction of agriculture on socialist lines'. Regrettably, he continued, the projected land socialisation law did but little, if anything, to further this objective. Even worse, it threatened to destroy whatever progress already had been made in this direction.[33] Convinced that large-scale agriculture was more productive than small-scale farming, he condemned the projected land law for its failure even to preserve the existing large estates:

> The protection of capitalist farms from disintegration and their transfer, intact, into the hands of the Soviets has not been envisaged. On the contrary, there is a point about rewarding the *batraki* with land ... which presupposes the breaking-up of such farms into small allotments. This is

both fundamentally reactionary from the economic point of view and deeply unjust to the agricultural proletariat.[34]

Developing his argument, rather ironically, in a manner reminiscent of that of Lenin in the spring of 1917, Preobrazhenskii proceeded to outline the economic consequences which he was certain would follow from land division. The majority of the peasants, especially the poor, had insufficient stocks of seed, tools and especially draught power to work effectively any allotments of land granted to them. If the large estates were parcelled out amongst them, there could be only one outcome – the precipitate fall in production in the countryside. In turn, urban Russia, already suffering hunger because of the destructive impact of war on agrarian productivity, would become threatened even more gravely with starvation. In these difficult circumstances, he concluded, the Soviet government 'could not allow itself the luxury of uncontrolled small-scale agriculture . . .'.[35]

Skvortsov-Stepanov shared, and later expanded upon, Preobrazhenskii's fears. Equalised division of the land amongst the peasantry, he agreed, would lead to an immediate fall in productivity. But in the longer term land socialisation would be economically retrogressive too. The modern equipment already present in the countryside, as well as any additional flow of machinery that might follow upon the demobilisation of industry when the war ended, could not be used optimally unless the existing large estates were preserved and new collectives created. The economies of scale that mechanisation promised could be achieved only on very large farms, not in a system of peasant small-holdings. Land socialisation, which amounted to the destruction of all the large estates, would not only bring back a considerably less efficient mode of production to rural Russia but also would thwart any technical advance there. Future progress towards a more efficient system of large-scale, mechanised agriculture would be precluded, and any potential for socialist transformation of the countryside virtually eliminated.[36]

The Left Communists' oppositions to land socialisation, however, was not simply the product of narrow economic concerns. Their fears of its political consequences were equally, if not more, pronounced, echoing the anxieties voiced by Bukharin at the Sixth Party Congress. Heirs to the virulent anti-peasantism embodied in Russian Marxism, they too mistrusted, even feared, the peasants, whom they considered to be inalienably hostile to socialism. As Preobrazhenskii rather scornfully claimed, the peasantry, comprising myriads of atomised small property-holders, could not be considered to be a socialist class, a theme echoed and expanded later by Bukharin in his major treatise on sociology, *Historical Materialism*.[37] They believed the peasants to be immured in 'the idiocy of rural life', in the main ignorant, politically naive and vulnerable to reactionary influences.[38] It was imperative, therefore, to resist land socialisation. If implemented, in the short term all that it would achieve would be to destroy the only reliable allies of the urban proletariat in the countryside, the *batraki*. The grant of land to these rural labourers would transform them into petty proprietors, opposed to further advances to socialism. The middle peasants too would gain land and would tenaciously defend their enlarged plots. In sum, the swelling in the ranks of the peasantry would so strengthen the forces of counter-revolution as to pose immense obstacles to the introduction of collective socialist agriculture in the future.[39]

In the long term the impact of land socialisation would be, if anything, more pernicious. Millions of peasants who would have been allotted land would be unable to work it as they would lack the means to do so. The government itself did not possess the equipment, livestock and seed to alleviate all the existing shortages. In consequence, the land would gradually fall into the hands of the more prosperous peasants who did have the wherewithal to work it. Land division, therefore, was a myopic policy. Rather than benefitting the poor and exploited peasants in the long term it simply planted the seeds for the eventual re-emergence of capitalism in the countryside.[40] Their socio-political objections to land socialisation have been reduced to the fact

> that the new law, impregnated as it is with individualism, disunites the labouring peasant masses, atomises them and opens the doors wide for the creation of a rural petty-bourgeoisie, which, economically backward and feeble, is a very reactionary class, *everywhere, always and in every respect*.[41]

To minimise the threat of peasant reaction and to promote the development of socialism in the countryside the Left Communists in the main – those in the Ukraine remained something of an exception, as we shall see in Chapter 7 below – defended what, with some justification, they believed party policy to have been in 1917. Their *Theses on the Current Situation* contained a bald statement of their continuing objectives, if one lacking in details of how they were to be achieved:

> The organisation in the countryside of an attack by the poor peasants on the rich, the development of large-scale socialised agriculture and support for modes of working the land by poor peasants which are transitional to socialised agriculture.[42]

Earlier, in January and February, in the midst of the controversy over the land socialisation law, Preobrazhenskii had begun to articulate what such a policy would involve. Developing ideas elaborated during 1917, he argued, first, that the large capitalist estates must be preserved intact. They were to be transferred to the control of the local soviets who were to make the necessary arrangements for their collective cultivation by the *batraki*. Second, poor peasants who lacked the draught power, equipment and seed stocks to work the land independently were to be organised into *artels*. The state would provide the means for cultivation and so check the tendency for the land of such peasants to fall into the hands of their richer neighbours. Third, migration was to be encouraged: specifically, the resettlement of poor peasants onto land especially prepared for them by the state. Again, they were to work this land collectively, with resources provided by the state.[43]

The Left Communists appear to have recognised that in themselves these measures would not be sufficient to transform the countryside along socialist lines. Certainly, the development of large-scale collective agriculture would increase productivity. But, as one of their critics repeatedly pointed out, socialism demanded more, that all production, agrarian as well as industrial, be regulated according to a general plan for the entire economy. He conceded that the more large estates there were, the easier it would be to plan for the agrarian sector. Nevertheless, if socialism was to be achieved the plan had to be extended to incorporate the remaining small peasant farms too.[44]

While aware of the need for this degree of planning, the Left Communists failed to explain quite how they envisioned achieving it. In a manner somewhat reminiscent of Hilferding, Bukharin expressed the vague hope that once Soviet control over industry was established, then 'the incorporation of even small peasant farming into the sphere of the general organisation of production' would inevitably develop.[45] Preobrazhenskii too recognised the vital role of planning. He argued for a strict state monopoly over all trade in grain. A crucial part of a more general scheme for planned distribution of all resources, he contended that such a system would serve to ensure that the economic interests of both the poor peasants and the proletariat were protected. He rather lamely concluded, however, that '[h]ere is not the place to talk of how to implement this plan . . .'.[46]

The Left Communists frankly admitted that implementation of their programme was dependent upon 'the organisation of socialist class struggle' in the countryside. It was essential to win over not just the poor peasant majority but also the bulk of the middle peasantry to undertake such a course of action. These peasants, they concluded rather sanguinely, would come to realise that the gains made by them during the revolution could only be secured by lining up firmly behind the urban proletariat and eliminating their capitalist, and counter-revolutionary, neighbours in the countryside.[47]

In sum, all these measures were seen to be the prerequisites for the 'socialist reconstruction of agriculture', guaranteeing the collectivism that Preobrazhenskii and others on the Left regarded as essential for socialism. Any other policy would simply create a fertile breeding ground for individual farming and the reinforcement of petty-bourgeois attitudes.[48] Not only was it inappropriate in principle for any socialist government, wittingly or unwittingly, to permit such developments to take place: more seriously, they would prove to be fatal for the revolution. As we have seen in Chapter 3, the Left Communists were terrified by what they saw as the corruptive influence of the peasantry on the prosecution of socialist objectives by the Soviet government. This influence was all-pervasive, not simply confined to the question of agriculture. For the Left, the preparedness of Lenin and his faction to accept a separate peace with Germany had been but one instance of a more general compromise of socialist principles to peasant prejudices. Even more troubling, they were certain that such sacrifices soon would extend further. In the spring Karl Radek rather gloomily reiterated their very worst fears:

> ... and the victory of proletarian revolution in Europe may allow the proletarian minority in Russia to place the peasantry on socialist rails. The absence of this revolution can cast the proletariat from power. If the Soviet government, standing on the point of view of a dictatorship of the proletariat and the peasantry ... takes into account the numerical and social preponderance of the peasantry, then it will proceed to a compromise with capital, a compromise acceptable from the point of view of the peasantry, but one which destroys the socialist character of the revolution and therefore unacceptable to the proletariat.[49]

\* \* \*

Many of the Left Communists' fears concerning the impact of the government's agrarian policy were well-founded. The economic criticisms which they levelled against land socialisation had considerable foundation. It finally destroyed the large estates which had produced, according to Malle, an estimated 70 per cent of all marketed grain before the war. Hence in the short run the potential surplus, at least the most easily attainable surplus, that hitherto had gone to feed the towns appears to have been significantly reduced, so exacerbating the already serious food crisis in urban Russia. This situation was made yet worse by the fact that livestock and farm equipment were not redistributed to the same extent as the land. Lack of these resources prevented many peasants in consequence from being able to work the land they had newly acquired, so diminishing vital production even further. In the longer term it also reduced what Lev Kritsman termed 'the agrarian base of industry and the towns'. What he meant was that peasant farming, particularly within the confines of the economically backward communes, now revived in larger numbers than ever, would produce much less of a surplus which could be tapped for the development of Russian industry than would large-scale agriculture.[50]

Politically, the short-term impact of equalised land division was to strengthen the ranks of the middle peasantry, with a corresponding reduction in the numbers of poor and land-less peasants – Siberia and much of the Ukraine remained exceptions, with marked inequalities in landholding persisting. Despite that fact that the bulk of the peasants received little additional land, in most instances less than one dessiatine (2.7 acres); despite the fact that livestock and equipment were not redistributed equally; nevertheless land socialisation, encompassing not just the estates of the gentry but also those *kulaks* who had set up large holdings outside the commune, had served to reduce differentiation within the peasantry.[51] Consequently, the villages were considerably more homogeneous than before, more united and resistant to Bolshevik efforts, rather utopian efforts as it transpired, to fan the flames of class war in the countryside in the spring and summer of 1918. Much of Bukharin's gloomy prophecy at the Sixth Party Congress seemed to have been fulfilled.[52]

During the spring and early summer of 1918 Lenin himself increasingly came to share many of their concerns, so much so that he again markedly changed the direction of Bolshevik policy towards the peasants. Increasing difficulty in keeping the towns fed were at the root of this change of tack, as he frequently professed. By early June he finally conceded that '[s]erious famine has driven us to a purely communist task ... a revolutionary socialist task' in the countryside.[53] Despite the swingeing losses of grain-producing areas flowing from the Brest peace, losses which greatly exacerbated the food crisis, he optimistically concluded that sufficient grain remained to feed the people, albeit 'only just enough'.[54] The problem, the cause of the food crisis, was the selfishness of the peasants, 'many millions of petty property-owners, the petty-bourgeois element, who look at everything from the standpoint of their own narrow interests', manifest in their unwillingness to surrender their grain surpluses.[55] His solution to this problem was to adopt what were essentially Left Communist policies. In a certain desperation, he now urged the intensification of the class struggle in the countryside. His intent was to win over the poor peasants, whom he alleged, with no small degree of exaggeration, in a letter of 26 July to Clara Zetkin, 'everywhere ... are for us',[56] to support the workers in attacking the *kulaks* and appropriating the surplus in their possession. At the same time, considerably more attention was to be paid to establishing collective forms of agriculture.[57] The period of compromise with the peasantry was over. In early July, at the Fifth All-Russian Congress of Soviets, he candidly conceded that the Bolsheviks 'may have made a mistake in embodying your [SR] socialisation of the land in our law....'[58]

It would appear that much of the Left Communists' critique of land socialisation had been vindicated. Yet the problem remains that their own policies could not be successfully implemented in the Russian countryside of 1918. Even disregarding the question whether Russia had the technology that their strategy demanded – and it is certain that it did not possess the equipment required for the extensive introduction of large-scale mechanised agriculture – there was also the intractable problem of peasant attitudes. Whatever the Soviet government, any government, might have desired, the overwhelming majority of the peasants desired the implementation of their long-sought *chernyi peredel*, the equal division of all the land, as Lenin had come to accept during the summer of 1917. No government then had the power to impose upon the peasants policies which they felt to be unacceptable, as the Provisional Government had discovered to its dismay in 1917. No government too could foment class war amongst the peasants, who in the main united to resist pressures from without the village. Bluntly, peasant attitudes were antipathetic to Left Communist visions of socialist agriculture. As Klementii acidly remarked, their programme simply was not feasible since 'the subjective conditions for the socialist reorganisation of agriculture ... have not yet appeared'.[59] V. Meshcheriakov elaborated upon this theme:

But was it really possible to undertake in November, as an immediate task, the bringing about of socialism – the system of socialised labour on socialised land? Everybody can understand that this was not possible ... The peasant masses have no idea what socialism means and want only a free additional allotment of land on egalitarian principles. We had to accept that programme as it was ...

Conceding that he still believed that land socialisation was 'a considerable improvement on the old order' he nevertheless concluded that regrettably there was 'not a grain of socialism in it....'.[60]

In these circumstances there was little likelihood of the Left Communists' own programme being accepted by the peasantry. Short of arresting the millions of peasants who did not realise where their true interests lay, as Bukharin was alleged to have professed on the morrow of the October Revolution,[61] a task well beyond the Bolsheviks' strength, they had little choice but to bow to the reality of the Russian countryside. Their continuing failure during the period of War Communism to mould the countryside as they desired led to further compromises with and concessions to the peasants in the NEP period – until in the late 1920s Stalin grasped the nettle and brutally coerced the peasantry into accepting a policy in many respects similar to that advocated by the Left Communists in 1918.

# 5 The Organisation of Industry

In the spring of 1918, the debate on agrarian policy became muted, and the focus of the conflict between Lenin and the Left Communists shifted to questions of political and industrial organisation. This chapter will concentrate on the latter issue. Again, the root of this conflict lay in Lenin's apparent apostasy, that is, his rejection of principles that the Left Communists believed to have become accepted Bolshevik policy in 1917. However, the matter is rather more complex as, in truth, the Bolsheviks self-professedly had failed to elaborate a coherent and unambiguous programme for industrial administration in 1917. Vladimir Smirnov conceded as much in the spring of 1918 when he admitted that 'at the beginning of the revolution we had given very little thought to the question ... of the organisation of production along socialist lines'.[1] In his major theoretical work of 1918, *Stroitel'stvo sotsializma*, Osinskii confirmed the substance of Smirnov's evaluation: 'But if we ask ourselves how, in the period before 25 October, we as a party envisaged the system of workers' control in its entirety and on what sort of economic basis we thought to construct it, then we shall find no clear answer anywhere.'[2] Moreover, several weeks before the October revolution, Lenin himself had insisted that it would be 'inexpedient' then to try to draw up too detailed a programme on such questions.[3] Shortly after the revolution he admitted that in fact '[t]here was not and could not be a definite plan for the organisation of economic life'.[4]

This *lacuna* in Bolshevik thinking made itself felt in the first weeks after October. The decree on workers' control of 14 November, based in large part on Lenin's draft, posited a radical devolution of power to the factory-plant committees at the enterprise level, with the proviso that they should be subject to control by regional councils, which in turn would be responsible to an All-Russian Council of Workers' Control (ARCWC). Whatever the difficulties of making such a complex hierarchical system work effectively may have been, in addition, so Steve Smith argues, 'the Decree did not spell out in detail how workers' control was to be implemented'.[5] Moreover, the ARCWC did not survive long. At the beginning of December it was absorbed into the Supreme Council of the National Economy (*Vesenkha*), established primarily to introduce planned regulation of the economy from the centre, an objective, as we shall see, that in the final analysis was to be incompatible with the decentralist spirit of the decree on workers' control.[6]

However, while the Bolsheviks may have failed to elaborate a 'well-defined program' for the organisation of industry before October,[7] the Left Communists clearly believed that certain general principles had been agreed upon by all, including Lenin. As we saw in Chapter 2, the prerequisite was the smashing of the existing state apparatus. Once it had been destroyed and replaced by a dictatorship of the proletariat, this new state must intervene to manage the economy in order to save it from total collapse. Any such attempts at regulation undertaken by the old regime had to be resisted since they would serve only to strengthen state capitalism which, to those on the Left of the Party certainly, was nothing but 'the cruellest form of class oppression'.[8] Once established, the proletarian state must first nationalise the finance-capitalist sector of the economy, that is, the large banks and industrial syndicates and cartels, which had grown so dramatically during World War I that, as the Left alleged, they dominated Russian industry.[9] Production in this sector then was to be organised according to the directives issued by a central planning agency, such as the *Vesenkha*. Central planning was an integral part of their vision of socialism, not an expedient.[10] Otherwise, only anarcho-syndicalism, to which they were vehemently opposed, would develop. Furthermore, to ensure that these central directives were carried out faithfully by management at the enterprise level – the precise composition of these basic units of industrial administration remained ill-defined, although a role for the existing technical personnel (*spetsy*) was implied – supervisory powers were to be devolved to the various local organs of workers' control, the factory-plant committees, the trade unions and the economic committees of the local soviets. Workers' control, organised 'from the bottom to the top',

Bukharin argued in the summer, was a vital part of the new order.[11] However, in the summer of 1917 Osinskii, 'implacable and extremist' in Cohen's opinion, went further.[12] Workers' control, he posited, would remain meaningless as long as the bourgeoisie retained any positions of authority in industry. It would abuse its power to sabotage production, so deepening the economic ruin gripping the country. Such mismanagement, experience to date suggested, could not be thwarted simply by workers' control. Moreover, the very concept of control would be redundant under a dictatorship of the proletariat since then the direct and active participation of the workers in the organisation of production would be the order of the day. In essence, the notion of workers' management had been mooted, even if the precise form that it would take still remained undefined, as Osinskii later acknowledged.[13]

Distribution was to be similarly regulated. All existing consumer goods, for example, were to be appropriated by the agencies of the new state and disbursed in a planned manner, especially amongst the peasants in return for grain to feed the towns. Again, control over this process was to be devolved to the local organs of the workers who were to take over the various distributive agencies set up by the state and the bourgeoisie during the war, notably the food committees and other *zemstvo* and municipal *duma* organisations.[14] Implicit in this vision of social regulation of distribution was the replacement of the market by the planned exchange of goods, as Lomov made explicit on the eve of the October revolution.[15]

Central regulation of industrial production and distribution, executed at the grass roots by local organs of revolutionary power, would serve, they believed, to overcome the disintegration and sabotage that increasingly were paralysing Russian industry in 1917. Equally, such a system, by ensuring a substantial degree of local autonomy for the workers, would be a giant step towards socialism.[16] The Left Communists repeatedly stressed that the diffusion of economic power was vital if the workers *en masse* were to achieve full emancipation. For this to occur they must have the opportunity to become active and conscious participants in the construction of socialism. The absence of such participation would threaten the very success of the socialist project, as Bukharin warned soon after the revolution:

Without the greatest self-activity [*samodeiatel'nost'*] of the masses, there will be no victory. And just as the proletariat in its armed struggle produced a Red Guard, so it must create a guard of organisers in the factories, the plants, the mines . . . and the offices. If it does this, then the victory of socialism will be assured.[17]

In 1918 the Left Communists were to elaborate upon the indispensability of such a system, in Sirianni's opinion essentially one of democratic self-management of the production process by workers at the enterprise level, if socialism was to be realised.[18]

In large part, their vision appeared to coincide with Lenin's own thinking on industrial organisation in 1917. He too called for the nationalisation of the banks and large industrial syndicates.[19] Moreover, he frequently emphasised the importance of workers' control as a mechanism to regulate production and distribution and prevent total economic collapse.[20] Indeed, there were times when Lenin's faith in the capacities of the workers seems to have been no less boundless than that of the Left Communists. While he may never have developed a consistent theory of workers' *management*, as several Western historians have argued, defined as the workers taking the fundamental decisions on what and how to produce, as opposed to workers' control, or supervision of decisions taken by existing managers,[21] on occasion he came close to advocating it. Shortly after October he unequivocally rejected the notion that 'the management of banks and factories were beyond the power of the workers', since factory life itself had provided them with 'the knowledge necessary for [its] accomplishment'.[22] The workers themselves, he soon added, had to organise industry from below, on their own initiative, relying on their own self-discipline, not on 'capitalist barracks room discipline'.[23]

However, Lenin's thinking in 1917 on this question was ambivalent. Another, less democratic and less participatory, model of industrial organisation co-existed with the one sketched above: the state capitalist model, or the programme of 'organic construction' as the Left Communists were to dub it in 1918.[24] The mechanics of this model were outlined most fully in his works of September and early October, *The Impending Catastrophe and How To Combat It* and *Can The Bolsheviks Retain State Power?*. This model also presupposed the nationalisation of the banks, and the existing syndicates in the sugar, oil, coal, iron and steel industries; the compulsory syndicalisation of other industries; and the organisation of the population into consumer societies.[25] The consolidation of these, the most advanced and progressive features of capitalist economic organisation, would serve two purposes. First, they would act as the economic framework within which the revolutionary government could regulate production and distribution and so save Russia from economic collapse and famine. Second, they would provide the foundations upon which the planned socialist economy of the future could be built.[26] However, if this economic apparatus was to be used effectively, then it was essential that the old capitalists, or bourgeois 'rascal[s]',[27] as Lenin later dubbed them, and their trained, technical elite, the *spetsy*, be employed to administer it, by high wages if possible, by coercion if need be. 'Comprehensive workers' control', he added, would ensure that they worked in the interests of the new order.[28] In a manner quite contrary to his professions of faith in the abilities of ordinary workers to run industry, in this instance he attested that it would be utopian to expect them to be able to do so immediately after the revolution.[29]

For this system to be effective, he continued, strict centralisation was essential, within the economy in general and in each branch of production in particular. In other words, the economic decision-making prerogatives of the factory-plant committees, the trades unions and the local soviets were to be tightly circumscribed. With power in the hands of the proletarian state, Lenin argued, 'we shall be fully and unreservedly in favour of a strong state power and of centralism'.[30]

In the spring of 1918 Lenin turned decisively to the state-capitalist model, claiming that it offered the only possible solution to Russia's calamitous industrial decline. His promotion of this system brought him into open conflict with the Left of the party on the whole issue of how industry ought to be organised in the post-revolutionary state. The failure of socialist revolution to engulf the rest of Europe was the immediate precipitant of this rift. Not only had it forced many Bolsheviks, impelled by Lenin's ruthless logic, slowly but surely to abandon the policy of revolutionary war and accept the punitive peace imposed by the Germans at Brest-Litovsk. But this peace, in turn, signalled a turning-point within Soviet Russia itself, a retreat in internal policy, as the Left Communists repeatedly charged.[31] The Bolsheviks found themselves in an unanticipated, and most unwelcome, quandary. Before October virtually none of them had imagined that they might have to proceed to lay the foundations for socialism in Russia alone.

In Lenin's case, it compelled him to reappraise what had to be done if the revolution in Russia was to survive until its final victory was secured by the eventual triumph of international revolution. In late February and early March he increasingly came to grasp that the restoration of the truncated Russian economy was essential if this end was to be achieved. But if economic reconstruction was to succeed, Lenin now believed, the libertarian post-revolutionary order which he had ostensibly depicted most fully in *State and Revolution*, and continued to defend in the first months after October, had to be renounced. No longer did he argue, as he had at the very end of December 1917, that 'every rank and file worker and peasant who can read and write, who can judge people and has practical experience, is capable of *organisational* work'.[32] The means by which he now sought to revitalise the economy, as soon became clear, were quite different. At the Seventh Party Congress in early March he emphasised discipline, organisation, efficiency as the watchwords for recovery.[33] Addressing the Bolshevik fraction on the eve of the Fourth All-Russian Congress of Soviets on 13 March, he hammered home that what was critical for the survival of socialism in Russia was 'discipline, discipline and discipline and in the struggle for ... this discipline we must adopt Draconic [sic] measures ...'.[34] Workers' control as it had existed hitherto, he alleged, with 'endless discussions and endless holdings of meetings',[35] had now ceased to play a positive role. If anything, it was exacerbating the economic chaos which had been bequeathed to the Bolshevik regime.

While continuing to pay heed to the need for such discussions to prepare 'the masses for participation in state and economic administration of all the affairs of society', in no way were they to be allowed at the expense of economic recovery. This above all required obedience to the orders of management, of 'one-man-managerial authority' if necessary, whose powers over the production process were to be restored.[36] A turning-point in the revolution had indeed arrived, as Lenin himself conceded at the end of March, a turning-point when the triumphal march of Soviet power had to give way to a new period of economic and social reconstruction.[37]

Then, in the spring of 1918, Lenin, as we saw in Chapter 2, if not the Left Communists, began to reappraise the extent of Russia's economic development before the revolution. State capitalism, 'the threshold of socialism', he now concluded, had not advanced sufficiently to permit an immediate transition to socialism in Russia. Economic recovery demanded that the Soviet government itself encourage its growth, so creating the bases for socialist economic construction in the future. In defence of his programme, he reminded his comrades at a session of the CEC on 29 April that he had elaborated such a strategy before October:

> I said that state capitalism would be our salvation; if we had it in Russia, the transition to full socialism would be easy . . . Allow me to remind you that I had occasion to write my statement about state capitalism some time before the revolution . . . in my pamphlet *The Impending Catastrophe*. . . .[38]

Lenin relentlessly repeated that the implementation of the system of state capitalism that he had sketched in the late summer of 1917 was the only means by which Soviet Russia could be saved from impending economic catastrophe. Equally, he emphasised the need to introduce specific measures to raise the productivity of labour. As well as the strict reimposition of the old, hierarchical forms of labour discipline, he looked to material incentives, notably, to piece work, and the 'scientific and progressive' elements of the Taylor system to achieve this goal.[39] Provided it was a proletarian state that constructed such a system, he con-

tinued, then all would be well. This state could use its
political power to prevent degeneration towards a genuine
state-capitalist system and ensure that 'a step towards Socialism' was in fact taken.[40] In his most sustained and trenchant
critique of the Left Communists, *'Left-Wing' Childishness and
the Petty-Bourgeois Mentality*, Lenin succinctly defended his
programme:

> In the first place, economically, state capitalism is im-
> measurably superior to our present economic system. In
> the second place, there is nothing terrible in it for Soviet
> power, the Soviet state is a state in which the power of the
> workers and the poor is assured.[41]

To the Left Communists this was arrant, and, even worse,
dangerous nonsense. They agreed with Lenin that measures
had to be taken to deliver Russia from an economic collapse
so total that there would be no foundations left upon which
to construct socialism.[42] However, they were equally convinced that the policy of 'organic construction' now being
advanced by Lenin and his allies in the Party would prove to
be fatal for the reconstruction of Russia on socialist lines.

In part, their opposition to Lenin's policies was rooted in
the seemingly determinist conviction that in the final analysis
'politics is founded upon economics, and whoever possesses
the power of command over production sooner or later will
lay hold of political power'.[43] Accordingly, they totally rejected Lenin's claim that the promotion of state capitalism in
the economy would not prejudice Soviet power. Bukharin
agreed with Osinskii on this issue, heatedly reiterating that
state capitalism, in any shape or form, was quite incompatible
with the survival of socialism. He painted a despairing
picture of what he foresaw to be the inevitable outcome of
Lenin's policy of 'organic construction':

> We [Left Communists] look at the matter concretely: let us
> suppose that Soviet power (the dictatorship of the proletar-
> iat, supported by the poor peasants), while organising in
> name . . . state regulation, in fact transfers the business of
> administration to the 'organisers of trusts' (i.e. to the
> capitalists). What happens in that case? The real power of
> capital in the economy grows and becomes consolidated.

Meanwhile the political superstructure either little by little degenerates beyond recognition, or at a certain point 'bursts', because the protracted 'command power' of capital in the economy is incompatible with the 'command power' of the proletariat in politics.[44]

It fell to Osinskii to develop the Left Communists' fears more concretely. Apparently voicing the opinions of many ordinary workers, Osinskii wrote that he doubted if the old capitalist 'captains of industry' would or even could allow themselves to be used to run the economy in the interests of the proletariat. They were so immured by the mores of capitalism that they could not but act in a counter-revolutionary manner. Accordingly, echoing the fears of many rank-and-file workers, he warned Lenin against granting them any positions of power in the new economic structure since '. . . the danger exists that our "teachers" will not help us to build socialism, but, on the sly, they will create a real capitalist trust, they will conduct their own *class* policy'.[45] 'As long as the Riabushinskiis and Meshcherskiis remained masters of and ran their banks and plants', he continued elsewhere, 'then they would possess the means to "organise" white guards, conspire with foreign invaders, secretly sabotage production . . .'.[46] The only possible outcome of such an equivocal policy, he concluded, would be the emergence of a real state-capitalist system. No longer would the October revolution remain socialist, but in fact it would be transformed into a bourgeois revolution, one which had served merely to sweep away all the vestiges of feudalism in Russia.[47] And this, of course, was unthinkable.

They also advanced a detailed critique of the precise measures which Lenin proposed to employ to ensure the success of the state-capitalist path to economic recovery. The restoration of one-person management at the enterprise level, with managers appointed from above regardless of the wishes of the workers, and of a hierarchically centralised system of economic administration generally, would breed nothing but a rebirth of the dictatorial and bureaucratic methods characteristic of capitalism. Such measures could only stymie the active participation of the proletariat in the organisation of production. Similarly, the employment of the other trappings of the old system of capitalist exploitation (namely, authoritarian discipline over the work-force; piece wages, which encouraged workers to pursue individual, not collective, rewards and so instilled petty-bourgeois values into them; and the Taylor system, which dehumanised workers by converting them into mindless appendages of machines, routinely performing fragmented tasks decreed from above) was all anathema to Osinskii and his comrades on the Left of the Party.[48]

In particular, they singled out two heinous consequences of these proposed measures. On the one hand, the unity and solidarity of the proletariat would be shattered and its collectivism, so vital to socialism, destroyed.[49] On the other hand, the proletariat would again be transformed into a passive cog in the production process, deprived of any opportunity to participate actively in the administration of industry. The recrudescence of this facet of the old order especially alarmed the Left Communists. They passionately defended the principle of the conscious participation of the proletariat in economic as well as political administration to be the *sine qua non* of its socio-political emancipation from the habits of the capitalist past, and thus the lifeblood of genuine socialist construction. In a manner reminiscent of Bukharin on the morrow of October, Osinskii elaborated on their understanding of this principle:

> We stand for the construction of proletarian society by the class creativity [*samodeiatel'nost'*] of the workers themselves, not by orders from on high issued by the 'captains of industry' . . . We proceed from faith in the class consciousness, in the active class initiative, of the proletariat. It cannot be otherwise. If the proletariat does not know how to create the necessary preconditions for the socialist organisation of production, then no one can do this for it nor compel it to do this . . . Socialism, and the socialist organisation of production, must be constructed by the proletariat itself, or not at all, and something else will be constructed – state capitalism.[50]

If this principle, essentially one of workers' self-management, was abandoned, then the Left Communists were certain that socialism was doomed and the state capitalism which they so much despised and feared would emerge triumphant.

Retrospectively, Lev Kritsman was to offer a more philosophical defence of the need for workers' participation *en masse* in the building of socialism. In language akin to that of the young Marx, he emphasised that the fundamental objective of socialism, 'the further conquest and transformation of nature (the progress of technology) ... and the further conquest and transformation of the nature of man himself ... [was] a creative task'.[51] In order to achieve this final goal it was imperative that the proletariat, consciously and collectively, undertake the socialist transformation of society. It could do so, however, only if it was given the freedom to exercise its latent creative abilities and learn how to harness them in the very process of socialist construction. For Kritsman, and arguably for his comrades on the Left of the Party, this 'mass creativity [was] the basic characteristic of communism'.[52]

They advocated a model of economic reconstruction quite contrary to that of Lenin, claiming that it alone would ensure that the path towards socialism at least remained open in Russia. In so doing they elaborated on the principles which, in a more rudimentary manner, they had espoused in 1917. To prevent the restoration of capitalism in Russia all the banks and large-scale enterprises were to be nationalised. However, nationalisation *per se*, or 'statisation', as Bukharin had termed it in 1917,[53] although a necessary precondition, was insufficient to ensure development towards socialism. After all, the railways in Prussia were state-owned, as Osinskii pointedly remarked, but no one would contend that in consequence Prussia was socialist. More was required: what might be called the 'socialisation' of these sectors of the economy. To achieve this end, the first precondition remained the complete expropriation of the capitalists in these key sectors, the 'commanding heights of the economy', so that the fundamental – economic – basis of their power was destroyed once and for all.[54] Such a policy, of course, precluded the toleration of any form of joint state-private capitalist trusts, as Lenin had been prepared to contemplate during the negotiations with Meshcherskii in the winter and spring of 1918.[55] But there was another precondition that had to be satisfied before industry could be considered to be fully socialised. The enterprises subject to nationalisation were to be managed 'on socialist principles' (*na sotsialisticheskikh nachalakh*). Osinskii explained what this meant at the first All-Russian Congress of Economic Councils in May–June 1918. 'The internal operations of the nationalised enterprise[s]', he argued, 'should be such that the very organisation of production provided ... the firm foundation for the political dictatorship of the working class ... [and] created the economic dictatorship of the proletariat.'[56] In brief, workers' management was considered to be vital. Ideological and philosophical justification apart, such a system increasingly came to be seen by the Left Communists as the only solution to the escalating decline in production which they largely attributed to sabotage by the remaining bourgeoisie, as Osinskii himself had maintained in the summer of 1917.

However, within this new system of socialised industry, they did accept, albeit grudgingly, that the old bourgeois *spetsy* – but not the 'captains of industry' themselves – still had a vital role to play. As yet the proletariat had not built up its own trained cadres of engineers and technicians with the expertise required to run modern, large-scale industry, Accordingly, the old *spetsy*, the majority of whom remained hostile to the Bolsheviks, would have to be enticed – or coerced, if need be – to give their irreplaceable services to the new regime. High wages, they conceded, would have to be offered to these *spetsy* to buy their cooperation; but on no account were they to be given any key positions of command in the economy lest they exploit them in the same way as their former masters, to subvert the socialist reconstruction of Russia. They were to remain strictly subordinate and answerable to the organs of workers' management.[57]

Similarly, the *spetsy* were to be deprived of their traditional methods, of material incentives or the knout, for the maintenance of productivity and discipline. New work practices were to be introduced by the workers themselves, in whose class consciousness the Left Communists had such 'faith'. Once industry had been reorganised on socialist lines, the workers, through the agency of their trades unions and factory committees, were to establish output norms, to be fulfilled in return for a 'normal' living wage. Non-fulfilment would be dealt with by workers' courts, so Osinskii argued, which would take whatever action they deemed to be necessary to punish recalcitrants who *de facto* were sabotaging the construction of socialism.[58]

Osinskii, it transpired, was also of a sufficiently bold – or temerarious – disposition to attempt to sketch out in detail how this system of workers' management was to be constructed. He unequivocally rejected the system of one-man management by centrally-appointed commissars, acerbically remarking that it would preclude what even Lenin had considered to be vital in 1917, that every cook should be given the opportunity to learn how to administer the state. This principle, he proposed, should be extended to the economy.[59] Actual workers' administration of industry, right down to the level of the enterprise, was to be introduced.

Despite their commitment to a devolution of authority to the enterprise level, Osinskii and his fellow Leftists continued to have absolutely no truck with the syndicalist sentiments evident among certain groups of the Russian workers.[60] They vehemently denounced as anti-socialist any efforts by organs of workers' management to convert enterprises into their own property and run them in their own interests. If unchecked, they would reduce Russia to nothing but a myriad of atomised, self-governing, anarcho-syndicalist communes.[61] It was Bukharin who developed this theme most cogently. In the final analysis, the basic distinction between Communists and Anarchists, he argued, was not their attitude to the state and its power. While they disagreed regarding the role it was to play in the transition period – the Communists ascribed to it a vital role – both sought its ultimate extinction. Rather, what fundamentally divided them was that Communists were convinced that only a centrally-planned economy, in which large-scale production was predominant, would be able to provide the material basis of abundance, on which alone socialism could be founded. Like the SRs' faith in land socialisation, so too the anarchist dream of sharing-out property was economically retrogressive. It would only lead, first, to the re-creation of a class of small proprietors and, ultimately, to the restoration of large-scale capitalism.[62]

What the Left Communists were seeking was the creation of a genuinely democratic centralist system, which would combine workers' management at the enterprise, or micro-, level with central control and planning of the economy at the macro-level. In *Stroitel'stvo sotsializma*, which synthetised ideas developed in his articles in *Kommunist* and in his speeches at the Congress of Economic Councils, Osinskii sought to reconcile these divergent requirements. At the grass roots, large enterprises were to be run by boards (*kollegii*), two-thirds of which was to be elected by the workers themselves – though, contrary to syndicalist ideas, these boards were *not* to be composed of a majority of workers employed in the enterprise itself, lest they develop a sense of property in it.[63] Above them was to be a tier of regional (*oblast'*) economic councils, in the main to be elected from below by plant administrations in each region. These councils were to be granted the right to affirm or to veto the elected plant administrations, once they had assured themselves of the capability, or otherwise, of the latter to organise production efficiently. At the apex, he envisaged a central economic council, such as the *Vesenkha*, composed largely of representatives from the regional councils.[64] To prevent deformations within this system, in the direction of either bureaucratic centralisation or anarcho-syndicalism, he stressed the urgency of 'a precise definition of the powers of the subordinate organs, both to protect their scope for self-activity and at the same time to prevent any arbitrary actions on their part'.[65] He attempted to proffer such a definition. The *Vesenkha* was to be responsible for the formulation and financing of the overall economic plan, and was to have general supervisory powers to ensure that it was carried out. Detailed administration was to be left to the regional councils which were to ensure that enterprises under their purview were supplied with the labour, materials and technical expertise that they required to continue in operation. Finally, the plant administrations were allotted purely 'technical executive functions'.[66] The need to tap mass initiative presumably would be met by this requirement, and by the participation of plant representatives at regional level.

But how were conflicts, real or potential, between these various tiers of administration to be resolved? Even with the best will and the best circumstances in the world they appear to be unavoidable, as Alec Nove has emphasised, given that organisations at the local level of necessity lack the information required to judge what the interests of society *in toto* would demand.[67] Given Russia's pitiful economic condition in 1918, conflicts were inevitable, as Skvortsov-Stepanov conceded. However genuine the commitment of the factory-plant committees and other grass-roots organs of the workers to pursuing the general interests of society and to supporting the central control required to achieve these, they would be forced to sacrifice this commitment to more immediate and narrower concerns. Shortages, of food, fuel and finance, Stepanov argued, would inexorably drive these workers' committees to strive to protect their own plants, so impelling them *de facto* in a syndicalist direction. Logically, he continued, production should be concentrated in the largest, most efficient enterprises. The question whether the workers in the plants due for closure in the interests of the greater productivity and economic efficiency of society at large would accept their fate passively remained unexplored and, as yet, unresolved.[68]

In Osinskii's model, it was assumed, rather optimistically, that conferences between representatives of the centre and the lower tier organisations would succeed in reconciling any such conflicts in the interests of society at large. However, if such a resolution was not forthcoming, then in the final analysis the authorities at the lower levels would have to be overridden.[69] Osinskii and his fellow-thinkers were compelled to assign the ultimate power of economic decision-making to the centre, as their conception of the economics of socialism demanded. Osinskii, it would appear, did not stand quite as 'uncompromisingly for the democratisation of industry' as Brinton has suggested. Nor was 'the triumph of centralisation' at the Congress of Economic Councils the total defeat for most of the Left Communists present that Kaplan has depicted it to have been.[70]

They now found themselves in a rather ironical position. Having accepted the principle that in socialist society the power of economic decision-making must reside ultimately in the hands of the central authorities, many of them continued to attack these authorities for over-reaching their competences, attacking the rights of the localities, and thus fostering the growth of bureaucratism. As V. N. Andronnikov, a representative of the Urals *sovnarkhoz* where a particularly virulent strain of Left Communism was to be found (see Chapter 7 below), sourly remarked at the Congress of Economic Councils, Osinskii's model, with its acceptance of hierarchical control over the composition of enterprise administrations elected from below, effectively vitiated workers' self-management.[71]

One can but presume that the Left Communists' 'faith in the class consciousness' of the proletariat led them to hope that such conflicts between local and central interests would not remain intractable. Theoretically, where the workers and managers of an enterprise possess a high degree of class consciousness, it is possible to imagine them disregarding their own immediate interests and bowing to central directives detrimental to themselves. Selucky is correct in concluding, however, that such an assumption is highly 'romantic . . . [and] scarcely realistic' and has not been borne out by any experience in peacetime.[72]

The remainder of their programme for industry can be dealt with in summary fashion, largely because they did not possess much of one, as we saw in Chapter 3 above.[73] The territorial losses suffered as a consequence of accepting the Brest-Litovsk peace precluded the restoration, let alone the development, of industry in Soviet Russia. In the meantime little could be done. The only areas remaining with any potential for industrial revival were the Urals and West Siberia. Accordingly, the limited resources that Soviet Russia did possess should be concentrated there to ensure that whatever industrial recovery was possible in these regions at least was achieved.[74]

The method by which the Left Communists proposed to finance even this limited programme of restoration, as well as maintain what other nationalised industries they could, was decried by E. H. Carr as 'fantastic'.[75] Whatever wealth remained in the hands of the bourgeoisie was to be confiscated. However, since this 'plunder' in itself would be insufficient to meet the financial needs of industry, the printing press would have to provide the remainder. Inflation would ensue, they admitted; but rather than seeing it as an evil they welcomed it, since it would facilitate the transition to the moneyless socialist economy of the future, where the ruble would be valueless.[76] Gukovskii's plan, in its main part supported by Lenin, to eliminate the budget deficit and stabilise the ruble was dismissed as a bourgeois 'opportunist deviation', which would lead only to the restoration of state capitalism.[77]

It was left to Vladimir Smirnov to develop the financial 'logic' of the Left Communists a little further. Totally planned distribution, he conceded, was still some time in the future, since it was impossible speedily to draw the millions of still uncollectivised peasants into such a system. In the interim money would be required to conduct exchange between socialised industry and individual peasant agriculture. Yet here lay an opportunity, so Smirnov added, to resolve, at least in small part, the problem of financing industry. The prices of goods produced by socialised industry were to be 'set as high as possible', in order to extract from the countryside a surplus which could be invested to stimulate the recovery and development of industry.[78] He was to develop this notion, as Bukharin duly noted, into the concept of 'primary socialist accumulation',[79] which was later elaborated upon by Preobrazhenskii, and implemented in an even more extreme manner, some might argue, by Stalin during the period of the first Five Year Plan.

*       *       *

In the sphere of industrial organisation, therefore, the conclusion drawn by Carr that the Left Communists 'shrank from producing any concrete programme' is not strictly tenable.[80] Nor was their programme as 'disappointingly sketchy' as Steve Smith has suggested.[81] Rather, the pertinent question is whether their programme was feasible. Certainly, their critique of the measures proposed by Lenin as essential to restore Russian industry was in many respects thorough and pertinent. In particular, Osinskii's critique of the consequences of these policies has been described by Smith as 'brilliant'.[82] They saw clearly that nationalisation *per se* would leave the workers with no more freedom 'to decide what and how to produce than before'. It would leave them as subordinated as before, as Mihaly Vajda has commented, but now to appointees of the state, if not to the bourgeoisie and its managers.[83] They perceived that the participation of the workers in economic decision-making, from the point of production upward, was vital if any genuine socialist reconstruction of industry was to be achieved.[84]

The problem was, however, that their own programme appears to have been patently ill-adapted to the political and social realities of Russia in the spring of 1918. Of course, the Left Communists themselves repeatedly claimed that their plans for the democratisation of industry were not unrealistic at all. The Russian workers, they argued, did possess the consciousness and acumen required to restore discipline and produce efficiently once they had taken over the management of their enterprises. Osinskii pointed to the experience of the Donets basin, which he had observed at first-hand in February, 1918, where bourgeois sabotage had compelled the workers to seize the mines. They had declared them to be state property and, more pertinently, succeeded in operating them by themselves.[85] Similarly, Lomov contended that production in many enterprises in the Central Industrial Region had actually risen after January 1918, largely as a result of the work-force independently nationalising and proceeding to manage them successfully. The same recovery, he argued on another occasion, could be observed in plants ranging from Petrograd to the Urals.[86] M. A. Savel'ev sketched a similar picture of the success of workers' management in the Urals, which he had visited in May, alleging that in many plants production had markedly improved as a consequence of this.[87] Any reductions in output that had occurred could not be blamed on the workers themselves, but rather was attributable to insufficient materials, the lack of finances to pay and of provisions to feed them, and, of course, to the impact of bourgeois sabotage.[88]

The usual dismissal of this defence of workers' management as simply utopian, a dismissal which rests on the familiar picture of the Russian proletariat as prone to anarchism and incapable of restoring discipline of their own accord, deserves some modification. Recently, several studies, most notably those of Smith and Carmen Sirianni, have indicated a greater awareness among many Russian workers of the need for discipline if their enterprises were to be able to continue functioning. Moreover, in many instances they also sought the active intervention of the government to assist them in organising production effectively. No doubt the Left Communists exaggerated the success of workers' management in overcoming industrial chaos. But it remains difficult to assess to what extent the workers' lack of success was the result of their own inabilities and foibles or of circumstances largely outwith their control, such as the lack of materials and food.[89]

At the same time, it would be unrealistic to deny that there were instances when workers' management proved to be disruptive. In a letter to his wife, written in May, 1918, Leonid Krasin, a rare figure amongst the Bolsheviks inasmuch as he was not only a qualified engineer but also an experienced manager, painted a grim picture of demoralisation and decay where the workers had taken over their enterprises and attempted to run them:

> The prospects for some categories of the urban proletariat are absolutely hopeless. The illusion of becoming masters where they were formerly slaves has demoralised the so-called working class. Nobody is getting any work done, and the railways and all productive machinery are rapidly falling into decay ...[90]

An even more damning condemnation of the workers' capacity to manage industry on their own came from Aleksandr Shliapnikov, then Commissar of Labour, yet, ironically, the champion of workers' management in the years after 1918. But in the first months of 1918 he attributed most of the disruption afflicting Russian industry to the chaos that ensued when workers seized their own enterprises. Too many workers, he claimed, were prone to anarcho-syndicalism, which thwarted any planned organisation of production.[91] One-man management, strict discipline over labour, material incentives – these were the methods that he then favoured to promote economic recovery.[92] Arguably, he was far from alone. Whatever the truth of the matter, attribution of the growing collapse of industry to the effects of workers' control in all probability struck a more responsive chord within Bolshevik ranks in the spring of 1918 than did the Left Communists' defence of the efficacy of workers' management.[93] In these circumstances it is far from surprising that Lenin's arguments in favour of a return to older, tried-and-tested methods of administration won the day.

At this point, discussions on this question usually end, with the conclusion that the perceptions of social reality held by the majority of leading Bolsheviks dictated the rejection of the Left Communists' model for the administration of industry. However, that is not all. Often we are left with the impression that the Left Communists were faithful defenders of a democratic socialist economic structure, in contrast to Lenin who still failed to grasp the crucial role of workers' self-management in such a system. Indeed, Sirianni has recently contended that '[t]he Left Communists ... developed the critical conceptions of Marxism itself on the issues of labour organisation and economic democracy'.[94]

Yet a more careful, and critical, analysis of their model for industrial administration reveals that such a conclusion is, bluntly put, unwarranted. Whatever their developments of Marxism may have been, they did not provide a blueprint for a viable economic democracy. The fundamental reason for their failure was rooted in their preconceptions of the economic essence of socialism. In common with the overwhelming majority of Marxists of their time, they believed that the transition to socialism must lead to the abolition of money, prices, and commodity production: in brief, all the characteristics of the market system that they detested and identified with capitalism.[95] Osinskii typified their thinking: '[t]he market is the seedbed of contagion from which the embryos of capitalism continually issue forth'.[96] Under socialism, the market was to be abolished, with production and distribution no longer regulated by shifts in supply and demand, manifest in changing commodity prices, but by the plan. The plan, however, if it was to satisfy the needs of society in general, rather than particular local demands, must be drawn up by a central authority which alone has the vision, and, no less important, the information to determine what these general needs might be. This central authority would then issue instructions to all enterprises under its purview regarding the nature and quantity of their production; it would distribute supplies of materials and labour amongst them to ensure that their production plans could be met; and it would distribute the goods finally produced.

In such a system of central planning, as Alec Nove has forcibly argued, there would not, and *could* not, be any scope for meaningful workers' democracy, in the precise sense of real shop-floor power over the production process.[97] Even if the workers did possess the 'romantic and scarcely realistic' levels of consciousness that would lead them to sacrifice their own particular interests for the sake of those of society at large, they simply would not possess the information necessary to take decisions which would achieve this objective. In a large and complex industrial economy, which the Left Communists believed to be an integral feature of socialism, production in all its component parts could be regulated through the market. If the market was to be abolished, then the emergence in its place of a centralised bureaucracy to regulate production would, as Nove remarked, become 'a *functional necessity*'.[98] In that case, '[b]elow the centre there are bound to be severe limits placed on the power of *local* or regional authorities, in order to ensure the priority of the general over the particular'.[99] The Left Communists themselves, as we have seen above, were forced, grudgingly, to concede that this in fact had to be the case, so vitiating their defence of workers' management from the point of production upwards. In all probability, therefore, a democratic form of socialism would not have been the outcome of their programme, since as Nove succinctly concluded 'the functional logic of centralised planning "fits" far too easily into the practice of centralised despotism'.[100]

# 6 Politics and the State

The clash between the Left Communists and Lenin that surfaced in the spring of 1918 over how the revolutionary state was to be constructed rather predictably mirrored the strands of the conflict already examined. Again, the Left Communists accused Lenin of reneging on the libertarian political principles on which, as he had argued repeatedly during 1917, the revolutionary state must be founded. They viewed with horror his preparedness to abandon this programme and to condone the reconstruction of a highly-centralised, bureaucratic dictatorial state to eliminate the chaos and anarchy that threatened the very survival of the infant Soviet republic. They were certain that his betrayal of the vision of 1917, described by Robert Daniels as the dictatorship of the proletariat in the form of a commune state administered from below by the workers themselves, could lead only to the degeneration of the revolution.[1]

One problem which arises in attempting to disentangle this particular debate between Lenin and the Left Communists, and a problem with which they had to grapple as a matter of political strategy, was that their mentors, Marx and Engels, had bequeathed them with no unequivocal blueprint for the construction of the revolutionary state. In fact, their writings on the state were both contradictory and sketchy, as Tony Polan wrily commented, lacking 'any rigorous exposition . . . of the institutions of an emancipated society'.[2] One interpretation of their thinking, then dominant among the socialists of the Second International, was that it was possible to employ the existing state in the construction of socialism. Based essentially on the message of *The Communist Manifesto*, the task of the proletariat was 'to win the battle of democracy', 'to raise [itself] to the position of ruling class'. Having done so, Marx and Engels apparently envisaged that the working class should employ the coercive organs of the state to crush opposition from the bourgeoisie and proceed to lay the foundations of the socialist economy and society of the future.[3] Ultimately, '[w]hen, in the course of development, class distinctions have disappeared', the need for a state of any sort, including a strong, centralised dictatorship of the proletariat, would vanish, they believed, since the state, 'political power . . . is merely the organised power of one class for oppressing the other'.[4]

However, the 'founding fathers' had left their followers with an alternative vision of the revolutionary state. In the preface to the 1872 German edition of *The Communist Manifesto*, following 'the practical experience' of the Paris Commune, 'where the proletariat for the first time held power for two whole months', they concluded that no longer could 'the working class . . . simply lay hold of the ready-made State machinery and wield it for its own purposes'.[5] In other words, the existing state could be employed neither to suppress the old ruling class nor to build a new, socialist society. On the contrary, it must be destroyed root and branch. In particular, the standing army and police, the essential purpose of which was to ensure the continued subjugation of the exploited majority of the population, were to be abolished. They were to be replaced by a popular militia, the people in arms, which alone could crush counter-revolutionary opposition. Similarly, the bureaucracy was to be dismantled and the work of administration thoroughly democratised. Democratically-elected representatives of the working population were to be granted the power to make and implement laws, that is, to combine the legislative and executive functions which had remained separated in the old state.[6] Presumably, Marx believed that this fusion of powers would contribute to the destruction of the bureaucratic professionalism characteristic of the old order as, to quote Richard Hunt, '[g]overnment by bureaucracy gave way to the authentic self-administration of the people'.[7] To ensure further against the recrudescence of bureaucratism, 'the officials of all other branches of the Administration' were also to be elected and responsible to the people and, as with the elected representatives, subject to instant recall. Lastly, all were to be paid only an average worker's wage to eliminate, it was hoped, the material bases of bureaucratic careerism.[8]

Consistent with the emphasis on popular participation in the administration of the revolutionary state, power was to be decentralised, into the hands of a myriad of local communes. Yet a central government of sorts, apparently to be composed of representatives from these communes, would remain necessary, to carry out 'the few but important functions which still would remain for [it] . . .'. What these functions were was never fully defined by Marx, but it is probable that the most important would be the central control of the economy, 'to regulate national production upon a common plan'.[9] Finally, as Polan again remarked, for Marx and Engels the commune state so organised was no longer 'a state in the proper sense of the word', conceived chiefly as an organ of coercion, of 'bodies of armed men' separate from the people and historically employed by the ruling minority to suppress the majority.[10] The commune, in which the vast majority of working people itself would exercise all coercive functions, would be quite different from all hitherto existing states. All remaining vestiges of traditional state power, as Engels argued in his 1891 preface to Marx's *The Civil War in France*, were to be 'lop[ped] off at once as much as possible until such time as a generation reared in new, free social conditions is able to throw the entire lumber of the state on the scrap heap'.[11]

That Marx himself never literally equated the Commune with the dictatorship of the proletariat is well-established. It fell to Engels to do so, again in his 1891 preface. Impatient at the 'superstitious reverence' in which many German Social Democrats, 'Social Democratic philistine[s]', held the existing state, he proclaimed: 'Dictatorship of the Proletariat. Well and good, gentlemen, do you want to know what this dictatorship looks like? Look at the Paris Commune. That was the Dictatorship of the Proletariat.'[12] Yet semantics alone are insufficient to resolve this problem. In October 1871, according to Hunt, in an article in the *New York World*, when describing it as 'a proletarian *dictature*', 'Marx all but called the Paris Commune a dictatorship of the proletariat'.[13] Moreover, in *The Civil War* itself, he candidly declared that its 'secret' was that it was 'essentially a working-class government . . . the political form at last discovered under which to work out the economic emancipation of labour'.[14]

Clearly, both models of the revolutionary state proffered by the founding fathers assumed the abolition, sooner or later, of state power *per se*. In Engels' famous maxim, 'the administration of men will be replaced by the administration of things'. Yet in other respects they were profoundly different. The first model stressed a continuing role for strong, centralised proletarian state power in the transition period, while the latter posited an immediate beginning to the dismantling of the state, by a radical diffusion of power into the hands of the working population organised in its local communes.[15] The problem, however, is not one merely of confusion. Marx's discussion of the commune state also suffered from a critical *lacuna*, singled out quite precisely by Hunt, in that he failed to provide any criteria 'to delineate exactly which functions should devolve upon which levels of the administration, or specify any overall degree of centralisation to be achieved, or suggest how the inevitable conflicts of and jurisdictional disputes among the various levels would be resolved'.[16]

A second, if less pressing, concern is to reconstruct in detail how the Left Communists conceived of the politics of the transition period. This task is complicated by the fact, to which Neil Harding has recently drawn our attention, that before the October Revolution none of them, not even their leading theorist on the state, Nikolai Bukharin, had drawn up a precise blueprint of 'the principles and forms of organisation appropriate to the construction of socialism . . .'.[17] Nevertheless, by drawing together the various references to this question made by them before and during 1917, supplemented by their political rhetoric in the spring of 1918 itself, it is possible to piece together their vision of the institutional framework upon which the revolutionary socialist state was to be built.

The first step in this investigation must, of necessity, refer again to their analysis of imperialism, in particular, to what they believed to be the socio-political ramifications of the development of finance capitalism. As we saw in Chapter 2, Bukharin and others on the Left had come to conclude that an integral part of, indeed the first essential stage in, socialist revolution was the smashing of the 'Leviathan' finance-capitalist state.[18] On this they were quite unequivocal. The question remains as to what they thought should take the place of the old state machine. In 1916 Bukharin began, so Michael Haynes has argued, to see a republic of soviets as the 'embryonic form of proletarian state power'.[19] During 1917 the Left generally was to advocate the transfer of power into their hands – despite some reservations in the summer when Bubnov condemned them as 'rotting' counter-revolutionary organs and Bukharin himself more cautiously urged re-elections in order to transform them from petty-bourgeois strongholds into genuine proletarian 'organs of class struggle', and, once victorious, 'organs of revolutionary power'.[20] Within the soviets the proletariat was to exercise the dominant role, albeit with the support of the poor peasants. Moreover, the soviets were to create a popular militia, so that the armed people would be able to exercise the coercive functions formerly performed by the old standing army and police.

Disclaiming any accusations that they were anarchists, they were adamant on the need for a strong state during the transition to socialism, until a classless – and consequently stateless – society would at last exist.[21] For them, the Soviet republic was to be this state, identified by Bukharin as 'the iron dictatorship of the proletariat'.[22] This dictatorship had two basic functions, one political, the other economic. First, it must consolidate the gains of the revolution by ruthlessly stamping out all counter-revolutionary opposition on the part of the old exploiting classes. At the same time, it had a more constructive role to play. It had to act to save the Russian economy from complete collapse and the population, especially in the towns, from starvation. The intervention in the economy required to prevent such a collapse – labour conscription was one measure necessary to achieve this end – if implemented by the Provisional Government, would serve simply to strengthen even more the development of state capitalism in Russia, and its 'Leviathan' state, and so only reinforce 'the cruellest form of class oppression'. If introduced by a dictatorship of the proletariat, however, in the form of Soviet power, the measures needed to preserve and expand industrial and agrarian production at the same time would help to establish the foundations of the socialist economy and society of the future, so 'bring[ing] Russia closer to socialism'.[23]

Rudimentary as the Left Communists' conception of the new political order then was, they were insistent on one point. While emphasising that some form of centralised administration would remain necessary in the revolutionary state, as their understanding of the economics of socialism unquestionably demanded, they also maintained, as Bukharin made clear, that 'it [was] totally without sense that one central "Soviet of Soviets" in St. Petersburg should control everything'.[24] On the contrary, they envisaged a radical decentralisation of power to the local soviets. Such a diffusion of power would serve two, inter-related purposes. It would help to destroy the highly centralised bureaucratic hierarchy of the old regime and the attitudes of deference nurtured by it. At the same time, it would provide the opportunity for the majority of the people to take an active part in the running of the new state and so to learn the art of administration, 'to use a slogan', Bukharin was sarcastically to remark in the spring of 1918, 'which was formulated so splendidly by Lenin'.[25] A rather optimistic evaluation of the class consciousness of the proletariat led them to conclude that the central 'guiding and unifying' institutions required in socialist society would emerge spontaneously from below as the workers themselves came to perceive the necessity of them.[26] But, as with their project for the organisation of industry, so too there were serious *lacunae* in their political thinking. Quite how this process of centralisation would occur; what was to be done should rank-and-file initiative fail to create the required central institutions; and how potential conflicts between the centre and the localities were to be resolved: the answers to these questions were not spelled out in detail.

*Lacunae* notwithstanding, in the spring of 1918 what the Left Communists understood to be essential to the politics of the transition period was much clarified. In the face of attempts by Lenin and his faction to limit the autonomy of the local soviets, the Left Communists' *Theses on the Current Situation* unequivocally defended the model of the '"Commune state" ruled from below' as the only possible form for a revolutionary socialist state to assume.[27] Bukharin was even more explicit, in his review of *State and Revolution*, published in the first issue of *Kommunist*. Effusive in his praise of the vision enshrined in it, he forthrightly concluded that 'the dictatorship of the proletariat is not a parliamentary republic with all its trappings. It is the commune state, without the police, the standing army, officialdom, etc.'[28]

To understand more fully, however, how the Left Communists conceived of 'the commune state' it is necessary to turn to Lenin himself who, as Harding has pointed out, during 1917 had come to articulate in a more comprehensive and systematic manner the principles on which such a state was to be constructed.[29]

Until the second half of 1916 he appears not to have given serious and consistent thought to the question of the form that the state must assume in post-revolutionary society.[30] Till then he had believed, like the majority of contemporary socialists, that '[t]he political form of society wherein the proletariat is victorious in overthrowing the bourgeoisie will be a democratic republic'.[31] During 1916 itself, in letters to A. G. Shliapnikov, G. E. Zinov'ev and Bukharin himself, he had repeatedly denied that an essential precondition for the victory of socialist revolution was the destruction of the bourgeois state machine. Such a conclusion was 'not thought out, useless', 'the height of stupidity, a disgrace', 'semi-anarchism'.[32] As late as December of that year, in direct refutation of Bukharin, he repeated that '[s]ocialists are in favour of utilising the present state in the struggle for the emancipation of the working-class...', that 'the bourgeois state [should be] utilis[ed] ... against the bourgeoisie to overthrow the bourgeoisie'.[33]

Yet, as intimated in Chapter 2, by February, 1917 Lenin had undergone a radical conversion. At the end of 1916, prompted primarily by what he believed to the grave errors in Bukharin's analysis of the imperialist state, he undertook an intensive study of the political prescriptions of the 'founding fathers'. His purpose, as he later admitted, was 'to re-establish what Marx had really taught on the subject of the state'.[34] Intending to deploy his conclusions in condemnation of Bukharin, a rather surprised Lenin found himself compelled to accept much of his protagonist's analysis. The thrust of his argument now was to be directed, generally, against the majority of socialists who thought to capture the old state machine, possibly in a peaceful, parliamentary manner, and employ it to introduce socialism by legislation. His particular target, as Alfred Evans recently re-emphasised, was Karl Kautsky, considered to be the greatest living authority on Marxism, but deemed by Lenin to be a 'renegade', guilty of betraying Marx's revolutionary *credo*.[35]

Lenin's new analysis of the nature of the state in the epoch of finance capitalism was almost identical to that of Bukharin. As is evident from *State and Revolution*, he had come to regard 'the state which is merging more and more with the all powerful capitalist associations...' as responsible for '[t]he monstrous oppression of the working people...'.[36] Violent revolution was necessary, to smash its power completely. From March, in his *Draft Theses* and his *Letters from Afar*, he began urgently to advocate such a course of action. He now bluntly denied that the bourgeois state, 'even a democratic bourgeois republican government' could be taken over intact by the proletariat and used to advance the cause of socialist revolution.[37] In his *April Theses* he was quite unequivocal, arguing that 'to return to a parliamentary republic ... would be a retrograde step...'. Casting aside whatever reservations he may have harboured about the soviets, he called for the creation of 'a republic of Soviets' as 'the only possible form of revolutionary government'. This new soviet state, he soon added, was to be built on the pattern of 'the commune in Marx's sense of the experience of 1871', and would serve as the dictatorship of the proletariat, with, of course, the support of the peasants.[38]

Throughout 1917 he continued to demand that the existing state be smashed and power transferred into the hands of the soviets – with the well-known exception of several weeks after the July Days when he was convinced that, in the thrall of the feckless Mensheviks and Social Revolutionaries, they had become nothing but 'organs collaborating with the bourgeoisie'.[39] But more than that, he also strove to expound on the political structures appropriate for the new revolutionary soviet state. He did so most fully in *State and Revolution*. Composed in the summer of 1917 while he was in hiding in Finland to escape the repression of the Bolsheviks for their part in the July Days, it was the fruit of his studies of the thinking of the 'founding fathers' on the state. Recognised in recent Western scholarship as neither an 'utopian fantasy' nor a purely anarchist treatise negating the need for strong centralised state power in the transition to socialism, nevertheless it 'does represent the high watermark of Lenin's optimism concerning the merits of mass initiative in building the new society'. As such it was also to bring him close to 'the aspirations of Left Bolsheviks' and in fact go beyond them, 'to specify the positive content of socialism itself'.[40]

A convoluted and repetitive work, replete with quotations from Marx and Engels, *State and Revolution* marked an attempt by Lenin to draw together ideas propounded at various times earlier in the year as he sought to define 'what was to take the place of the state machine to be destroyed'.[41] Reiterating that the prototype of the '"specific" form of the proletarian, socialist republic' was the Paris Commune, he again called for the abolition of the oppressive agencies of the old state, the police and the standing army. They were to be replaced by a popular militia drawn from the workers and peasants. Similarly, the 'privileged' civilian bureaucracy, separate from and standing above the people, was also to be dismantled root and branch. In its place, the working people, 'each in turn', was to take a direct and active part in running the new state and in so doing 'learn the art of administration'. The institutional mechanism for popular participation on this scale was to be the soviets. Conceived after the model of the commune, they were to be composed of democratically-elected and revocable representatives performing executive as well as legislative functions.[42]

Mass participation, Lenin optimistically added, was not at all utopian. Capitalism in its contemporary imperialist form had developed sufficiently to create 'the *preconditions* that *enable* really "all" to take part in the administration of the state . . .'. In particular, the positive functions of the state, the administration of

> large-scale production, factories, railways, the postal service, telephones, etc., and *on this basis* the great majority of the functions of the old 'state power' have become so simplified and can be reduced to such exceedingly simple operations of registration, filing and checking that they can be easily performed by every literate person, can quite easily be performed for ordinary 'workmen's wages', and that these functions can (and must) be stripped of every

shadow of privilege, of every semblance of 'official grandeur.'[43]

The emphasis here on mass initiative appears also to have been based on Lenin's growing appreciation during 1917 of the potential abilities of ordinary working people – and on his increasing antipathy to '[f]oolish bureaucratic prejudices, tsarist red-tapism, reactionary professorial ideas as to the indispensability of bureaucratism . . .'.[44] During the April Conference, for instance, he singled out for praise the example given by a group of miners who had proved themselves to be perfectly capable of maintaining production on their own initiative. Both before and, as we shall see, after October he was to return to this theme, frequently defending the competence of rank-and-file workers, and peasants too, to run the state and the economy. Their talents to do so, admittedly, still lay 'dormant', but they would blossom once they were given the opportunity to exercise them.[45]

In keeping with his new-found faith in 'the direct initiative of the people from below, in their local areas',[46] *State and Revolution* also posited a radical devolution of power to the local soviets of workers and peasants. Such a diffusion of power, however, would not be tantamount either to federalism, or to the elimination of centralised state power which would remain an essential feature of the revolutionary dictatorship. Yet, like those on the Left of the party, he too was rather vague about how the central organs of the new state would emerge, rather lamely concluding that they would be created spontaneously from below, on the initiative of the proletariat and poor peasants. This system of 'voluntary centralism', 'of the voluntary fusion of the proletarian communes', he insisted, would 'not in the least preclude . . . broad local self-government'.[47]

The revolutionary dictatorship so constituted, 'the proletariat armed and organised as the ruling class', had two principal functions: the first, to 'crush' the inevitable opposition of the old 'exploiters';[48] the second, more positive task, 'to lead the enormous mass of the population . . . in the work of organising a socialist economy', which alone, so Lenin was convinced, could combat the growing economic chaos within the country.[49]

While conceding that of necessity the revolutionary dictatorship would persist throughout 'the entire *historical period*
which separates capitalism from "classless society", from
communism', he hastily added that it would no longer be 'the
state proper', a 'special force' of the 'privileged minority' for
the suppression of the majority of the people.[50] Following in
the tradition of the 'founding fathers' on the nature of the
state, he argued that the majority could not suppress itself.
In post-revolutionary society, which would witness the gradual transcendence of class antagonisms, there would ultimately be no need for any form of state at all. Consequently,
even the revolutionary state itself would begin to wither
away. And, he emphasised, 'so constituted [as the commune
state] it begins to wither away immediately'.[51]

Yet, even in *State and Revolution*, he displayed some hesita-
tion. For Lenin, there could 'be no question of specifying the
moment of the *future* "withering away", the more so since it
[would] obviously be a lengthy process', of a 'protracted
nature'. The final 'withering away' of the state required that
the economy develop to such levels that 'the antithesis
between mental and manual labour disappears . . . one of the
principal sources of modern social inequality . . . which
cannot on any account be removed immediately by the mere
conversion of the means of production into public property,
by the mere expropriation of the capitalists'.[52] Similarly, he
qualified his remarks regarding the abolition of bureaucracy.
It too was destined to experience 'a gradual withering away
. . . to the gradual creation of an order . . . under which the
functions of control and accounting, becoming more and
more simple, will be performed by each in turn, will then
become a habit and will finally die out as the *special* functions
of a special section of the population.' But again he insisted
that the immediate elimination of all bureaucracy was utopian. While capitalism had 'simplifie[d] the functions of
"state" administration' he was emphatic that some form of
'administration' and 'subordination' remained vital since
'people as they are now . . . cannot dispense with subordination, control and "foremen and accountants"'. A role clearly
remained for 'state officials . . . as responsible, *revocable*,
modestly paid "foremen and accountants" (of course with the
aid of technicians of all sorts, types and degrees)'.[53] Reiterat-

ing several times the indispensability of a 'scientifically
trained staff' of administrators in the post-revolutionary
state, he nevertheless insisted that they be paid only 'work-
men's wages', to remove the material bases for bureaucratic
careerism. Equally they were to remain responsible for their
actions 'to the armed vanguard of all the exploited and
working-people, i.e., to the proletariat', and subject to instant
dismissal for any malfeasance.[54]

In light of the above, one can readily accept Evans'
conclusion that *State and Revolution* was not simply a
work of 'quasi-anarchic utopianism' but, on the contrary,
itself was 'filled with ambiguities, equivocations and
inconsistencies...'.[55] Yet it was not necessarily viewed as
such at the time, or for long thereafter. To Lenin's contem-
poraries its emphasis was understood to be on the necessity
of smashing the old political order, and all the features
characteristic of it, such as the centralised and hierarchical
bureaucratic system of administration. This was to be replaced by self-administration by the majority, the only means
whereby it would gain the requisite experience to run the
state. It was this image of *State and Revolution* that the Left
Communists lauded, as it coincided with their own vision of
the extensive diffusion and decentralisation of power in
socialist society.

The problem, however, that confronted the Bolsheviks
after they assumed power was that political reality within
Soviet Russia in the months following the revolution belied
the hopes that they had pinned on mass initiative in the
construction of the new revolutionary state. Far from leading
to the spontaneous creation of an 'iron dictatorship of the
proletariat', the transfer of power to the soviets, on the
contrary, had resulted, as Anweiler pointed out, in 'the
formation of semi-independent republics, autonomous regions, etc.'.[56] In face of the grave threats to the infant Soviet
republic posed by ever-growing economic disintegration and
military opposition, internal and external, the absence of any
'kind of effective central authority', so E. H. Carr argued,
jeopardised the very survival of the revolution. In these
circumstances its restoration seemed to be imperative.[57]

Initially, Lenin's own response to this situation was hesi-
tant. In the first months after the October Revolution, in the

main he appears to have kept faith in the capacities of rank-and-file workers to administer the state. In January 1918 at the Third Congress of Soviets he continued to defend the model of the commune state as appropriate for Soviet Russia. 'Of course', he admitted, 'the working people had no experience in government but that does not scare us ... for in them lie dormant the great forces of revolution, renascence, renovation'.[58] At that time he continued to attribute the bulk of the problems, especially the economic problems, afflicting the country to counter-revolutionary sabotage, not to the foibles of 'the working people'.[59]

Yet gradually his attitude to the role of mass initiative became considerably more ambivalent. In early March, at the Seventh Extraordinary Party Congress, on one occasion he summoned the 'Party ... the entire vanguard of the class conscious proletariat' to be ruthless in its efforts 'to create everywhere soundly coordinated mass organisations held together by a single iron will'. He quickly qualified this call to the vanguard, however, stressing the need 'to draw literally working people into the government of the state. It is a task of tremendous difficulty. But socialism cannot be implemented by a minority, by the Party. It can be implemented only by tens of millions when they have learned to do it themselves'.[60]

Soon afterwards, however, in face of virtual anarchy in much of the country, his position was to become markedly less ambivalent. At the end of March, just as he had regarding the administration of industry, he demanded a return to 'businesslike methods' in state administration too, an end to 'the overlapping of authority and irresponsibility [within the Soviets] from which we are suffering incredibly at the present time ...'. This confusion had transformed 'the dictatorship of the proletariat ... [into] something as amorphous as jelly'.[61] Coercion was required, not just against 'our enemies' but also 'all waverers and harmful elements in our midst' if order and discipline were to be restored. '[T]he revolution', he concluded, would be crushed 'if we do not counter ruin, disorganisation and despair with the iron dictatorship of class conscious workers'.[62]

Lenin had now begun to distance himself quite self-consciously from the vision of popular participation in the

administration of the revolutionary state that he had profer-
red in *State and Revolution*.[63] He reverted to a more authoritarian strand also present, even in *State and Revolution* itself, in
his political thinking in 1917, if then in largely muted form.
Most clearly evident perhaps in *Can the Bolsheviks Retain State
Power?*, Lenin there posited a rather different, more circumscribed role for mass initiative. He dismissed as quite
utopian the idea 'that an unskilled labourer or cook [could]
get on with the job of state administration'. The best that
could be achieved, he claimed, was that 'a beginning be made
at once in training all the working people, all the poor, for
this work'.[64] Again emphasising the vital need in the post-
revolutionary period for a centralised, dictatorial state, on
this occasion he omitted any discussion of 'voluntary centralism', of centralised power being constructed from the grass
roots up on the initiative of rank-and-file workers and
peasants.[65] The leading role in establishing this dictatorship,
and in educating the majority in the work of administration,
was assigned to the 'class conscious workers and soldiers'.[66]
As he began to despair increasingly during the spring of
1918 of the abilities of ordinary working people to participate effectively in the work of state administration, even
complaining of their 'timidity', their belief that 'the only
people capable of governing [were] their "betters"', he again
elevated 'the disciplined and class conscious vanguard of the
proletariat' – the party – to the leading role within the
revolutionary state.[67] It alone, he now asserted, had the
political *nous* to run the state.

Yet reliance upon the 'vanguard' raised another problem.
The party itself simply did not possess skilled administrators,
political as well as economic, in sufficient numbers to cope
with the range of tasks before it.[68] Consequently, Lenin was
forced to concede that there was little choice but to employ
the bureaucracy from the old regime to assist the party in
restoring order to the state administration. The need to do so
was so great in Lenin's eyes that despite bitter criticisms from
the Left Communists, he professed his willingness to 'compromise ... the principles of the Paris Commune' and 'pay a
very high price for the "services" of the top bourgeois
experts', a clear retreat from the egalitarianism enshrined in
*State and Revolution*, but one which had been hinted at in *Can*

*the Bolsheviks Retain State Power?*[69] Rather ironically, Lenin's renewed concern for efficient administration, and his determination to restore it at virtually any cost, was to lead him to preserve the old bureaucratic apparatus in substantial part intact. The eventual outcome of his emphasis on restoring order and authority within the Soviet republic was to be an ever greater centralisation of power in the hands of the *Sovnarkom*, dominated by the party leadership, and of the spawning bureaucracy that it was to control. This concentration of power, of course, as Carr aptly commented, could only take place 'at the expense of the All-Russian Congress of Soviets and V.Ts.I.K. ... [and] of the local soviets and congresses of soviets and their organs ...'.[70]

The Left Communists themselves were all too aware, as their *Theses* made clear, that the conduct of politics within Soviet Russia in the spring of 1918 was increasingly diverging from the vision of Soviet power that they had nurtured in 1917. Unlike Lenin, however, they remained vehemently opposed to the all too perceptible trend towards the recrudescence of a hierarchical, centralised bureaucracy, in large part drawn from the old officialdom, which was unreflective of and unresponsive to rank-and-file aspirations. If continued, this trend could only stifle local initiative and deny the workers the opportunity 'to learn the art of administration'. Effective mass participation in administration, as essential politically as economically for the construction of socialism, would be stymied, with only one possible outcome – the degeneration of the revolution.[71]

Of all the Left Communists, it was perhaps Vladimir Sorin who presented the most compelling analysis of the roots of the political degeneration evident within the infant Soviet republic. Given the paucity of experienced administrators amongst party members, and the working class more generally, many who staffed the new state administration of necessity, he conceded, had to be drawn from the ranks of the old bourgeois intelligentsia. Moreover, it had been necessary too to seek recruits from the 'semi-intelligentsia', of 'clerks, secretaries, minor officials and others', who had played little prominent role in the old regime, since a substantial part of the better-trained personnel had refused to work for the Soviet regime. Imbued with the habits of the past, they had agreed to serve the revolutionary state solely from motives of personal gain. They were driven primarily by the desire to preserve their positions and the material privileges which flowed from them, such as higher salaries, and, not the least important in the spring of 1918, an adequate supply of food. The politics of socialism, which demanded that they should be responsible and accountable to the soviets *per se* was complete anathema to them. Hence they sought every opportunity to escape such accountability and to return to their traditional authoritarian and bureaucratic ways. Sadly, and much more disturbing, the experienced party workers who had been recruited in droves to man the new state apparatus, in order to provide it with at least a leavening of revolutionary consciousness, had been unable to counter these forces of reaction entrenched within it. Worn out by the travails of revolutionary life, all they sought now was peace and quiet, the opportunity to relax and enjoy the fruits of their labours. Misguidedly they believed that the new direction in Lenin's overall policy, one of compromise if possible with the bourgeoisie, promised to ensure that this was possible. For them, the heroic period of revolutionary assault and socialist construction was over.[72]

The solution to this problem of the revival of bureaucratism proposed by Sorin was two-fold. First, the soviets themselves, the institutions deemed to be representative of the 'broad working masses', were to be reinvigorated – precisely how was not explained in detail – on the assumption that they, more than the officials employed by them, were more reliable repositories of revolutionary *élan*. The strengthening of their authority and control over their bureaucracies would ensure, he believed, that the latter served the revolution, and not their own narrow self-interests. One particular measure which would help to realise this end, Sorin added, very much in the spirit of the Paris Commune, was the elimination of all 'privileges' for 'public workers'.[73]

Sorin, however, was not yet finished. 'The Left Communists', he continued, '[were] the most passionate proponents of soviet power, but ... only so far as this power does not degenerate ... in a petty-bourgeois direction'. The soviets themselves, he argued, were representative of the working people in general, including 'the petty-bourgeois peasantry' as well as the proletariat. As such, they were vulnerable to corruptive and demoralising influences that might dilute their socialist zeal. The only true bastion of the interests of the proletariat was the party which '*is in every case and everywhere superior to the soviets*'. Its role was to act as the watchdog which would ensure that the soviets in fact 'implemented an undeviating proletarian line in foreign and domestic policy', a line presumably identical with that advocated by the Left Communists themselves. Ironically, Sorin's call for a revived soviet democracy was becoming vitiated by the dominant role assigned, in the final analysis, to the party. And in practice, according to one Menshevik observer, David Dallin, some of his comrades, such as those in Saratov, sought to purge the soviets of all non-Bolshevik, 'petty-bourgeois' elements, actions which are difficult to reconcile with a 'passionate' defence of real soviet power.[74]

Sorin's reliance on the party to safeguard the integrity of the revolution, however, did not go unchallenged. A number of his comrades, including leading Left Communists such as Bukharin, Osinskii and Radek, as well as less prominent figures from Petrograd and the northern region, expressed grave reservations regarding the condition of the party itself. No longer was it solely a party of the proletariat. Rather, as it had grown rapidly during 1917, especially after the Kornilov affair, it had degenerated into a 'national party', permeated with non-proletarian elements – in particular, peasants and soldiers, 'peasants in uniform' – considered by the Left Communists, as we have seen in Chapter 4, to be hostile to socialism. Moreover, it had also been weakened by the exodus of a vast number of old party workers who had left to take up positions within the state administration. The only solution in these circumstances, if the party was to be able to ensure that 'undeviating' socialist policies were put into practice, was in effect to purge it of all these alien elements and restore it to its pristine condition.[75] The problem remained, however, of defining what were proletarian and, conversely, what were non-proletarian elements. Social origin or former occupation were clearly insufficient, as the Left Communists were critical of the conduct of many worker Bolsheviks who had entered the state administration, as we have just seen. Ultimately, the only criterion that they appeared able to offer was to define 'proletarian' in terms of adherence to their own policy prescriptions and 'non-proletarian' by non-adherence to them.[76] In consequence, all who dared to oppose them could be accused either of being non-proletarian, or at the very least of suffering from some form of 'false consciousness' – and in the interests of building socialism must recant or be purged from the party. Rather ironically, beneath the surface of their fine rhetoric in defence of the soviets, and of the party as 'a forum for all of proletarian democracy',[77] there lay a political philosophy that was arguably as authoritarian as that of which they accused Lenin and his faction.

The purge of the party that the Left Communists demanded was in fact initiated by the Central Committee in the latter half of May. In this case the irony was that in part it was directed against the Left Communists themselves, who were accused of contributing to the disorganisation evident within the party by their continuing opposition. And, as we have seen in Chapter 1, an indeterminate number of their supporters were expelled in consequence.[78]

\* \* \*

Intimately related to the Left Communists' opposition to the re-emergence of a hierarchic, centralised bureaucratic state was their criticism of what they also saw as 'a deviation' in the military policy that the Soviet government began to introduce in the spring of 1918.[79] Then Lenin abandoned his oft-repeated commitment to the creation of a popular militia, one of the foundations on which he had claimed Soviet power was to be built.[80] Now he came round to support Leon Trotsky, who insisted that any realistic defence of the revolution demanded the re-creation of a new regular conscript army and, even more heinous from the point of view of the Left, one staffed by appointees from the old officer corps willing to collaborate with the Soviet regime.

Harsh reality again lay at the root of Lenin's apostasy. The old imperial army, while broadly sympathetic to Soviet power, was fast disintegrating, the result of war weariness, the burning desire to return to the countryside to share in the new land settlement, and of Bolshevik anti-militarist propaganda itself. As a fighting force it was useless. But the expectations of the Bolsheviks that a new volunteer army, drawn from the ranks of the workers and poor peasants, would soon form were to be disappointed. The reliance on the volunteer principle failed in the main to produce the anticipated results, despite a perceptible, if still modest, rise in recruits in face of the renewed German advance in the final days of February.[81] Moreover, the effectiveness of the units that did exist was vitiated both by the lack of effective leadership, and by the absence of any overall command structure, as the local and regional soviets resisted the efforts of the centre to coordinate the activity of their forces on a national scale. The result, unsurprisingly, was one of virtual military anarchy and weakness, as witnessed by the ineffectual resistance to the German advance both on the western front and into the Ukraine.[82] Fear of a fresh attack by German or Allied imperialism, as well as the threat posed by the growing forces of counter-revolution organising across Russia itself, made continuation of this situation untenable.

The appointment of Trotsky, as president of the Supreme War Council on 4 March, and then as Commissar for War on 8 April, signalled a new departure in military policy. During the spring of 1918 he strove to build a new, regular army, organised on conventional lines, which alone, he was convinced, could provide an effective defence for the revolution. This required the gradual introduction of conscription; the creation of a single, unified, hierarchical command structure; and the replacement of elected officers by military *spetsy*, officers of the old imperial army, to provide efficient, professional leadership.[83]

This new orientation in military policy provoked great furore amongst the Left Communists, and also, it seems, within many units of the then slowly forming Red Army, which continued to insist that a truly socialist army could be built only on the volunteer principle, the election of officers and a decentralised command structure. They were certain that general conscription, especially combined with the re-employment of the old officer corps, could only lead to the degeneration of the army into a weapon of counter-revolution.[84] Indeed, even during the parlous days of the renewed German advance into Russia, they had disclaimed the need to create a regular army to defend the revolution. Instead, the Soviet government should call to arms revolutionary detachments [*otriady*], of workers and peasants, to wage a guerrilla war behind the lines of the advancing Germans and so, they rather blithely claimed, after the first inevitable defeats, halt them.[85] Osinskii developed this strand in the Left Communists' thinking to its logical, if extreme, conclusion. In the course of civil war, he contended, be it against the forces of world imperialism or of counter-revolution within Russia, a partisan army would arise spontaneously from the ranks of the workers and peasants. This army, he was confident, would suffice in the interim, until the revolution became victorious internationally, whence the need for an army of any sort, as for the other trappings of state power, would wither away.[86]

In the spring the Left Communists continued to rail against the creation of a new regular army constructed on conventional lines, as Trotsky was proposing, alleging that the Soviet government remained trapped by bourgeois conceptions of war which were quite inappropriate for a revolutionary socialist state.[87] Radek, perhaps, elaborated most fully their objections to Trotsky's plans. He began on a conciliatory note, conceding that Trotsky was correct in urging the establishment of a much larger army. This was vital not so much to combat counter-revolution within Russia itself – partisan detachments would be sufficient for this purpose, provided the mass of the population continued to support the Bolshevik government – but to defend the revolution against the pretensions of world imperialism, most recently evidenced in Japan's thrust into Siberia. Moreover, when the much-heralded European revolution did in fact break out, then the 'Red revolutionary army' must be ready to advance to assist its comrades there. For Radek the issue was not one of building a new army or not, but the question of '[h]ow to construct the Red Army?' He welcomed the decision of the government, on 22 April, not to mobilise the bourgeoisie for military service, as Trotsky and N. I. Podvoiskii had proposed. To do so would not only have armed potential opponents of the revolution but would also have eroded the revolutionary class character of the new army. But, he warned, the construction of a regular army, even one composed solely of workers and peasants, had its own perils. Any regular army had the tendency to become 'detached from its social base' and transformed into a 'special caste', with its own particular 'psychology' and special interests. Even a new, class-based Red Army would not be immune from this tendency. The danger would be even greater if it was staffed by members of the old officer corps. By no means convinced that they had been won over to the side of the revolution, he feared that they would subvert its revolutionary ethos and convert it into a conventional army of the 'old' bourgeois variety and divert it from its revolutionary tasks. To prevent such 'degeneration' it was essential to train officers from the ranks of the proletariat itself as quickly as possible, a training which he admitted required the cooperation of the old military *spetsy*. But this measure was in itself still insufficient to counter the possible growth of military separatism. To ensure that the newly-forming army remained true to its revolutionary purpose and maintained its links with the working population, its 'chief purpose' must be to educate the workers and peasants in the arts of warfare, to act as the cadres around which a genuine, trained people's militia would grow. Then, of course, it would be feasible to rouse the population *en masse* to wage a really effective partisan war, in the final analysis the only sure means to secure the revolution against any military threat.[88]

Lenin, it appears, was totally unconvinced. Sceptical of the virtues of partisan war during the Brest-Litovsk debate, he became more and more certain that it was 'absurd' to rely on guerrilla war to defend the revolution.[89] The continuing isolation of the revolution and the growing range of military challenges facing Soviet Russia from within and without led him to have little patience for the solutions proposed by the Left Communists. Increasingly, he threw his political weight behind Trotsky and supported the rapid build-up of a conventional army. As with the economy and the state, so too the army was to become highly centralised, with control in the hands of the government in Moscow.[90]

*       *       *

Just as the exigencies of burgeoning civil war and intervention militated against the adoption of the militia model in the organisation of the Red Army, so too one must concede that Soviet Russia in the first half of 1918 was not the ideal laboratory in which to experiment with a participatory democratic form of socialist politics. The proletariat remained a minority, in a vast ocean of peasants. Of the proletariat itself, a substantial part remained politically and culturally backward. Moreover, it was increasingly prey to the growing shortages of food and fuel, which accelerated the disintegration of the urban economy already in evidence before the revolution. Hunger, cold and unemployment contributed to the 'declassing' of the Russian proletariat, as workers, in their tens and then hundreds of thousands, fled back to the shelter of the countryside where subsistence, at least, promised to be secured more easily. Moreover, many others, often young workers, recruited mainly from the ranks of the most skilled and politically conscious who had been the most active supporters of the Bolsheviks in 1917, were mobilised into the Red Army to combat the growing threat posed by the forces of counter-revolution and intervention. In these circumstances of the increasing fragmentation of the working-class, any attempts to devolve power into the hands of the proletariat would have proved to be problematic.[91]

However, the failure of the Bolsheviks to construct a democratic polity cannot be attributed simply and solely to socio-economic obstacles, no matter how real they were. First, and the issue perhaps most easily dealt with, there was a glaring contradiction in their overall conception of how socialism was to be constructed. As we saw in the preceding chapter, their understanding of the economics of socialism inexorably demanded that the regulation of production be placed in the hands of a centralised bureaucracy. The question of how their commitment to economic centralisation was to be reconciled with a highly decentralised political system was never adequately answered. Again, the logic of their thinking, the Left Communists' as well as Lenin's, pointed in the direction of the circumscription of the powers of the local soviets when they failed, as they must, to act in accord with the interests of the 'general will'.[92]

But there were other reasons why the Bolsheviks would

have found it difficult to devolve power fully to the soviets. Even had Russia been an advanced capitalist society, with an extensive and highly-developed industry and a large, educated, cultured working class, not one in which the proletarian base of the regime was rapidly eroding, problems would have remained. In particular, the historical record indicates that nowhere has a unified, homogeneous proletariat appeared, conscious of its mission to bring about socialist revolution and so liberate all humanity from its chains. As Edward Thompson has remarked, the proletariat, as a 'real, observable . . . historical' phenomenon, rather than an 'analytic category', has remained divided into divergent strata, most of which have lacked the revolutionary consciousness imputed to them by Marxist tradition.[93] At best, this class consciousness has been the property of a particular group within the proletariat as a whole, which can only realise the libertarian vision of socialism depicted in Marxism by imposing its will on its more 'backward' comrades – and, as Mihaly Vajda wrily commented, forcing them to be free.[94]

The Bolsheviks themselves proposed no practical solution to this dilemma, or, more precisely, no democratic solution. At first sight, *State and Revolution,* and many other of Lenin's writings in 1917 and early 1918, emphasising the vital role of mass initiative in the administration of the revolutionary state, appear to offer what Sirianna has characterised as a 'profoundly popular and participatory' model for the politics of the transition period.[95] But as well as severely underestimating the complexity of administration in modern industrial society, the talent for which all do not share equally as yet, even at this time Lenin's subscription to a seemingly ultra-democratic form of politics is deceptive. As Polan recently reminded us, 'administration concerns the carrying out of an already determined policy; politics involves the discussion and negotiation of such policies'.[96] Arguably, steeped in Marxist tradition, his understanding of politics led him to conclude that the political sphere proper was confined 'to the struggle between classes'.[97] If so, there could be no genuinely political differences within the proletariat itself. This view helps explain why he failed to address adequately the real problem of proletarian heterogeneity, the fact that the proletariat has not been a united, politically-conscious 'class for itself' collectively capable of articulating an agreed set of policies. This failure in its turn meant that he neglected the need to elaborate an institutional model which could resolve in a democratic manner the inevitable conflicts over policy that would arise within the ranks of the proletariat itself. The problem then remains to determine who – or what – was ultimately to decide policy. As 1918 unfolded, Lenin's answer, as we have seen, was to become clear, Harking back to the philosophy expounded in *What Is To Be Done?* – and to the one fleeting reference in *State and Revolution* – decision-making power was to be concentrated in the hands of the party, as the constitution of the Russian Socialist Federal Soviet Republic adopted in July, 1918, so Marc Ferro pointed out, recognised.[98] As the future of Soviet Russia was to reveal, this answer would lead in practice to a party-dominated, bureaucratic dictatorship over the proletariat. It was to be a dictatorship, moreover, whose powers were untrammelled as 'the conflation of politics and administration' which flowed from Lenin's advocacy of the fusion of legislative and executive functions meant that there could be no checks on it from the autonomous forces of civil society.[99]

The notion still persists that somehow the Left Communists were different, less authoritarian, more democratic. Lenin's most savage critic of late, Polan, has praised them for their opposition to the substitution of party for class, while conceding that this choice doomed them to '"utopian" politics and historical "irrelevance"'.[100] Yet as we have seen, such a conclusion is simply wrong. Despite their professed commitment to mass participation in state administration and to democracy within the soviets and party, the Left Communists too failed to provide a blueprint which could reconcile disputes within the proletariat in a democratic manner. Implicit in their critique of the political degeneration evident within the infant Soviet republic was the suggestion that only 'true' proletarians, organised in a cleansed party and elevated above the soviets, could in the final analysis be entrusted with power. Otherwise, the construction of socialism would be perverted. Within two years, in his seminal work, *The Politics and Economics of the Transition Period*, Bukharin was to take this suggestion to its logical and explicit conclusion. Recognising that in truth the proletariat was not a 'cohesive', class-conscious monolith, he frankly admitted that its less advanced elements would have to be subject to some form of coercion by the state, until such time as it was re-educated politically to the requisite level of consciousness by the Communist vanguard. Despite tendentiously arguing that such 'compulsion' was equivalent in fact to 'the self-coercion of the working class',[101] the conclusion is inescapable. At the heart of the politics of the Left Communists, with a few honourable exceptions such as Preobrazhenskii, who apparently argued in the late spring of 1918 that the party be disbanded,[102] lay an authoritarianism no less profound than that which they imputed to Lenin.

# 7 The Strength of the Left Communist Movement: Moscow, the Urals and the Ukraine

How strong was the Left Communist movement in Russia in the first half of 1918? Surprisingly, little detailed attention has been paid to this question, particularly in Western studies. Admittedly, some generalisations have been put forward. For example, Leonard Schapiro remarked that in January and February of 1918 the Left Communists 'enjoyed considerable support in the rank and file . . .', while Stephen Cohen has gone even further, claiming that 'at the peak of their political strength against the peace treaty, the Left Communists represented an enthusiastic mass movement, probably a majority in the party'.[1] Little more substantial evidence has been offered. Even less has been said about the support that they possessed in the months after the peace was signed when they were in marked decline, apart, that is, from broad allegations that they retained strongholds in the Moscow industrial region, the Urals and the Ukraine.[2] Questions of the actual extent of their support and why it should have survived in these regions have remained basically unexplored.

Soviet historians have contributed considerably more to our knowledge of popular support for the Left Communists. As we noted in the introduction, several of them have established in some detail that they won substantial support, within the party and the soviets across Russia, in the period before the impact of the renewed German advance in mid-February made itself felt. Moreover, they have also made some progress in delineating the areas where the Left Communists continued to find some favour in the spring of 1918, although they too have not provided any convincing explanation as to why this was the case.[3] The purpose of this chapter, drawing upon a range of

145

local sources hitherto relatively untapped, is to attempt to advance this particular area of study further. Its particular focus will be to test existing assumptions that the Moscow region, the Urals and the Ukraine were bastions of Left Communism and remained so longer than other parts of the country, and where this appears to be the case to suggest possible reasons why this should have been so. At the same time, in pursuing this objective, the rather skeletal depiction of the rise and fall of the movement given in Chapter 1 will be given more depth as we shall discover to what extent the arguments of the Left Communists struck a chord at the local level and also fathom more fully the reasons for their decline.

## THE MOSCOW REGION

Both Western and Soviet studies have long portrayed the Moscow region as a stronghold of Left Communism in the winter and spring of 1918. To a degree this interpretation is correct. Many leading Left Communists were to be found in the various Moscow party organisations, and, more significantly, the Moscow Regional Bureau has been singled out as the 'organisational centre of Left Communism'.[4] On closer examination, however, it transpires that significant modifications to this picture are required. In Moscow, as in much of Russia, the Left Communists enjoyed considerable, in all probability majority, support within the party, the soviets and possibly even among ordinary workers until early March. Then, after the Treaty of Brest-Litovsk was signed and ratified, they managed to retain control of the Moscow *Okrug* Committee for a brief period and of the Regional Bureau for rather longer, as well as mobilising some support within several local organisations. Yet what is most striking is not the grass-roots strength of the Left Communists, but their weakness. What distinguished Moscow, if anything, was that it remained one of the very few regions where they succeeded in retaining an organisational footing at all.

But let us begin at the beginning. As we saw in Chapter 1, the resolution of the plenary session of the Regional Bureau on 28 December 1917 witnessed the emergence of the Left

Communists as a sharply-defined faction within the party. They quickly mobilised considerable rank-and-file support within the city. On 11 January 1918, a joint session of the Moscow City Committee and the *Okrug* Committee, with representatives of the Red Guard and the leading Bolshevik paper in the city, *Sotsial-Demokrat*, in attendance, received Emelian Iaroslavskii's report on the hotly-disputed question of a separate peace with Imperial Germany. With the active support of G. Ia. Belen'kii, Timofei Sapronov and Aaron Sol'ts, Iaroslavskii won the meeting over to oppose the continuation of the peace negotiations. Two days later a City Party Conference, confident of imminent revolution in Europe, overwhelmingly endorsed this policy, with only two delegates voting against it and two abstaining. In fact, it accepted the most pessimistic conclusions of those Left Communists who spoke – Iaroslavskii, S. Fel'dman, Sol'ts, Iliushin, Konstantin Maksimov and Sapronov – that it was preferable to fight for the cause of international socialism, even at the risk of the defeat of the revolution, than to betray it by consenting to an ignominious peace with Germany. Allegedly, it also approved a decree forbidding Lenin's supporters to argue their case before the rank-and-file of the party.[5]

In the regional and city Soviets a similar picture emerged. On 12 January the presidium of the regional Soviet passed a resolution against peace. Two days later the executive committee of the city Soviet accepted the resolution proposed by Maksimov who argued in typical Left Communist vein that revolutionary war alone could bring a truly democratic peace by promoting the victory of socialism within and without Russia. Even the breakdown of negotiations with Germany appeared to cause little immediate concern. Speaking before the regional Soviet on 30 January, Grigorii Usievich sanguinely insisted that there was no reason for any anxiety, as the growing revolutionary movement in Germany would foil any renewed attack against Russia.[6]

Within days Usievich's prediction was shown to be utterly mistaken. However, even in the face of the rapid German advance, the leading party organs still denied the need to accept a separate peace. On 20 February the City Committee restated its commitment to revolutionary war. Its stance was strongly endorsed when it met with representatives of the district organisations on 24 February, and then by an almost two-thirds majority at the City Conference held the following day.[7] The Regional Bureau too remained implacably opposed to peace, passing on 24 February a resolution of no confidence in the CC, which had just voted for its acceptance.[8] On 2 March, at an expanded session with delegates from many organisations in the region present, the Regional Bureau remained intransigent. Stukov's derisive condemnation of Brest-Litovsk as a '*muzhik* peace', the inevitable consequences of which would drive the revolution from the path of socialism into a compromise with the aspirations of the petty-bourgeois peasantry, won overwhelming support. Varvara Iakovleva, Vladimir Smirnov and Stukov himself were mandated to defend revolutionary war as the only possible salvation for Russia at the forthcoming Party Congress. Within the *Okrug* Committee too the Left Communists prevailed, but only after a fierce internal struggle at the end of February.[9]

The mood within the soviets mirrored that of the leading party organs. For instance, at the end of February the executive committee of the regional Soviet adopted, by a large majority, the resolution proposed by E. N. Ignatov. In it he urged that the new, more punitive, peace terms dictated by the Germans had to be rejected. If accepted, they would frustrate the future economic development of Russia and thus destroy any prospects for socialist construction within it.[10]

At lower levels in the city and region attitudes appeared to be equally militant, at least until the beginning of March. Many of the district soviets within the city unequivocally supported revolutionary war. On 15 January the Presnia soviet debated the issue. It concluded by adopting the resolution passed the day before by the executive committee of the city Soviet, denouncing separate peace with Germany as a fatal blow to socialism both in Russia and in West Europe. War had to be waged, to help kindle the flames of revolution in Germany itself. The soviets in the Alekseevsko-Rostokinskii, Sokol'niki and Vsekhviatskii districts soon followed suit.[11] The German advance produced no immediate change of heart among the district soviets but rather the reaffirmation of their faith in revolutionary war, the Western proletariat and international revolution. In the last week of February the soviets in the Khamovniki, Rogozhskii, the City (Gorodskoi), Sokol'niki, Dorogomilovo, Basmannyi, Sushchevo-Mar'iniskii, and Vsekhviatskii districts all resolved to fight on. Similar levels of militancy were reported from the Blagushe-Lefortovo, Zamoskvorech'e and Simonovo districts.[12]

Moreover, evidence culled from reports in the contemporary press suggests that commitment to revolutionary war remained strong, for a time, at the grass roots. Even after the Germans began to advance on Russia again *Pravda* described the attitude of the majority of workers, and soldiers, in the city as 'resolute and cheerful'. In justification it referred, somewhat exaggeratedly as we shall see, to the apparent ease with which the district soviets and Red Guard had been able to mobilise detachments of volunteers to send to the front.[13]

Certainly, the central workers' organisations in Moscow were bellicose. The Third City Conference of factory-plant committees, which convened on 17 February, unequivocally denounced all thought of separate peace with Germany. Only revolutionary war, to spark off socialist revolution on an international scale, could beget a genuine democratic peace. It was to be accompanied by an intensified assault against all remaining vestiges of capitalism within Russia itself, to advance the construction of a socialist economy. Soon afterwards, on 23 February, the Union of Unions called on the workers to resist peace on German terms. Next day a meeting of the metal workers' union defended the same policy, followed the day after by the Union of Unions again, which now raised the dismal spectre that the Brest peace would gradually starve Soviet Russia of food and fuel, and so of all hope of salvation.[14]

Their appeals apparently found a widespread response among the ordinary workers. The Union of Young Workers in particular rose to the challenge by volunteering in such numbers for the detachments to be sent against the Germans that it had disintegrated by the end of February.[15] Many other workers, in a variety of industries, expressed a similar resolve. A general meeting of the metal workers of the Gakental' plant on 24 February concluded that the choice before them was simple: fight in the hope of igniting socialist revolution in Europe, or perish at the hands of German imperialism and their reactionary Russian allies. On 27 February the textile workers of the Semenov factory too demanded that all vacillation cease and revolutionary war be vigorously prosecuted, while next day a 4000-strong meeting in the Bogatyr' chemical works, denouncing the acceptance of peace as a victory for counter-revolution, called for the rapid organisation of a revolutionary army to fight the Germans.[16] Mass endorsement of resolutions in favour of war can, of course, be somewhat misleading as in fact few workers, it seems, were ultimately prepared to take up arms.

In the Moscow region too there had been widespread support for the revolutionary war, as Fel'dman reported on the eve of the Fourth Congress of Soviets.[17] Kaluga province, to the south-west of Moscow, was a case in point. On 25 February the Third Provincial Party Conference reaffirmed that the position adopted by the party in mid-January, when it had subscribed to the policy set out by the Left Communist-dominated Regional Bureau, was the only correct one. Those present at the conference professed that it was preferable to perish honourably in war with Germany rather than to accept a servile peace which would destroy the conquests of the revolution. Further, it mandated its delegate to the Seventh Party Congress, Kh. I. Tsukerberg, to oppose to the bitter end any such capitulation. Such intransigence in defence of revolutionary war, Tsukerberg himself alleged, mirrored the attitudes not just of the party rank-and-file but also of the majority of the population in the province. Lending some credibility to his assessment was the fact that the last Provincial Congress of Soviets to meet had committed itself to prosecute revolutionary war against world capitalism.[18]

To the north-east of Moscow, in Vladimir province, clear divisions on the issue of war or peace existed. The delegate to the Seventh Party Congress from Aleksandrov, M. S. Griundbaum, reported that the local party organisation had condemned both the CC and the SNK for their readiness to conclude a separate peace with Germany, whose objective above all else was to crush the revolution in Russia. Despite the renewed German attack the local party organisation remained convinced that the European proletariat would rise very soon to aid its beleaguered Russian comrades. However, the workers and peasants in the district fervently sought peace at any price and, according to Griundbaum, this pressure had impelled the party to reverse its policy on the eve of the Seventh Congress. Similarly, V. I. Dolbilkina, from Kovrov, claimed that the local party organisation had repeatedly supported the policy of revolutionary war, with the Bolsheviks in the local soviet being the first to volunteer for the new Red Army. The attitude of the local workers and peasants remained unclear, though the *uezd* soviet, as its counterpart in Shuia, saw no alternative but to fight if the revolution was to be saved. The situation in the city of Vladimir itself was quite different, as N. I. Danilov reported. There both the party and the most workers and peasants had urged the rapid conclusion of peace whatever it cost.[19]

Opposition to the Brest peace could be found elsewhere in the region. The delegate to the Seventh Party Congress from the Nizhnii Novgororod provincial organisation, M. S. Sergushev, himself a staunch defender of peace, admitted that many leading Bolsheviks bitterly rejected peace, citing as one example the stand taken by the Bolshevik fraction in the provincial soviet in late February. In Kostroma too the city soviet and the executive committee of the provincial Soviet staunchly upheld revolutionary war, while in Orel the Left Communists won over certain key localities, Briansk being the most important, closely followed by Mtsensk. And in Ivanovo-Voznesensk the executive committee of the provincial Soviet swung its forces behind the opposition to peace.[20]

In provinces such as Iaroslavl' there appears to have been but little enthusiasm for continuing the war, both within the leading provincial institutions and at the grass roots. The representative of the city party at the Seventh Party Congress, O. I. Rozanova, claimed that for the most part the local party had come round rapidly behind the peace policy advocated by Lenin, a shift which had won the approval of the factory-plant committees. Moreover, on 25 February a joint meeting of the city Soviet and the executive committee of the provincial Soviet categorically came out in favour of peace. At lower levels across the province the same configuration of forces was reported, with the noted exception of Rostov where the local soviet championed revolutionary war.[21] Other provinces within the region, Voronezh, Tambov and Smolensk, also soon shed any illusions about the feasibility of waging revolutionary war.[22]

In early March disillusion with revolutionary war spread rapidly, to encompass the majority of organisations which hitherto had firmly defended it. Moscow itself was a case in point. On 3 March, heeding Grigorii Zinoviev's arguments on the necessity of peace, the Soviet, with representatives of the factory-plant committees, the trades unions and the district soviets in attendance, voted to accept peace. The continued opposition of the Left Communists, led by Pokrovskii and Usievich, who repeated that peace would be tantamount to the political and economic suffocation of the revolution, cut little ice, despite the support of the Mensheviks and Left SRs present.[23] Next day the executive committee of the provincial Soviet followed suit. While Sapronov and Shternberg continued to challenge the view that peace would allow Soviet Russia any real breathing-space in which to rebuild its strength for a future struggle, even they were forced to admit that attitudes among the rank-and-file had shifted in favour of retreat. At best the workers and peasants were split on the question of peace or war, with the majority wavering in their resolve to continue to fight. I. I. Min'kov, the *Okrug* Committee's delegate to the Seventh Party Congress and himself a Left Communist, confirmed this gloomy picture of grass-roots sentiment in the province. Party activists and other conscious proletarians still supported revolutionary war, he claimed, but the masses, who were 'not conscious, [did] not understand the gravity of the current situation and [were] becoming increasingly demoralised ... [were] for peace at any price'.[24]

The same transformation could be observed within the city party. On 4 March, apparently in response to rank and file pressure, the City Committee voted by ten to seven to accept peace. That night a City Conference revealed the extent of the decline in Left Communist support. The impassioned pleas of Osinskii not to lay down arms before the forces of counter-revolution led by Germany gathered only five votes. Zinoviev, who had come to Moscow with Sverdlov to win the party over to the cause of peace, emphasised the futility of prosecuting a war when Russia had no effective army and was in the throes of economic collapse and hunger. Bellicose resolutions were not enough, he concluded, caustically pointing out that less than 3000 workers had volunteered for the new Red Army.[25]

Disillusion with revolutionary war had also penetrated to the grass-roots within the city. In comparison with the final days of February, early March witnessed few reports of enthusiasm for revolutionary war in the districts or among rank-and-file workers. Apparently the last major report of support for war came from a 2000-strong meeting of workers on 3 March, the day the peace treaty was signed, organised by the Union of Unions and the textile workers' union, which called on the proletariat to rally behind Soviet power and defend the conquests of the revolution, whatever the cost.[26]

Support for the Left Communists also disintegrated rapidly in the region. Fel'dman reported that even those provinces, such as Vladimir, which had formerly possessed substantial enclaves of militancy, now witnessed an almost universal groundswell in favour of peace at any price. The same pattern was to be found in Nizhnii Novgorod where both party activists and ordinary workers and peasants now almost all endorsed peace, and in Kostroma where a bitter rearguard action in favour of war, in this instance fought largely by the Left SRs, came to naught. Where widespread scepticism about the feasibility of revolutionary war had surfaced earlier, as it had in Voronezh, Smolensk and Iaroslavl', the first half of March simply saw a consolidation of this attitude. In Iaroslavl', for example, by the middle of the month the Second Provincial Conference of trades unions and factory-plant committees overwhelmingly approved acceptance of peace, while numerous reports from the countryside indicated that the peasants bitterly opposed any continuation of the war.[27]

As we saw in Chapter 1, it is over-simplistic to explain the rapid dissolution of support for revolutionary war by reference to Leninist, or Sverdlovean, 'bludgeoning' of the party or the soviets. Admittedly, Sverdlov and Zinoviev did put the case for peace in Moscow itself, but they appear to have won on the strength of their arguments. Beyond that, it remains doubtful if Lenin and his allies possessed sufficient able orators, or manipulators, to effect conversions on such a broad scale across the region. Moreover, Pokrovskii's suggestion, that the workers of Moscow – and the central industrial region more generally – abandoned revolutionary war because they were less militant than their Petrograd comrades, is equally simplistic.[28] On the contrary, Moscow did witness every sign of militancy amongst the party and ordinary workers in February, if a militancy that was not always translated into effective, and sustained, mass action, as Zinoviev had pointedly argued. What remains to be explained is the reason for this disparity between words and deeds. Part of the answer is given by Vindzberg, a member of the volunteer detachments sent from Moscow, first, to fight opponents of Bolshevism in the Ukraine, and then the Germans:

> The negotiations at Brest . . . animated the workers and drove them to adopt a militant attitude. The majority . . . did not approve of the position taken by the Soviet government . . . and willingly volunteered [to fight]. Only later, when we discovered what the real situation in fact was, the impossibility of waging war against a German army that remained organised and disciplined, only then did our jingoism begin to dissolve and we saw that [our] leaders had calculated quite correctly . . . and concluded the Brest peace [even though] it imposed Draconian conditions on us.[29]

The growing realisation that the German advance would be halted neither by revolutionary propaganda, nor by the hastily-assembled forces available to Soviet Russia, appears to have had the same demoralising impact throughout the region. There too economic disintegration, unemployment, food shortages, especially in the towns, and the exhaustion caused by these problems and the preceding three and a half years of war meant that any surviving will to resist quickly crumbled in face of the apparently unstoppable German juggernaut.[30]

After the Seventh Party Congress, the Left Communists' decline in Moscow and the central industrial region accelerated at all levels. On 10 March, the Bolshevik fraction at the Third Regional Congress of Soviets conceded that given the relative economic and military strength of Germany and Russia peace was vital. The breathing-space so won must be used to consolidate the revolution and to prepare for the inevitable renewal of battle on an international scale.[31] By the end of the month the Left Communists had also lost their control of the *Okrug* Committee. On 24 March the Seventh *Okrug* Conference rejected the pleas of Bukharin, Radek and their allies to condemn the CC for accepting a peace which had reduced Soviet power to no more than 'a scrap of paper'. Only the representatives from the Orekhovo-Zuevo industrial district supported them. Rather, the Conference resolved to use the current respite from war to complete, in a vaguely defined manner, the construction of socialism within Russia, and to organise a volunteer army of workers and peasants, to resist future attack by the forces of world imperialism.[32] Four days later, a Congress of Soviets of Moscow and region, with representatives of the district soviets and the factory-plant committees present, affirmed that the current exhaustion of the country meant that peace had been the only realistic policy to follow.[33]

Despite their decline, the Left Communists retained control of the Regional Bureau, notwithstanding the refusal of an expanded plenary session of the Bureau to adopt the resolution proposed by its Left-dominated core in the second half of March.[34] They continued to use it as a base from which to launch a sustained offensive against the policies of Lenin and his allies, until the Fourth Regional Party Conference, convened in the middle of May, when they lost their hold on the Regional Bureau. Lomov's motion, condemning Lenin's foreign and domestic policies, was rejected decisively in favour of the latter's own theses. The Left Communists won the votes of only nine of the fifty-six delegates present, though Iakovleva disgustedly remarked that the extent of their defeat was in good measure the product of the packing of the Conference with Lenin's supporters.[35]

In all probability there was an element of truth in Iakovleva's charge,[36] but it was by no means the sole, or most important, reason for their defeat. More to the point, the Left Communists' domination of the Regional Bureau was not justified by the amount of rank-and-file support that they possessed in the spring of 1918. This support, indeed, had become very limited. In the city itself a meeting of delegates from the various party cells that convened in April expressed a general sympathy for their critique of Lenin's domestic programme. It called instead for the more consistent implementation of 'the principles of Communism, in the economy and in politics'. To achieve this objective greater efforts would have to be made to 'straighten out' the policy of the *Sovnarkom*, which had deviated to the right, in order to bring it closer to the principles of the 'proletarian communist programme'.[37] Later, on 8 May, a meeting of party activists from the districts of the city came close to endorsing a Left Communist resolution condemning the peace, and the pernicious consequences that had flowed from it. The workers and peasants were to be mobilised to renew revolutionary war against German imperialism, while internally the consolidation of the revolution demanded the root and branch expropriation of the bourgeoisie. Sadly for the Left Communists, they narrowly failed to win a majority, by a vote of thirty against twenty-seven.[38]

Yet several district organisations continued to provide them with some solace. In April and May a significant 'group of Bukharinists' was active in Rogozhko-Simonovo district, bitterly attacking the 'bankrupt' central authorities for their isolation from the masses and their betrayal of the workers' revolution. Defying the directives of the City Committee, it allegedly conducted a campaign of intimidation against the bourgeoisie and the old *spetsy*, openly declaring that 'a deviation to the left was better than one to the right'.[39] Similarly, in early May the party in the City (Gorodskoi) district passed a resolution which demanded 'straightening both the internal and external policies of the *Sovnarkom* and bringing them nearer to the principles of the proletarian Communist programme'. On 9 May the party committee in Basmannyi district, in joint session with representatives from various party cells and the Bolshevik fraction of the district soviet, took much the same line. After protracted debate, Stukov's report was endorsed, condemning the policy of concessions to foreign imperialist and the native bourgeoisie alike. It too advocated a return to 'proletarian Communist' principles, calling for a renewal of war to defend the revolution, aid to the Ukrainian proletariat to rise against its

German occupiers and their collaborators, and an end to all compromises with the bourgeoisie.[40]

Such support within the city, sparse as it was, also proved to be ephemeral. Lenin and his faction tightened their hold at the City Conference on 13 May. Despite vitriolic attacks by Bukharin, Osinskii, Stukov, and M. P. Ianishev (who had the temerity to liken Lenin to the renegade Plekhanov and accuse him of creating a dictatorship within the party to match the dictatorship of finance capital that he was constructing within the country at large), Lenin's theses were approved by an overwhelming majority of 126 to thirty-four. Next day the *Okrug* Conference also endorsed Lenin's strategy, but by the bare majority of thirteen to twelve.[41] At the same time the Bolshevik fraction in the Soviet supported, virtually unanimously, the policy of the *Sovnarkom*.[42] Subsequently, on 16 May the Left Communists lost their control of the party organisation in the City (Gorodskoi) district. An open meeting of party members adopted the motion proposed by V. N. Podbel'skii approving the foreign and domestic policies of the CC and *Sovnarkom*.[43] Yet they succeeded in maintaining their position a little longer in Basmannyi district. On 20 May the district Soviet approved their resolution calling for the 'active defence' of the revolution and the immediate end to all compromises. On 31 May the district committee of the party adopted Stukov's resolution criticising the delay in implementing the programme of the October Revolution, particularly in carrying out the complete nationalisation of industry.[44]

Support for the Left Communists was similarly meagre in the region. The Left Communists themselves could find only three instances to report. On 28 April, the City Conference in Ivanovo-Voznesensk approved the theses of the Regional Bureau as outlined by Lomov, while on 10 May the *Okrug* Conference followed suit, adopting the resolution proposed by Bukharin by a vote of twelve to nine, with four abstentions.[45] On 13 May the City Conference in Iaroslavl' unanimously passed the resolution proposed by Iakovleva on behalf of the Left Communists. Within two weeks, however, the provincial party had overturned this decision, despite bitter protests by Babich and Panin against Lenin's continuing compromises in foreign and domestic policy.[46]

Finally, the Left Communists found considerable sympathy at the First Regional Congress of metal workers held between 19 and 22 April. Here a clear majority opposed the application of the Taylor system and the introduction of piece rates, as they themselves did. Moreover, a decisive majority rejected Lenin's policy of seeking agreements with the 'captains of industry', such as Meshcherskii. Instead, it demanded the rapid nationalisation of industry which alone would lay the foundations for the construction of socialism in the economy and ensure that the interests of the working class were safeguarded.[47]

The implication, it would appear, that the Moscow region was a bastion of Left Communism is rather exaggerated. Admittedly, the Left Communists enjoyed a substantial body of support within the city and across the region in the first two months of 1918, but as we saw in Chapter 1 this was in no way exceptional. Thereafter, from early March, it again proved to be no exception, with whatever grass-roots strength the Left Communists had possessed rapidly melting away. Their control of the Moscow Regional Bureau then did not reflect their continued popularity within the region.

THE URALS

In the Urals too, comprising the provinces of Orenburg, Perm', Ufa and Viatka, the Left Communists appear to have won much support, especially in the winter of 1918. Whatever indecision and confusion on the question of peace or war that reigned in the central organs of the party and government, here at least there seemed to be little doubt that the 'obscene peace' should be rejected and revolutionary war fought.

Within the party, the Third Regional Conference in early January set the tone. It categorically refused to consider separate peace with Germany, which would bring nothing but the destruction of all the gains of the revolution. The only possible alternative was to wage revolutionary war. The Regional Committee clung doggedly to this position, which met with considerable sympathy at lower levels in the party throughout the Urals. In the key industrial city of Ekaterinburg, the Party Conference that convened on 2 March demanded that the forthcoming Party Congress reverse 'the policy of capitulation' being pursued by the CC, reflecting, it appears, the opinion of the district organisations that revolutionary war be waged. Earlier, in Zlatoust *uezd* a Party Conference on 25 February had similarly protested bitterly against accepting annexationist peace and adopted the resolution critical of it proposed by Evgenii Preobrazhenskii, who, with Nikolai Krestinskii and Georgii Safarov, directed the Left Communist movement in the Urals.[48] On the same day the Bolsheviks in Nizhnii Tagil' came out against peace. Other organisations, in the Cheliabinsk district (*okrug*), Izhevsk, Lys'va, Perm' and Votkinsk, and in Viatka province, also swung their support behind the advocates of revolutionary war.[49]

The weight of opinion in the soviets mirrored that of the party, although here one must add that in many of them the still considerable SR and Menshevik contingents added their voices in protest against peace. For example, in the provinces of Perm' and Ufa the Left SRs then remained as strong as, if not stronger than, the Bolsheviks while in Zlatoust and Nizhnii Tagil' the Mensheviks and SRs in general equalled them.[50] At the end of February the executive committee of the regional soviet, in tune with the attitude of many lower-level soviets, repudiated the separate peace with Germany.[51] For instance, on 23 February the Ufa soviet had urged mobilisation in defence of the revolution against the threat posed by German imperialism, a position it reaffirmed on 2 March.[52] Similarly, on 25 February a joint session of the provincial and city soviets in Perm' condemned peace as tantamount to 'the suicide of Soviet power'. At the same time, it would betray the European proletariat, first of all in the Baltic provinces which in effect would be sentenced to brutal domination by the Germans. An honourable death in battle was to be preferred to the shameful compromise of the ideals of international socialism.[53] Other local soviets followed suit. On 26 February, the Troitsk soviet rejected peace and, with apparent equanimity, was prepared to surrender most of western Russia if that was the price of waging revolutionary war. On 27 February, a conference of soviets in Zlatoust *uezd* adopted a similar resolution. On 28 February, the Nizhnii

Tagil' soviet likewise denounced peace. On the same day the soviets in the Simskii mining district assembled and demanded that the *Sovnarkom* abandon its policy of peace in favour of one of revolutionary war. The soviets in Sterlitamak, Mariinsk, Okhansk, Nadezhinsk, Cheliabinsk, Neviansk, Revda, Lys'va, Sysert', Tobol'sk and Shadrinsk also came out against peace. Finally, the provincial soviet in Viatka too argued that peace on German terms would be suicidal and began to mobilise detachments to wage a partisan war.[54]

The views of ordinary workers and peasants in the Urals, as elsewhere in Russia, are difficult to ascertain with the desirable degree of certainty. Nevertheless, the existing evidence suggests that amongst them too there was much sympathy for the opponents of separate peace. Certainly, a series of meetings in the factories and plants of Ufa at the beginning of March reportedly supported the decision of the soviet to mobilise to fight the Germans. The Perm' soviet also claimed that it had the backing of the majority of workers in the city for revolutionary war. In the Simskii mining district, the trades unions and plant committees rallied behind the policy of revolutionary war, as did meetings in the Simskii plant itself on 1 March and in the Asha-Balashevskii plant on 3 March. Moreover, V. A. Shumailov, present at the Seventh Party Congress as the delegate of the Votkinsk and Izhevsk organisation, claimed that the majority of the 60 000 workers in the region were resolute in their readiness to wage a revolutionary war, for all their uncertainty as to whether it would be successful or not. Finally, so great was the antipathy of the workers of the Zlatoust plant to peace that they struck in protest at its conclusion, although in this case the Mensheviks and SRs, not the Left Communists, are credited with responsibility for inciting such opposition.[55]

It was with no mean degree of justification, then, that in early March Safarov claimed that across the Urals antipathy to a peace that was at one and the same time disgraceful and self-destructive was prevalent. Defending the resolution of the Regional Committee of the party, unanimously endorsed by an extraordinary meeting of the Urals *Sovnarkom*, the executive committee of the Ekaterinburg soviets, the regional union of metal workers, and the Ekaterinburg Committee at the end of February, he demanded that the Brest-Litovsk treaty be annulled. Revolutionary war, in the form of a class-based, partisan war against the forces of international imperialism, remained vital to advance the cause of world revolution, itself the sole guarantee of the salvation of the revolution in Russia. Should Petrograd and Moscow have to be surrendered in order to continue the struggle in the east, then such a price would have to be paid. Even ultimate defeat, he concluded, would inflict less harm on the cause of international socialism than the surrender of revolutionary socialist principles for the sake of a base and, in the final analysis, unworkable peace with German imperialism.[56]

However, as Safarov was writing, so the situation in the Urals was changing. Many party organisations and soviets rapidly came to accept the Brest peace as a *fait accompli*. On 6 March, a general meeting of party members in Ufa rejected the impassioned defence of revolutionary war mounted by El'tsin. By a substantial majority it endorsed Iur'ev's and Sviderovskii's resolution approving peace. In the circumstances, of general economic chaos and exhaustion, and of the lack of any effective army, it agreed that peace had been the only realistic policy to pursue, to win a respite during which the revolution could consolidate itself internally and, consequently, be able to give real assistance to the European proletariat when it rose in the future.[57] Several other organisations, in Beloretsk, Kotel'nich and Satka, too had come round to support peace before the Seventh Party Congress convened.[58]

Once begun, the rot spread rapidly. On 7 March, the Bolshevik-dominated Min'iarsk plant soviet conceded that there had been little choice but to accept the dictated peace. On 9 March, the party organisation in the Ust Katavsk plant followed suit.[59] By 13 March, the Nizhnii Tagil' organisation, where Grigorii Usievich had been active earlier in the year, also abandoned its opposition to peace. In the face of growing economic ruin, it conceded that a breathing-space of any sort was vital if the revolution was to survive.[60] On 23 March the Alapaevsk organisation accepted that peace had been inevitable, to be followed the next day by the Bolsheviks of Cheliabinsk. Party organisations in Orenburg, Kushva, Krasnoufimsk, Verkhne Ufalei, Novaia Liaglia and the Simskii plant followed suit. On 14 April a conference of Bolshevik organisations in Ufa province underlined rank-and-file disillusion with the whole idea of revolutionary war when it concluded that the Brest peace had been a necessary, albeit most painful, retreat.[61]

Within the soviets the same decline in support for revolutionary war was evident. Before the Fourth All-Russian Congress of Soviets began in Moscow, the soviets in Orenburg and in Orlov, Viatka province, had come round to favour the ratification of the peace treaty. After the Congress, many more shifted their ground. On 23 March the Gubakha soviet abandoned its advocacy of revolutionary war as utopian. Similarly, the Ufa soviet, apparently influenced by reports from the countryside that under no circumstances could or would the peasants continue any war, executed a *volte face* and approved ratification of the peace. At the beginning of April the Cheliabinsk soviet, after heated debate, also welcomed the peace by the narrow majority of sixty-six to sixty-four. The same reversal took place within the Ekaterinburg soviet itself.[62]

Dramatic and rapid as their loss of support was, the Left Communists were not yet beaten in the Urals. They continue to dominate the Regional Bureau of the party, from where they sought a union with the Moscow Regional Bureau in order to be able to resist more effectively the whole tenor of the policies advocated by Lenin and his allies. Moreover, they still possessed strongholds within the party in Ekaterinburg and Perm'. To take one instance, in Ekaterinburg a party conference on 21 April adopted the resolution proposed by Safarov. Again castigating the Brest peace as fatal for the survival of socialism in Russia, he called for the renewal and uncompromising prosecution of revolutionary war. Whether this policy struck the same chord in the ranks of the workers of the city remains open to some doubt, but the lack of evidence permits no definitive answer to the allegation, repeated several times by the Ufa party organisation, that the Ekaterinburg Bolsheviks were a group of 'intellectual ultra-Communists' who had no right to speak for the proletariat itself.[63]

At the Fourth Regional Conference of the party that convened in Ekaterinburg on 25 April the Left Communists again emerged triumphant. Over 130 delegates, representing more than seventy organisations allegedly comprising about 35 000 workers, were present. Safarov, ably abetted by I. Ia. Tuntul' and Vorob'ev, renewed his attack on the Brest peace as marking the capitulation of the revolution, its surrender into the hands of world capitalism. At the same time, the Left Communists denounced the domestic policies of the *Sovnarkom*, railing in particular against Lenin's attempts to reach some agreement with the bourgeoisie whose assistance he sought in restoring Russia's shattered economy. If implemented, such a policy would stymie the construction of a genuine socialist economy which, they continued to assert, could be built only by the initiative of the proletariat from the grass roots up. In fact, the conference even resolved to create an autonomous Urals commune within which authentic socialist policies could be introduced.[64]

There is little evidence, however, to substantiate Preobrazhenskii's contention that the majority of party organisations in the Urals supported such a programme, which lends some credence to accusations that the Left Communists themselves had packed the conference.[65] One notable exception was the city of Perm'. On 12–13 May a joint conference of the Perm' and Motovilikha organisations assembled, with Gabriel Miasnikov in the van of the Left's campaign. After fiery speeches by Borchaninov and Miasnikov himself condemning the Brest peace – for its failure to provide any real breathing-space and for the retreats from socialist policies that flowed from it – a resolution in support of the Regional Conference's decisions was adopted by a vote of thirty to twenty.[66] But this case appears to have been an isolated instance, as the majority of party organisations in the Urals – those already mentioned as well as organisations in Zlatoust, Sysert, Orenburg province and the Ziamskii district in Perm' itself, and the Balashov and Niaze-Petrov plants – rallied behind the policies of Lenin and the CC. What role the re-registration of party members ordered by the CC in May played in the Left Communists' failure to regain support at these lower levels of the party remains unclear. What is more certain is that many organisations saw this process as an integral part of the struggle to restore party unity in which the Left Communists' followers presumably suffered.[67]

The only other instances, it appears, of unequivocal support for the Left Communists came, on the one hand, at a session of the executive committee of the Regional soviet on 21 May when the resolution unsuccessfully put forward at the inter-district meeting in Moscow on 8 May was adopted, and, on the other, at the congress of workers of the Zinger company in mid-May, attended by thirty-three delegates from plants throughout the Urals. This congress approved the resolution by Iushkov, from the Regional soviet, castigating the Brest peace in typical Left Communist fashion for providing no genuine respite from war and destroying any prospects for socialist reconstruction in Russia.[68]

The spring of 1918, it would appear, saw the same disintegration of support for the Left Communists on the question of war or peace as had occurred in the Moscow region. The party leadership and the rank and file within and without the party diverged more and more as news filtering east of the rapid and largely unchecked German advance convinced the latter of the foolhardiness of any attempt to pursue revolutionary war. The Germans were not the relatively easy meat that Dutov and his Cossacks had been, whom locally-organised detachments of workers had succeeded in defeating in February, 1918.[69] The renewal of civil war in May, possibly combined with a purge of Left Communist sympathisers within the party, brought to an end any debate on this question. Reality now demanded that the Bolsheviks fight, if not against the Germans, then against the Czech legions and the forces of counter-revolution rallying behind them in Siberia. However, the Left Communists were not yet completely crushed. Their ideas on the organisation of industry met with considerably greater sympathy. In particular, their stubborn opposition to any agreements with the bourgeoisie, to experiments in state capitalism and to one-man management, and their call for nationalisation of industry, subsequently to be administered by elected representatives of the workers, found a fertile soil among very many Urals workers. Indeed, Paul Flenley has concluded that the Urals witnessed perhaps the most thorough-going experiment in workers' management in the first half of 1918.[70]

Early in 1918 the Third Regional Congress of Soviets, echoing the resolution of the First Regional Conference of Factory-Plant Committees, endorsed the implementation of workers' management in an organised and coordinated manner throughout the Urals. Industry, from the level of the plant itself up to that of the region, was to be administered by elected boards (*delovye sovety*) in which the workers would have a two-thirds majority.[71] Even after Lenin began his attempt to limit the scope of workers' control in the spring, support for workers' administration remained strong in the Urals. In mid-May the Second Regional Congress on the administration of nationalised enterprises firmly defended such a system, contending that it alone could prevent the re-emergence of a self-seeking 'administrative aristocracy' at the plant level. The same sentiments were to be found in the Ekaterinburg soviet and among many rank-and-file workers, for example, in the Zinger company and in Nev'iansk.[72] Moreover, at a conference on the administration of nationalised enterprises held in Moscow in May the delegate from the Urals, allegedly to thunderous applause, launched into a familiar leftist assault on those *spetsy* who denied the workers any role in the running of industry.[73] Finally, in late May, at the First Congress of Councils of the National Economy, the delegates from the Urals, with V. A. Andronnikov, the Commissar of Industry in the Urals region, in the van (as we saw briefly in Chapter 5) argued that the actual experience of trying to maintain production in the region had clearly demonstrated the need for a system of workers' management, and one radically more decentralist in spirit than that advocated by leading Left Communists such as Osinskii and Smirnov.[74]

The question that remains is why the Urals should have proved to be such a bastion of radicalism, since the recent economic and social history of the region might have suggested otherwise. For long it had been something of an industrial backwater, dominated by a multitude of small, technologically backward enterprises often located in isolated settlements in the countryside. The character of much of its work force had matched the backward state of its industry, composed in its larger part of unskilled 'peasant proletarians' who laboured two-thirds of the year in industry and spent the summer working on their farms. Episodes of militancy notwithstanding, in the main they had shown themselves to be politically passive and resistant to organisation.[75] The expansion of the rail network in the Urals after 1908, however, was followed by an influx of investment which saw the founding of new enterprises, as well as the concentration of existing production in modernised plants to meet the competition of the rapidly developing Donets basin. In turn, the years immediately preceding World War I also had witnessed the attraction of skilled labour, yet still in insufficient numbers to radicalise the region, which remained relatively quiescent in the period when militancy rose rapidly in the other industrial areas of the country.[76]

World War I itself produced marked changes in the Urals. Then a substantial migration of workers, from Petrograd, Riga, Revel, Warsaw and elsewhere in the west, swelled the work-force. In their ranks were politically active workers fleeing the repression of the authorities. These newcomers, arguably, brought with them what the hitherto depressed and down-trodden workers in the Urals had lacked, what Stephen Berk described as 'a core of class-conscious proletarians capable of providing revolutionary leadership under the right circumstances'.[77] The right circumstances soon emerged. Inflation well in excess of wage rises, a marked deterioration in working conditions, and the heavy-handed suppression of all protests provided the bases for a wave of strikes in the first half of 1916. By the winter of 1916–17 food and fuel shortages had exacerbated an already inflammable situation, although as yet this had not been translated into a mass influx into Bolshevik ranks.[78] These developments, however, were not peculiar to the Urals, and in themselves are insufficient to account for the broad support for extreme left economic policies evident in 1918. What also must be taken into account, as Preobrazhenskii claimed, were the particular experiences of many Urals workers in 1917 and early 1918, experiences which radicalised them and drove them to support economic strategies similar to those of the Left Communists.[79]

The cruel exploitation and repression of the workers in

the region did not diminish with the fall of the autocracy. Even the Provisional Government conceded that economically the position of the workers 'had become more parlous in the Urals ... than in the other regions of the state'.[80] All attempts to improve conditions, for example, by the introduction of workers' control, faced bitter opposition. The industrialists, supported by the majority of their *spetsy*, threatened to close down production and so deprive workers of their livelihood in response to attempts to institute even minimal levels of workers' control. The Bolshevik seizure of power made the industrialists, if anything, even more determined to resist any encroachments upon their traditional prerogatives. Hopes of any compromise between capital and labour in the Urals simply did not exist. As A. A. Andreev avowed in December 1917, the sheer intensity of the economic struggle in the Urals had radicalised many workers and heightened their political consciousness, so much so that at the grass roots they were intent on introducing workers' control and were even prepared to take over the running of industry should this prove to be necessary. Lenin himself acknowledged the gravity of the situation in the region, urging Shliapnikov and Dzerzhinskii in a letter of early December 1917, that 'all works in the Urals should be *confiscated*'.[81]

As the problems of maintaining industrial production, already jeopardised by food and fuel shortages and the accelerating breakdown of the transport system, were compounded by the sabotage of the owners, so soon after October the workers were forced to turn to nationalisation as a solution to this disruption. The refusal of the industrialists and their *spetsy* to cooperate in the operation of the nationalised enterprises soon placed the whole issue of workers' administration, not just control, on the agenda.[82]

In these circumstances, the Left Communists' programme for the reconstruction of industry on socialist principles coincided in large part with the actual experiences of many Urals workers. For them, the former's call for the widespread nationalisation of industry and its administration by elected workers' councils seemed neither outrageously radical nor impractical. Rather it accurately reflected what had increasingly been seen to be the only feasible strategy to keep the factories and plants working and the proletariat employed.[83]

## THE UKRAINE

As the Urals, so the Ukraine frequently has been depicted as a particularly fertile region for the Left Communists. Indeed, John Bushnell has even singled it out as 'the most important center of Left Communist strength'.[84] Admittedly, there is some substance to such an interpretation, as the Left Communists did dominate the leading organisations of the Ukrainian party in the spring and summer of 1918. On closer examination, however, we shall discover that the configuration of forces within the party, and in the Ukraine more generally, was considerably more complex that the above conclusion suggests.

But before we can proceed, we must delineate what is understood by the Ukraine. In 1917 and 1918 it had no universally accepted boundaries, as the Right SR M. A. Likhach remarked at the Fourth All-Russian Congress of Soviets. Then, apparently, the very name, according to Richard Pipes, 'was used loosely . . . to denote the region in the south-western part of the Russian empire'.[85] At its narrowest, it was taken to include the five provinces of Kiev, Podolia, Volhynia, Poltava and Chernigov, while the Rada envisaged it encompassing nine, or even twelve, provinces – the above, plus Khar'kov, Ekaterinoslav, Kherson and Taurida (inclusive of the Crimea), and the Ukrainian-populated parts of Kursk, Khol'm and Voronezh.[86] The picture is complicated further by the fact that the Bolsheviks in the Ukraine, broadly defined, were not united in a single organisation. Since July 1917, two major organisations had existed. One centred on Kiev and embraced the provinces of Podolia, Volhynia, Chernigov and Poltava. The other encompassed the more industrial and proletarian, and demographically more Russian, provinces of Kharkov and Ekaterinoslav, including the 'Ruhr' of the Ukraine, the Donets basin. This disunity was compounded by the refusal of the Odessa Bolsheviks to unite with the Kiev organisation after the

October revolution, as the formerly autonomous organisations of Nikolaev and Poltava had done, while the Bolsheviks and their Left SR allies in Taurida set up an independent Soviet republic.[87] The fundamental division, between the Kievan organisation on the Right Bank (west of the Dnepr) and the Left Bank, was consolidated early in 1918 when the Bolshevik-dominated Fourth Congress of Soviets of the Donets-Krivoi Rog region established its own separate Soviet republic. It did so seemingly to escape any contamination flowing from the peasant-dominated Right Bank which it feared might dampen the revolutionary struggle for the Donets proletariat.[88] Despite these complexities, the logic of the following discussion, as we shall see, warrants adopting a broad definition of the Ukraine.

Another complication is the fact that it is incorrect simply to equate the Ukrainian variant of Left Communism with its Great Russian counterpart. Admittedly, some of 'the most extreme supporters of Left Communism of the All-Russian [species]' operated in both areas in 1918, particularly Iurii Piatakov, Andrei Bubnov, Stanislav Kosior and Karl Radek, but this was not universally the case. As Vladimir Zatonskii, himself on the Left in 1918, recalled:

> 'Right' and 'left' Ukrainian Communists were not at all the same as 'right' and 'left' Russian Communists. At least among the left Ukrainians were those (I include myself in that number) who in the Russian context were considered to be on the right (they defended the signing of the Brest peace, etc.). Among the 'right' Ukrainians far from all of them, especially the rank and file, were to the right to the same overtly opportunist extent as comrade Epshtein (Iakovlev).[89]

One reason for this divergence, Zatonskii suggested, was the question of peace. Some Bolsheviks in the Ukraine agreed that Soviet Russia had but little choice to accept the Brest peace, yet insisted that the same policy was not at all appropriate for the Ukraine, given the quite different political conjuncture there. Another difference was to emerge with respect to the peasantry. In the Ukraine the Left Communists persistently advocated immediate action to oust the German imperialists, and their Ukrainian puppets, and in so doing ignite revolution in the West. Yet if this strategy was to be carried out successfully, they believed that it was critical to mobilise the peasantry *en masse* in the struggle, as Bukharin and Bubnov had fleetingly suggested during the debate over Brest-Litovsk. But if the peasants were to be mobilised, concessions – temporary concessions – were inevitable, as even a radical proletarian internationalist such as Piatakov conceded. For example, he was prepared to let the peasants keep the land they had won in the revolution even at the expense of establishing collectives. In this respect the Left Communists in the Ukraine were different from their counterparts in Russia who, as we have seen, opposed any conciliation of the peasantry that it despised and feared, attributing most of the compromises that the Soviet government had made to its pernicious, petty-bourgeois influence. Ironically, the conciliatory attitude of the Ukrainian Left to the peasants provoked Epshtein, the right 'opportunist', to accuse them of representing the interests of not the proletariat but the middle peasants.[90]

Finally, Pipes has suggested that the Left Communists in the Ukraine came close to Lenin in recognising the sensitivity, and potential power, of the national sentiments and were ready to compromise with these too. Certainly, they did support autonomy for the Ukraine and independence for the Ukrainian party. Yet it is doubtful if their proposals were anything other than expedients, whereby they could secure an organisational and territorial base from which to continue to push for revolutionary war. After all, Piatakov, the most influential leader of the Ukrainian Left, was renowned for his vitriolic attacks against any concessions whatsoever to national aspirations. As Kviring aptly remarked, '... any Communist who knew the position on the national question adopted by comrade Piatakov, both in that period [1918] and even earlier, [could] not reproach him for his nationalism'.[91]

But let us return to the primary objective of this chapter, to an examination of the strength of the Left Communist movement itself. In the early months of 1918 the picture in the Ukraine was not dissimilar to that in the rest of Russia, with opposition to peace widespread. There, too, in face of the renewed and seemingly irresistible German advance, a noticeable groundswell in favour of peace emerged. However, here this groundswell died away, not just because of the opposition, or machinations, of the Left Communists but largely because the circumstances pertaining in the Ukraine were markedly different than in the north.

On the Right Bank, in the Ukrainian Soviet Republic which centred on Kiev, opposition to the whole idea of separate peace with Germany was prevalent at the beginning of 1918. Having returned from Khar'kov to Kiev at the end of January, when the *Rada* was overthrown, the CEC of the Republic, and its executive organ, the People's Secretariat, issued an intransigent proclamation on 23 February in defence of partisan-based revolutionary war, which, in combination with a scorched-earth policy, it hoped would halt the Germans. Stressing the counter-revolutionary character of German imperialism, as well as its conviction that revolutionary pressure within Germany would preclude a large scale attack, it summoned the Ukrainian workers and peasants to resist at all costs. If they did, then revolution would soon spread to the West and rescue them from danger once and for all. There was no alternative since the Germans would never permit a socialist regime to survive in the Ukraine, or in Russia itself for that matter. On 6 March, in *Vestnik Ukrainskoi Respubliki*, the official government newspaper, the CEC and Secretariat reaffirmed their opposition to peace and bitterly condemned as spurious all Lenin's arguments in favour of peace.[92]

In the southern, or 'maritime', provinces, Kherson and Taurida, there was also considerable opposition to peace. In Odessa, the soviet called for revolutionary war, arguing that the bourgeoisie should be expropriated completely to pay for it. They found strong support among the Bolshevik-dominated union of young workers.[93] In Nikolaev, the party considered Trotsky's policy, of 'no war, no peace', to be correct, but on 25 February resolved to prepare to wage partisan war should propaganda and revolutionary contagion fail to stop the German advance.[94] In Berdiansk, on 3 March the soviet, supported by the local trades unions and factory-plant committees, condemned peace as fatal for the revolution and advocated revolutionary war.[95] Similarly, at the end of February the Military Revolutionary Committee of the Feodosiia soviet sought to mobilise rank-and-file support for revolutionary war.[96]

On the Left Bank too there was much pressure for revolutionary war, and more uncompromising socialist economic policies, in February and March.[97] In late February a conclave of the Khar'kov and Donets-Krivoi Rog Regional Committees, the Bolshevik fraction of the *Sovnarkom* of the Donets Republic, the Bolshevik fraction of the Regional Congress of Economic Councils, and other party activists witnessed a decisive victory for the Left Communists. Valerii Mezhlauk, Sudik and Osinskii, the last present on a mission to restore vital fuel supplies to Russia, strongly defended the by now familiar Left case. Peace on German terms, they contended, would consign all of Russia, including the Ukraine, to long years of reaction. At the same time, it would demoralise the Russian and West European proletariat and so deliver a mortal blow to the cause of international revolution. These fears, and the same sanguine belief as their comrades on the right bank that the Germans would find it impossible to send large forces against the revolution, convinced many of the necessity, and the feasibility, of armed resistance.[98]

Moreover, revolutionary war against the German imperialists was to be accompanied by a radical attack on the indigenous bourgeoisie, involving the complete nationalisation of large-scale industry and the expropriation of its other property. As in the Urals, the main impulse behind what amounted to a policy of workers' management was the industrialists' resistance to workers' control and their subsequent attempts to sabotage production.[99] Those who protested against these decisions, as Voroshilov did, found little sympathy and were shouted down. Osinskii's resolution was adopted by a crushing majority of fifty-four to ten, with one abstention.[99]

On 28 February, at the Regional Committee of the Soviets of the Donets Republic, S. F. Vasil'chenko spoke for the Bolsheviks. He reiterated the Left Communists' arguments that peace would be tantamount to the suicide of the revolution and would douse the growing flames of revolution in the West. His call for partisan war was accepted by a majority of four.[100] Later, on 6 March, the *Sovnarkom* of the Donets Republic issued a proclamation very much in the same spirit, above the signatures of Vasil'chenko, Mezhlauk and Rukhimovich. Summoning the workers, soldiers, poor peasants and even Cossacks to fight, it was sufficiently realistic to accept that revolutionary war might end in defeat. But there was no choice in the matter, it hastened to add, as the Brest peace itself would destroy the revolution.[101]

Important industrial centres and lower-level party organisations endorsed this policy. In the largest industrial city of the Ukraine, Khar'kov, a mass meeting held in the People's Hall on 27 February to commemorate the first anniversary of the revolution denied that a real democratic peace was possible with Germany. War, to defend the revolution and extend it to the rest of Europe, was the only way forward. At the same time, it too called for more radical socialist policies within the country, including 'the comprehensive nationalisation of production' and the expropriation of the personal property of the bourgeoisie.[102] In Ekaterinoslav, too, on 26 February, the soviet, with representatives from the soldiers' committees, the factory-plant committees and the trades unions in attendance, unequivocally condemned peace, arguing it would convert Russia into nothing more than a colonial appendage of Germany. The only way to avert this fate was to fight, both the Germans and their Ukrainian 'Junker' allies.[103] The same attitude was to be found in the well-organised Gorlovo-Shcherbinsk industrial region where a party conference on 24 February adopted the resolution proposed by the Left Communist, S. A. Gruzman. The district committee reaffirmed its commitment to revolutionary war on 28 February, while at the Seventh Party Congress the delegate from the district, V. F. Stozhok, alleged that the mood of the masses was equally 'bellicose'.[104] The soviets in Bakhmut, Izium, Kupiansk, Liman and Pavlograd were equally militant.[105]

Early March, however, saw signs of growing uncertainty about the wisdom of revolutionary war. In face of the swift German advance a groundswell in favour of peace emerged across the Ukraine. Even the Left Communists, Bubnov in particular, conceded that in fact 'a move towards peace' had grown there, ascribing it to the fact that the decision of the

Russian Republic to sign the Brest treaty had undermined the will to resist in the Ukraine itself.[106] Not surprisingly, the CEC of the Ukrainian Soviet Republic was among the first to succumb to this loss of will. Compelled by the advancing Germans to flee from Kiev at the end of February, in Poltava on 8 March it abandoned its opposition to peace. It mandated its delegates to the Fourth All-Russian Congress of Soviets to accept that the Russian Republic had no choice but to ratify the peace treaty if it was to preserve itself as a base from which to aid world revolution in the future. Even more, it was now prepared on behalf of the Ukraine to endorse the peace concluded between the *Rada* and the Central Powers on 9 February, provided that the latter did not intervene in internal Ukrainian affairs, in other words, provided they did not assist the *Rada* in its efforts to overthrow Soviet power.[107]

Doubts also emerged in Taurida about the sense of revolutionary war very soon after the Germans renewed their attack. In Sevastopol on 21 February the party committee and later, on 25 February, the soviet acknowledged that Russia had been correct to accept peace, given its manifest inability to mount any effective resistance. Implicit in this admission was their own preparednesss to do the same. Indeed, as late as 22 March, the *Sovnarkom* of the Taurida Republic, in apparent contradiction then to attitudes across the province, continued to advocate peace, not revolutionary war.[108]

The same uncertainty appears to have made its presence felt on the Left Bank too. Artem (F. A. Sergeev), a committed Leninist, who chided all who argued for revolutionary war for their foolishness, claimed to have won widespread support, within the party, the soviets and the population generally, in Khar'kov and elsewhere in the Donets basin.[109] Party organisations in Enakievo and the Iurevskii metallurgical plant bluntly stated that neither they nor the majority of workers and peasants in their environs had the will to continue the war.[110] The Lugansk soviet too voted to accept peace.[111] On 3 March, a congress of peasants in Ekaterinoslav also passed a resolution in favour of peace, contending that the Ukraine, just as Russia, required a breathing-space in which to organise its forces for the inevitable final confrontation with world imperialism. The miners and other workers in the Ol'khovskii district were now convinced of the futility of revolutionary war too.[112] Indeed, the advocates of peace appeared to have won an even more significant victory in Ekaterinoslav on 5 March. Then a meeting of the City Committee, with delegates from the districts, the Bolshevik fraction of the soviet and representatives of the factory-plant committees present, conceded that the Russian Republic had no alternative but to accept the Brest peace and so gain the respite that it needed to consolidate itself and rebuild its strength. Significantly, however, it added that what was true for Russia was not necessarily so for the Ukraine, where Soviet power had been given no breathing-space by the German imperialists and their Ukrainian allies. This crucial difference dictated that there was no choice but to continue to wage revolutionary war, accompanied, of course, by more radical socialist policies directed against the indigenous bourgeoisie.[113]

Indeed, the continued German advance best accounts for the transient character of the movement in favour of peace in the Ukraine in the spring of 1918. It also was at the heart of the heated debates that took place at the Second Ukrainian Congress of Soviets that convened in the still Soviet-held city of Ekaterinoslav on 17 March. Many delegates who gathered there mirrored the attitudes of their counterparts at the All-Russian Congress and with no little passion defended the policy of revolutionary war, allegedly professing that 'we shall die or we shall emerge victorious.' Although their protests against peace were finally rejected by the Congress, they represented a still substantial and reviving current of opinion in the Ukraine.[114]

Moreover, on the Left Bank Artem's success in winning converts to Lenin's policy of peace appears to have been incomplete and but short-lived. On 11 March the *Sovnarkom* of the Donets Republic, supported by the Regional Committee of the party, again came out unequivocally in support of revolutionary war. On 28 March it repeated that there was no alternative if the conquests of the revolution were to be saved. At the same time, it resolved to liquidate rapidly any vestiges of capitalism remaining within the Republic and to introduce universal labour conscription.[115] At lower levels a similar hardening of resolve to stand against the Germans could be observed. On 19 March the Bolsheviks in the Khar'kov soviet repeated that the continuing offensive by the forces of counter-revolution, foreign and native, meant that the only possible policy to pursue was one of revolutionary war against 'the armed White Guards of international imperialism'. Equally, measures to socialise the economy were also to be introduced immediately, amounting predictably to the nationalisation of all sizeable industrial enterprises and the confiscation of the personal property of the bourgeoisie.[116] A 7000-strong meeting of the workers of the General Electric Company's plant in the city endorsed this policy of 'merciless revolutionary war' on 24 March, while the post and telegraph workers of the city and its environs concluded that there was no option left but to fight capitalism at the front or in the rear.[117] In Lebedin and Mariupol' the party, apparently with the support of many workers, also agreed that circumstances dictated that the only path before them was to fight to defend the revolution against its external and internal enemies.[118]

In the south too there was a comparable rise in militancy. The German advance dispelled all illusions about the possibility of gaining any breathing-space and generated risings, albeit ultimately unsuccessful ones, in Odessa, Kherson and Nikolaev.[119] In Taurida the situation was much the same. O. Aleksakis, chairman of the Sevastopol soviet and himself an advocate of revolutionary war, admitted that in late February and early March there had been growing pressure from the grass roots to accept peace as a tactical expedient. The growing realisation that this policy had brought no respite led to the revival of pressure in favour of revolutionary war. On 30 March the Bolsheviks in Sevastopol resolved to fight the Germans 'to the last drop of their blood', and with the aid of the Left SRs began to arm partisan detachments. On 10 April the Military Revolutionary Committee of the Taurida Republic took up the mantle of revolutionary war again.[120]

Finally, the CEC of the now defunct Ukrainian Soviet Republic changed tack yet again. On 19 April it abandoned all hopes of accommodation or compromise with the Germans and instead called anew for mass worker and peasant insurrection against *Rada* and its German imperialist masters.[121]

Across the Ukraine, therefore, the grim warnings of the Left Communists that there could be no breathing-space from the crushing tentacles of German imperialism were vindicated in practice. Driven by a desperate need for grain the Germans ruthlessly swept through the Ukraine, restoring behind them puppet regimes – first, the *Rada*, soon to be replaced by the Hetmanate of Skoropadskii when the former was deemed to be insufficiently compliant – with whose aid they sought to ensure the flow of supplies back to Germany.[122] The reactionary nature of these regimes soon became clear: the working day was lengthened; wages were reduced; requisitioning of the peasants' grain was introduced; and in places the land gained by the peasants was returned to its former owners. All thoughts of possible agreement with the Germans soon vanished, and the movement in favour of peace disappeared. Opposition mounted and became manifest in a series of risings in the towns and countryside. Here at least Left Communist, and SR, calls for partisan war fell on fertile soil, but with no lasting success as the sheer weight of German forces crushed all such resistance.[123]

Yet despite this renewed preparedness to wage revolutionary war, the idea that the Ukraine remained a hotbed of Left Communism is simplistic. Admittedly, the leadership of the embryonic Communist Party of the Ukraine (CP(b)U) which fled to Moscow in late April was firmly in Left Communist hands. It was, however, largely isolated from, and far from wholly reflective of, the real state of affairs in the Ukraine itself in the later spring and summer of 1918.

The collapse of Soviet power in the Ukraine in March and April, and the persisting fragmentation of the party, led the surviving Bolsheviks to convene a conference in Taganrog on 19–20 April. Present were representatives of the now deposed CEC, as well as activists from Kiev, Khar'kov, Ekaterinoslav, Poltava, Chernigov, Kherson and the Donets basin, sixty-nine in all. Its main objective was to create one united organisation for the Ukraine which would be able better to direct Bolshevik activities in the region.[124] The conference itself for long has been seen as a clear-cut victory for the Left Communists. Certainly, by a vote of thirty-five to twenty-one their resolution in favour of the creation of an independent Ukrainian Communist Party was adopted, a decision which led Kviring and others on the right to fear that they would dominate the new party and use it for clearly factional ends. Moreover, the Organisation Bureau (*Orgburo*) elected by the conference to take responsibility for convening a congress of this new independent party was almost totally Left Communist in composition, comprising Bubnov, Ia. B. Gamarnik, Zatonskii, Kosior, I. M. Kreisberg (Isaakov) and Piatakov, with the centrist, Skrypnik, the sole exception.[125]

But in fact the conference was not an unqualified triumph for the Left Communists. Piatakov's theses, calling for an immediate mass rising by the Ukrainian proletariat and peasantry against German imperialism, were rejected. Such a rising, Piatakov argued, would act as the spark to international revolution and so help to salvage Soviet power in the Russian Republic itself as well as the Ukraine. Instead, the theses proposed by Skyrpnik, the 'Brest Communist' as Piatakov sardonically described him, were adopted by a narrow margin. In them he insisted that an immediate attempt to oust the Germans was premature and predicated the very success of any such policy on the prior outbreak of revolution in the West.[126]

Forced to flee Taganrog on 21 April, the *Orgburo* took up residence in Moscow where it began publication of its own journal, *Kommunist*, edited by Bubnov, Piatakov and Zatonskii. This journal reflected the Left Communist views dominant within the *Orgburo*. In its theses of 18 May it called upon the workers and poor peasants of both the Ukraine and Russia to unite to wage revolutionary war against the German imperialists and their indigenous capitalist and petty-bourgeois lackeys.[127]

Yet while the leadership of the emerging CP(b)U was clearly dominated by the Left Communists, this is not to say that they possessed much conscious support within the Ukraine itself. On the contrary, the available evidence suggests that there was little for the Left Communists to base themselves upon, as the occupying German forces had repressed almost the entire Bolshevik network that previously had existed there. Answering the anxieties of those who feared that the Ukrainian party would split on the same factional lines as its Russian counterpart. Zatonskii rather wrily summed up the situation. Such a split, he remarked, was simply out of the question as there was virtually no party left to split.[128] His judgement was soundly based. At an underground conference of Bolsheviks still active in the Ukraine that took place in Kiev on 26 May, all who spoke reported that the party had all but been wiped out. For example, there was no organisation to speak of left in the towns of Khar'kov, Chernigov, Kremenchug, and Poltava. In Ekaterinoslav, Kiev and Odessa the rudiments of an organisation had re-emerged, but the absence of politically-conscious activists remained a serious obstacle to further recovery. Moreover, the delegate from this conference who reported on the state of affairs in the Ukraine to the *Orgburo* confirmed that at the grass roots the party had been so shattered that any rapid revival was out of the question. Even more significantly, he also protested that little was known in the Ukraine of the situation within the party in Russia. What had transpired in detail at the Seventh Party Congress remained vague, and only recently had news filtered through of the renaming, from Social Democratic to Communist, of the party. Left Communism had remained something of a mystery throughout April and most of May, until recently an unnamed comrade had returned from Moscow bearing two issues of *Kommunist*.[129] In light of this evidence, the proposition that the Ukraine remained a stronghold of Left Communism in the spring of 1918 appears to require considerable qualification.

Indeed, the *Orgburo* itself was unsure of the mood of the Bolshevik rank and file left in the Ukraine. Skyrpnik evidently feared that at the forthcoming party congress the Left Communists would secure a majority. Bubnov, however, was not so confident, suggesting that the delegates from the Donets basin and Odessa might well tip the scales to the centre.[130]

The congress itself, the First Congress of the CP(b)U, duly took place in Moscow from 12–15 July. No single faction, however, could claim to have dominated it entirely. Certainly, the Left Communists did not possess an in-built majority.

Of the thirty-five organisations which responded to a questionnaire circulated by the *Orgburo*, thirteen reported that the Left was dominant, six were professedly under the control of the Right, seven claimed to be Centrist, while five appear to have adhered to no particular current.[131] This complex configuration of forces was reflected in the debates and decisions taken during the congress. Piatakov's resolution on the current situation, in which he argued, against Kviring and Epshtein, that the party, though not yet fully revitalised, should nevertheless prepare for an immediate insurrection against the Germans and their native puppets, was adopted, at the second count, by a bare majority of thirty-three to thirty-two. Similarly, Bubnov's resolution in favour of insurrection just prevailed, by a vote of thirty-one to thirty, over the counter-proposal that an immediate rising would be premature and contaminated by petty-bourgeois peasant influence.[132] However, on the question of the independence of the CP(b)U the Left Communists suffered a clear defeat. By a vote of thirty-three to five, with sixteen abstentions, Kviring's resolution was adopted and the decision of the Taganrog conference reversed.[133] Moreover, Skrypnik's resolution in which Soviet Russia's acceptance of the Brest peace was defended was approved by a vote of forty-three to six.[134] Some solace for the Left Communists was the fact that they achieved a majority on the newly elected CC of eight to seven and also controlled the newly-established Military Revolutionary Committee, which was given the task of preparing for revolutionary war in the Ukraine.[135] But even these successes might exaggerate the strength of the Left Communists within the Ukrainian party. They were certainly accused of abusing their control of the *Orgburo* to pack the Congress with delegates favourable to their position, or so a group of twenty representatives from the Donets basin alleged.[136] Unfortunately, the existing evidence allows no definite conclusions to be drawn on this issue.

As the summer advanced, so the Left Communists lost even more ground. The insurrection that they had long desired did break out, begun in Chernigov province on the initiative of the Nezhinsk Military Revolutionary Committee. The Military Revolutionary Committee of the CP(b)U in

Moscow responded to what essentially was a *fait accompli* by calling for a general rising on 8 August. The response to this call was pathetic. Several largely uncoordinated attempts were made but they were quickly and easily crushed by German troops.[137] The Left Communists' analysis of the situation in the Ukraine appeared to have been quite unrealistic. Even where they claimed to have local support, as they did in Khar'kov, they proved unable to do anything effective to promote partisan war, as Gruzman admitted at a session of the CC on 8 September.[138] After this costly fiasco, the Left Communists within the CP(b)U found themselves on the defensive. At the Second Party Congress, again held in Moscow between 17–22 October, the Right assumed the leadership. However, the eclipse of the Left was to be temporary. With the collapse of the German Empire, a new conjuncture again emerged in the Ukraine. The re-establishment of Soviet power now became realisable and allowed the Left to make a strong comeback. What happened thereafter is another story, more properly told as part of the history of subsequent intra-party opposition groups.

\* \* \*

What emerges from the preceding analysis in large part confirms much of the account presented in Chapter 1. Support for the Left Communists' call for revolutionary war was widespread in the first two months of 1918, but, with the notable exception of the Ukraine, rapidly disintegrated thereafter in face of the apparently omnipotent German military machine. Moreover, in the spring it also appears that the Left Communists won relatively little support for their own programme for the transition to socialism. However, in this respect the Urals remained an exception, where the question of workers' management continued to be an issue on which their views struck a responsive chord. Here the experiences of much of the organised work force belied Lenin's hopes of any compromise with the industrialists to restore production. On the contrary, the Left Communists' pleas for the extension of workers' participation in the administration of industry alone seemed to offer any hope of economic survival. Finally, the case of the Ukraine adds an

# Conclusion

At many points in the preceding study, major challenges have been made to the Left Communists' image of themselves as representatives of an alternative, a democratic socialist alternative, to Leninism. That is not to say, however, that their ideas should be dismissed as totally lacking in value. They did possess a certain strength, but of a negative rather than positive character. Their strength lay in their recognition of the threats to the construction of socialism in Russia posed by the policies that Lenin began to pursue after the revolution. In a sense, the Left Communists' were akin to that other great champion of democratic socialism, Rosa Luxemburg, in that they had a much greater awareness than Lenin of 'more or less what [socialists] must eliminate at the outset' if the path to socialism was not to become strewn with virtually insurmountable obstacles.[1] It is to the strength of their critique that we should turn first.

Their opposition to the 'shameful peace' of Brest-Litovsk was based not simply on a romantic defence of the principle of proletarian internationalism, but also on arguably realistic fears of its potential dangers for the revolution. Had it endured, it would have spelled the end of any prospect of socialism in Russia, with the country becoming at least a semi-colonial appendage of Imperial Germany and its workers and peasants victims of imperialist exploitation. That such a fate was avoided was no thanks to their advocacy of revolutionary war to ignite a socialist revolution that would sweep across Europe in one mighty wave and so eliminate, *deus ex machina*, the problems of building socialism in Russia. If carried out, such a policy would arguably have brought the full weight of German military power to bear down on Russia to crush the revolution. To their surprise, it was Germany's defeat in the West, for which neither they nor Lenin bore any responsibility, which 'saved' Soviet Russia from such a fate.

Equally, their critique of the domestic policies introduced by Lenin and his faction in the first half of 1918 also demands serious attention. Let us start with agriculture. In the short term, 'neutralising' the peasantry was probably the

183

only feasible strategy for the Bolsheviks to pursue when they took power. Yet the means by which Lenin sought to achieve this objective, essentially by the division of the land among the peasants, was to create grave economic and socio-political problems for the regime in the future, as the Left Communists predicted. Land division increased the very numbers, and power, of a small, land-holding peasantry which proved resistant to the eventual transformation of agriculture along collective, socialist lines, and, more immediately, to Bolshevik policies which threatened to strip it of the fruits of its newly-won land. For example, at the end of the Civil War much of the peasantry, with the defeat of the Whites now secure in the gains that it had made during the revolution, rose in opposition to Bolshevik requisitioning of grain, and forced the party to 'retreat' again. The New Economic Policy – 'the peasant Brest-Litovsk' – was introduced in 1921 essentially to 'neutralise' peasant opposition again and ensure the survival of the Communist regime. Yet this too proved to be a temporary palliative. Only six years later the regime was again threatened by the peasantry's unwillingness to market sufficient grain, an unwillingness in large measure caused by the prevailing pricing policy of the government and compounded by uncertainty about the future. On this occasion the crisis was resolved by brute force, with the dominant Stalinist faction coercing the peasants into collectivisation at a staggering cost in human life, and in the long term at the expense of agrarian productivity. The fears of the Left Communists in large part appear to have been vindicated.

Moreover, their forebodings that the recrudescence of authoritarian, bureaucratic practices in the administration of industry and the state encouraged by Lenin's policies could only lead to the degeneration of the revolution from the democratic, egalitarian and collectivist goals of socialism were equally well-founded. More than Lenin, they were conscious of the fact that ends and means were inextricably inter-related. In particular, they perceived that a vital element in the construction of socialist society was mass participation in economic and political administration. Otherwise, how could the workers begin to learn these vital arts and liberate themselves from the tutelage of their old masters and the ideology of the old order? If they failed to do so, then traditional forms of domination would revive. Indeed, in criticising Lenin's call for the reintroduction of one-person management in the spring of 1918, Evgenii Preobrazhenskii developed this strand in their thinking to its logical and uncannily prescient conclusion. Echoing Leon Trotsky's earlier diatribe against the potential for dictatorship in Lenin's theory of class consciousness, and his concept of party organisation based upon it, he prophetically warned:

> The party apparently will soon have to decide the question as to what degree the dictatorship of individuals will be extended from the railroads and other branches of the economy to the Russian Communist Party.[2]

In the 1930s the vast majority of former Left Communists were to fall victim to this party dictator, Joseph Stalin.

The acuity of their critique remains striking. Yet when we turn to examine their own prescriptions, serious misgivings begin to arise. No doubt, they attempted to construct their own programme for the transition to socialism, but whether it was the 'relatively coherent and articulate alternative to Lenin's' that Sirianni suggests is open to question.[3] Of course, they were operating in something of a vacuum. Their mentors, Marx and Engels, themselves offered little specific and unequivocal guidance on this matter. As Rosa Luxemburg once remarked, no 'ready-made prescriptions' for building a socialist society existed.[4] In common with most socialists, before 1917 the Bolsheviks had given little thought to elaborating a blueprint for the construction of socialism. Reviewing Aleksandr Bogdanov's *Questions of Socialism* in the spring of 1918, Bukharin conceded that no such plan existed. It could be formulated only '*in the very process* of the revolutionary struggle of the proletariat, it itself depends on the changing conditions of this struggle and can be worked out in detail only after the victory of the working class on a global scale'.[5] Perhaps we should credit them for their efforts to provide some content for this *lacuna* in Marxist thinking. But whatever credit they are given must be qualified in light of their failure to articulate a path to socialism which would in fact have devolved power to the workers. At the root of their failure lay the fact that their conception of socialism remained constrained by a series of assumptions which inevitably precluded the realisation of this goal.

In a rather inchoate way the Left Communists arguably enunciated the desires of many ordinary workers who sought control over their own lives. As Rudolf Bahro has argued, they 'expressed in some way or other the disillusion of those strata of the workers who saw themselves robbed of their birthright, a disillusion which was by no means focused simply on the particular problem of supply, but was ultimately related to the renewed subaltern role that the majority of workers had in society'.[6] Yet their proposals to transfer power into the hands of the workers foundered on a shibboleth of Marxism of that time, that socialism demanded the abolition of the market and its replacement by a centrally-planned economy. They did not comprehend that their conception of central planning was incompatible with the devolution of authority to the shop floor that they aspired to. Their failure perhaps was unsurprising. After all they were pioneers, the first in practice to engage in experiments in the construction of socialism, with no historical experiences to alert them to deficiencies in their theory.

Equally, their solution to the problem of burgeoning bureaucratic authority evident in the infant Soviet republic was fatally flawed by their conceptions of socialist politics. As much as Lenin they saw politics *per se* as the sphere of conflicts between classes. As such it would become redundant in socialist society where it would be replaced by the 'administration of things'. Hence they shied away from contemplating the creation of an institutional nexus both to mediate any disputes that might arise and to check the untrammelled power of the bureaucracy. Instead, they sought the solution to bureaucratic abuse in what Thomas Remington has described as 'class purity in the composition of the state'.[7] In other words, the workers were to be promoted to run all administrative organs. Yet their idealisation of the capacities and consciousness of the workers to do so proved to be a chimera, as they soon perceived. Then they looked to the most advanced element of the proletariat, supposedly represented by the party. But even the party, in their eyes, had become insufficiently pure to solve the problem of bureaucratism. Their solution was to purge it of its non-proletarian or weary and declassed members, whereafter all would be well. In fact, what this meant was the elimination from all positions of power of those who thought or acted contrary to their particular prescriptions of how they should behave. Ironically, the victims of the first of many such purges (in May, 1918) were the Left Communists themselves, soon to be followed by the various Left factions after the Tenth Party Congress in 1921, and ultimately and more violently, all real, potential or imagined oppositionists in the time of Stalin.

Even worse was their attitude to the peasantry. Even had world revolution occurred, the problem of how to deal with the peasantry in Russia, the overwhelming majority of the population, would have remained. But for the Left Communists, as for the majority of Russian Marxists, the peasants were a cancer, corruptive of socialism. Their objective was to transform them from petty proprietors into rural proletarians working in large, collective farms. But what was to be done should the peasants oppose the fate that the Left Communists ascribed to them? Implicit in their programme was the idea that force, if necessary, would have to be used to achieve this end. Here, most clearly of all, the anti-democratic character of Left Communism becomes apparent. In all, Ernst Haberkern's savage critique of another alleged prophet of democratic socialism, Jan Machajski, seems to be equally germane to the Left Communists. Beneath their radical democratic façade 'the authoritarian nature of their politics has tended to remain hidden'.[8]

And yet the legacy of the Left Communists endured in Soviet Russia, and even beyond. Their defeat at Lenin's hands in the late spring of 1918, and even the subsequent victory of the Bolsheviks over their opponents in the Civil War, did not resolve the questions that they had asked of the nature of development in post-revolutionary Russia. Survival in power was one thing, but not necessarily synonymous with the creation of a socialist society. Soon other factions emerged, the Democratic Centralists, the Military Opposition and the Workers' Opposition, to raise again the criticisms of the Left Communists that the revolution was degenerating from its libertarian goals.[9] Pragmatism and compromises may have contributed to Bolshevik success in retaining power, but had not assured many in the party that all was for the best in the best of all possible socialist worlds. However, the proper study of these oppositions is the subject of another book in itself.

Finally, since history arguably is present politics, and the Russian Revolution remains perhaps the most politically contentious subject of the twentieth century, what lessons, if any, can be drawn from this investigation? For those studying the Revolution in the hope of finding in Left Communism a model for democratic socialism that was prevented from coming to fruition either by the exigencies of the Civil War, isolation or economic backwardness, the prospects are indeed gloomy. Even had the Left Communists triumphed in 1918, even had Russia been spared the horrors of Civil War, and, *mirabile dictu*, even had the workers of the world come to its aid, it remains doubtful if socialism with a human face would have flourished. The ideological preconceptions of the Left Communists would have spawned a centralised, bureaucratic system, not an emancipated society in which power was diffused to the workers. But there are more fruitful lessons to be drawn. Just as the Left Communists had some appreciation of what socialists must avoid lest their goals be perverted, so too their failures can alert us to the shibboleths to be destroyed if there is to be any prospect of winning the battle for socialism and democracy – for indeed they are inextricably linked, as Sirianni has argued[10] – in the future. Perhaps Mikhail Gorbachev, and other advocates of *perestroika*, have recognised this fact, but at the time of writing it remains uncertain how far, or how fast, the Soviet Union in fact will evolve in the direction of a democratic, market socialist society.[11]

# Appendices

## APPENDIX A: LIST OF THE MORE IMPORTANT LEFT COMMUNISTS IN 1918

Abramovich, R.; Antonov, N. (Lukin); Arkady (Krumin); Baryshnikov, V.; Bela-Kun, K.; Bobinsky, S. I.; Bogolepov, D.; Boky, G.; Bronsky, M.; Bubnov, A.; Bukharin, N. I.; Fenigshtein, Ya. (Doletsky); Inessa (Armand); Ivanov, Vladimir; Kossior, S.; Kollontay, A.; Kritsman, L.; Kulibyshev, V.; Lensky, Yu.; Lomov, A. (Oppokov); Lukina, N. (Bukharina); Min'kov, I.; Muralov, N.; Myasnikov, V. G.; Osinsky, V. (Obolensky); Pokrovsky, M.; Preobrazhensky, E.; Pyatakov, G.; Radek, K.; Ravich, S.; Safarov, G.; Sapronov, T.; Saveliev, M. (I. Vetrov); Shternberg, P.; Skvortsov-Stepanov, I. I.; Smirnov, V. M.; Sol'ts, A.; Sorin, Vl.; Spunde, A.; Stukov, In.; Unshlikht, I.; Uritsky, M.; Usievich, G.; Vardin-Mgeladze, I.; Vyborgskaya, A.; Vasiliev, M. (Saratov); Yakovleva, V. N.; Yaroslavsky, Em.; Zul', B. G.

Source: L. B. Schapiro, *The Origin of the Communist Autocracy* (Cambridge, Mass., 1955), p. 366.

## APPENDIX B

Signatories of the declaration of the group of Left Communists at the Fourth Extraordinary All-Russian Congress of Soviets, 15 March 1918.

| | |
|---|---|
| Nikitin | member of the Mytishchi district Soviet of Workers' and Peasants' Deputies, Moscow *uezd* |
| P. K. Zarin | Perm' provincial and city Soviets of Workers', Soldiers' and Peasants' Deputies |
| M. V. Frunze (Mikhailov) | Ivanovo-Voznesensk provincial and Shuia *uezd* executive committee |

189

| | |
|---|---|
| Pavel Dybenko | CEC |
| A. Kollontai | CEC |
| G. Oppokov (A. Lomov) | CEC |
| N. Bukharin | CEC |
| T. Sapronov | (Moscow) provincial Soviet |
| V. Baryshnikov | |
| V. Obolenskii [Osinskii] | CEC |
| I. Armand | CEC |
| A. P. Stankevich | Ivanovo-Voznesensk provincial and Shuia *uezd* Soviet |
| S. Kosior | CEC |
| I. Unshlikht | CEC |
| G. Usievich | member of the presidium of the Soviet of Workers', Soldiers' and Peasants' Deputies of Moscow and region |
| Vlad. Sivkov | member of the Chusovoi executive committee of the Soviet of Workers', Soldiers' and Peasants' Deputies |
| A. Dugin | Alapaevsk Soviet of Workers', Soldiers' and Peasants' Deputies, Perm' province |
| Satin | Kamyshlov Soviet of Workers' and Peasants' Deputies |
| Vasia T. Biderman | Kostroma Soviet |
| Gurvich, Evsei | Pavlograd, Ekaterinoslav province |
| Katenev, Andrei | Nev'iansk, Ekaterinburg [province] (*sic*) |
| T. Mikhelovich | Aleksandrovka Soviet of Workers' and Soldiers' Deputies (Ekaterinoslav province) |

| | |
|---|---|
| M. Gimov | from Simbirsk, in a personal capacity |
| O. Aleksakis | Sevastopol' Soviet of Soldiers', Workers' and Peasants' Deputies |
| Ia. Klys | Luga Soviet of Workers' and Soldiers' Deputies, Petrograd province |
| G. K. Shchenin | Staryi Oskol' Soviet of Workers' and Soldiers' Deputies, Kursk province |
| V. F. Logginov | Kiev executive committee of the Soviet of Workers' and Soldiers' Deputies |
| V. A. Pokrovskii | Penza Soviet of Workers', Soldiers' and Peasants' Deputies |
| I. Burluev | Epifan' soviet, Tula province |
| G. A. Glikin | representative of the united Ivanov, Khrustal' and Shterov Soviets of Workers', Soldiers' and Peasants' Deputies of Ekaterinoslav province and the Don region |
| G. Safarov | Ekaterinburg Soviet of Workers' and Soldiers' Deputies |
| V. Kuibyshev | Samara Soviet of Workers' and Soldiers' Deputies |
| S. V. Sarychev | [Kolomna Soviet] |
| I. Krainiukov | Samara Soviet of Workers' and Soldiers' Deputies |
| E. Zhdanov | Lys'va Soviet of Workers' and Soldiers' Deputies |
| I. Z. Tkachenko | from the executive committee of the Soviets of the Kuban' region |

| | |
|---|---|
| N. Rychkov | Nadezhdinsk district Soviet |
| L. D. Sokol'skii<br>O. P. Sokol'skaia | Bugurslan Soviet of Workers', Soldiers' and Peasants' Deputies |
| V. Korneev | Saratov Soviet of Workers', Soldiers' and Peasants' Deputies |
| G. N. Gusev | Balashov executive committee of the Soviet of Workers' and Peasants' Deputies |
| Erman | Tsaritsyn Soviet of Workers', Soldiers' and Peasants' Deputies |
| V. Goriachev | Iuzov Soviet of Workers' Deputies |
| Churkin | Iuzov Soviet of Workers' Deputies |
| Paramonov | Khoperskii *okrug*, the Don region |
| D. Bulatov | Korchevskii *uezd* executive committee of the Soviets, Tver' province |
| Vl. Voznesenskii | member of the executive committee of the Liskov Soviet |
| Ivan. Mikh. Egorov | Tsaritsyn Soviet |
| A. F. Borman | Tsaritsyn Soviet |
| Mikhailushkin | Cossack military section, Tsaritsyn |
| Pokrovskii | Moscow Soviet |
| S. P. Kesarev | Usol'skii *uezd* |
| P. Pentsev | Khrustal', the Don |
| Iv. Kazakov | Bel'skii *uezd* Soviet, Smolensk province |
| P – | south-eastern army staff |

| | |
|---|---|
| M. Vetoshkin | CEC |
| M. Sedov | Shuia *uezd* Soviet |
| Sh – | Perm' province |
| V. Lochakov | Olonets *uezd* Soviet |
| P. Gureev | Khanzhenkovo, the Don region |
| Banatov | Sapozhkov Soviet |
| Kuznetsov | Briansk district Soviet, Orel province |
| Shan'gin | Perm' province, Irbit *uezd* Soviet of Workers', Soldiers' and Peasants' Deputies |
| Bryzgalov | Perm' province, Irbit *uezd* Soviet of Workers', Soldiers' and Peasants' Deputies |
| A. Bubnov | CEC |

N. Temezhnikov requested that his name be added to the above list.

Source: *Sed'moi ekstrennyi s"ezd RKP(b), mart 1918 goda: stenograficheskii otchet* (Moscow, 1962), pp. 294–6.

# Notes

## INTRODUCTION

1. S. F. Cohen, *Bukharin and the Bolshevik Revolution. A Political Biography* (Oxford, 1980), p. 63.
2. Ibid.; among many other studies, R. V. Daniels, *The Conscience of the Revolution. Communist Opposition in Soviet Russia* (Cambridge, Mass., 1960); B. Farnsworth, *Alexandra Kollontai. Socialism, Feminism and the Bolshevik Revolution* (Stanford, 1980); L. Schapiro, *The Origins of the Communist Autocracy. Political Opposition in the Soviet State. First Phase: 1917–1922* (Cambridge, Mass., 1955); R. Service, *The Bolshevik Party in Revolution, 1917–1923* (London, 1979).
3. Daniels, *Conscience*, p. 88; Schapiro, *Autocracy*, p. 141; Service, *Bolshevik Party*, p. 79.
4. Daniels, *Conscience*, pp. 4–6.
5. Ibid., pp. 6–7; for his diagrammatic illustration of his thesis, pp. 435–8. In diagram 3d, p. 437, the Democratic Centralists are located just to the hard side of mid-point of his hard-soft axis, yet in the text, p. 218, he clearly assigns them to the 'Ultra-Left' of the party. Presumably, then, Daniels would categorise the Left Communists within this tendency too.
6. J. C. McClelland, 'Utopianism versus Revolutionary Heroism in Bolshevik Policy: The Proletarian Culture Debate', *Slavic Review*, 3 (1980), p. 404.
7. Ibid., p. 405.
8. J. C. McClelland, 'The Utopian and the Heroic: Divergent Paths to the Communist Educational Ideal', in A. Gleason *et al.* (eds), *Bolshevik Culture: Experiment and Order in the Russian Revolution* (Bloomington, 1985), p. 114.
9. McClelland, *Utopianism*, p. 405.
10. T. F. Remington, *Building Socialism in Bolshevik Russia. Ideology and Industrial Organisation, 1917–1921* (Pittsburgh, 1984), pp. 115–16, 136–45.
11. Ibid., pp. 116–17.
12. McClelland, *Utopianism*, pp. 405, 418–19; Daniels, *Conscience*, p. 7.
13. Daniels, *Conscience*, pp. 218, 227, 330.
14. V. Serge, *Memoirs of a Revolutionary* (Oxford, 1963), pp. 228, 254.
15. McClelland, *Utopianism*, p. 420.
16. Schapiro, *Autocracy*, pp. 265–6, 295; D. M. Crowe, Jr., 'Preobrazhenskii, Evgenii Alekseevich', in J. L. Wieczynski (ed.), *Modern Encyclopedia of Russian and Soviet History*, 29 (Gulf Breeze, 1982), pp. 189–91.
17. Schapiro, *Autocracy*, p. 144.
18. McClelland, *Utopianism*, p. 407.

19. Z. A. Sochor, *Revolution and Culture. The Bogdanov-Lenin Controversy* (Ithaca, 1988), p. 179.
20. McClelland, *Utopianism*, pp. 418–19; Cohen, *Bukharin*, pp. 14–15.
21. N. Osinskii, 'Avtobiografiia', *Deiateli S.S.S.R. i Oktiabr'skoi Revoliutsii*, 2 (Moscow, 1927–9), columns 89–98; B. Clements, *Bolshevik Feminist. The Life of Alexandra Kollontai* (Bloomington, 1979), pp. 72, 181; also Farnsworth, *Kollontai*, pp. 40–1.
22. Remington, *Building Socialism*, pp. 138–9; Sochor, *Culture*, pp. 204–5.
23. V. Sorin, *Partiia i oppozitsiia. Iz istorii oppozitsionnykh techenii, 1. Fraktsiia levykh kommunistov* (Moscow, 1925), p. 7.
24. Ibid., p. 180.
25. Ibid., pp. 8, 27–41, 178–81.
26. Ibid., pp. 80–6.
27. Ibid., pp. 94–6.
28. Daniels, *Conscience*, pp. 89–91; Schapiro, *Autocracy*, pp. 143–6.
29. A. S. Bubnov, *VKP(b)* (Moscow, 1931), pp. 513–14.
30. Em. Iaroslavskii, *Istoriia VKP(b)*, 2 (Moscow, 1933), pp. 95–6; also M. G. Gaisinskii, *Bor'ba s uklonami ot general'noi linii partii. Istoricheskii otchet vnutripartiinoi bor'by posle oktiabr'skoi revoliutsii* (Moscow, 1931), pp. 28–9.
31. Bubnov, *VKP(b)*, p. 516.
32. *History of the CPSU(b)* (Moscow, 1938), pp. 216–18; R. C. Tucker, S. F. Cohen, *The Great Purge Trial* (New York, 1965), pp. 29–33, 341, 398–405, 416–23.
33. Daniels, *Conscience*, p. 90; Schapiro, *Autocracy*, pp. 143–5.
34. R. I. Markova, 'Bor'ba V. I. Lenina s trotskistami i "levymi kommunistami" v period Bresta', *Voprosy Istorii K.P.S.S.*, 5 (1959); Z. I. Berlina, N. T. Gorbunova, 'Brestskii mir i mestnye partiinye organizatsii', ibid., 9 (1963); D. V. Oznobishin, 'K istorii bor'by partii protiv "levykh kommunistov" posle VII s"ezda RKP(b)', ibid., 10 (1969) and 'K voprosu o bor'be s fraktsiei "levykh kommunistov"', *Voprosy Istorii*, 9 (1971); V. I. Tkachev, 'Bor'ba s "levymi kommunistami" v period Brest-Litovskikh peregovorov. (Na materialakh partiinykh organizatsii Povolzh'ia)', *Voprosy Istorii K.P.S.S.*, 6 (1986); and A. O. Chubar'ian, *Brestskii mir* (Moscow, 1964).
35. G. S. Ignat'ev, *Moskva v pervyi god proletarskoi diktatury* (Moscow, 1975), pp. 19–20, 111–12; K. I. Varlamov, N. A. Slamikhin, *Razoblachenie V. I. Leninym teorii i taktiki 'levykh kommunistov'* (Moscow, 1964), p. 391, claim that 'I. Armand, A. Bubnov, A. Kollontai, V. Kuibyshev, S. Kosior, N. Krestinskii, R. Zemliachka, M. Pokrovskii, V. Shumiatskii, G. Oppokov (Lomov), E. Iaroslavskii and others' performed valuable work for the party after they had acknowledged their errors.
36. R. C. Tucker, 'Stalin, Bukharin and History As Conspiracy', in *Great Purge Trial*, p. xxv; L. H. Siegelbaum, 'Historical Revisionism in the USSR', *Radical History Review*, 44 (1989), pp. 38–9; Ignat'ev, *Moskva*, p. 19, acknowledged that the whole concept of a Left Communist conspiracy contained in the Short Course was a crude distortion.

37.   Varlamov, *Razoblachenie*, p. 7.
38.   Ibid., pp. 6–8, 13, 69–73, 142, 190, 216, 363. Ignat'ev, *Moskva*, p. 110, appears to rise above this glibness, arguing that it was incorrect to equate the Left Communists and the Trotskyists, yet promptly, p. 111, proceeds essentially to do just that.
39.   I. E. Gorelov, *Nikolai Bukharin* (Moscow, 1988), pp. 4–5; I. M. Taranev, 'Diskussii v RSDRP(b)-RKP(b). Mart 1917–1920gg.: novye podkhody', *Voprosy Istorii K.P.S.S.*, 10 (1989), p. 146.
40.   Siegelbaum, '*Revisionism*, pp. 33, 38–9, 48.


CHAPTER 1:   THE RISE AND FALL OF THE LEFT
COMMUNIST MOVEMENT

1.   Varlamov, *Razoblachenie*, pp. 42–5; Sorin, *Partiia i oppozitsiia*, p. 14.
2.   *The Bolsheviks and the October Revolution, Minutes of the Central Committee* (London, 1974), p. 193; F. N. Dingel'shtedt, 'Iz vospominanii agitatora Petersburgskogo Komiteta RSDRP(b) (S sentiabria 1917g po mart 1918g.)', *Krasnaia Letopis'*, 1 (1927), pp. 65–6; *Leninskii sbornik*, XI (Moscow, Leningrad, 1929), p. 41; Z. L. Serebriakova, *Oblastnye ob"edineniia Sovetov Rossii, mart 1917–dekabr' 1918* (Moscow, 1977), p. 89.
3.   V. I. Lenin, *Collected Works*, 27 (Moscow, 1964), p. 99 (hereafter CW).
4.   Service, *Bolshevik Party*, p. 79.
5.   A full analysis of the rise and fall of the Left Communist movement in Moscow, as in the Ukraine and the Urals, will be developed in Chapter 7 below.
6.   Varlamov, *Razoblachenie*, p. 83.
7.   *Pravda*, 22 February 1918. The Central Committee of the Metal Workers' Union shared similar misgivings about revolutionary war, ibid.
8.   *Pravda*, 23 February 1918; for Volodarskii's report on general attitudes in Petrograd, ibid.; for Korchagin on the Peterhof district, Buron on the Rozhdestvennyi district, among others, ibid.; for the Nevskii district, ibid., 24 February 1918; for the Moscow district, ibid., 27 February 1918; and *Kommunist*, 5 March 1918.
9.   *Pravda*, 26 February 1918; D. Mandel, *The Petrograd Workers and the Soviet Seizure of Power* (London, 1984), p. 388. D. Fedotoff-White, *The Growth of the Red Army* (Princeton, 1944), p. 31, confirms that a readiness to fight to defend the revolution did exist, at least till 1 March, by which time he reckons that 15,300 volunteers had come forward in Petrograd.
10.   *Kommunist*, 5 March 1918. K. I. Shelavin, 'Iz istorii Petersburgskogo Komiteta bol'shevikov v 1918g', *Krasnaia Letopis'*, 2 (1927), p. 106. His claim, and that of Dingel'shtedt, *Iz Vospominanii*, pp. 66–7, that these delegates no longer represented rank-and-file attitudes appears to be somewhat exaggerated.
11.   Markova, *Bor'ba V. I. Leninym*, p. 56; Berlina, Gorbunova, *Brestskii*

*mir*, pp. 40–3; *Istoriia KPSS*, 3 (Moscow, 1967), p. 528; *Stenograficheskii otchet 4-ogo Chrezvychainogo S"ezda Sovetov Raboch., Soldatsk., Krest'iansk i Kazach'ikh Deputatov* (Moscow, 1920), p. 119 (hereafter *Otchet*); *Kommunist*, 6 March 1918; I. Getzler, *Kronstadt 1917–1921*. The fate of a Soviet democracy (Cambridge, 1983), p. 184.

12.  *Izvestiia Saratovskogo Soveta*, 21, 26, 27 February 1918, 1, 3 March 1918; *Kommunist*, 12 March 1918; *Istoricheskii arkhiv*, 4 (1958), p. 30; V. I. Tkachev, *Bor'ba s "levymi kommunistami"*, pp. 59–61, and p. 62 for peasant aspirations for peace.

13.  *Kommunist*, 14 March 1918; *Saratovskii sovet rabochikh deputatov, 1917–1918: Sbornik dokumentov* (Moscow, Leningrad, 1931) p. 394.

14.  Ibid.; *Izvestiia Sovetov Rab., Sold., i Krest., Deputatov gorod a Moskvy i Moskovskoi oblasti*, 28 March 1918 (hereafter *Izvestiia Moskvy*); Chubar'ian, *Brestskii mir*, pp. 225f. Kuibyshev and Krainiukov signed the declaration of the Left Communists at the Congress (see Appendix B) but there appears to be no record of what Kuz'min and Kazakov did. Kuibyshev also had been the delegate of the provincial party organisation at the Seventh Party Congress where he claimed a majority for revolutionary war in the Samara party. *Istoricheskii arkhiv*, 4 (1958), p. 29.

15.  *Otchet*, pp. 118, 128, 133; Varlamov, *Razoblachenie*, pp. 103, 129; Chubar'ian, *Brestskii mir*, pp. 229f.; Tkachev, *Bor'ba s "levymi kommunistami"*, p. 64; *Pravda*, 5 March 1918; Service, *Bolshevik Party*, p. 81, for Tsaritsyn in particular.

16.  *Kommunist*, 5 March 1918; *Pravda*, 20 January, 5 March 1918; *Vpered* (Ufa), 2 March 1918; *Otchet*, pp. 120–1, 131; *Izvestiia Moskvy*, 28 February 1918; Varlamov, *Razoblachenie*, pp. 103, 327; P. Dotsenko, *The Struggle for Democracy in Siberia, 1917–1921* (Stanford, 1983), pp. 18–19; R. Snow, *The Bolsheviks in Siberia, 1917–1918* (London, 1977), pp. 16, 221, where he also isolates Krasnoiarsk as a bastion of Left Bolsheviks during 1917.

17.  O. Anweiler, *The Soviets: The Russian Workers', Peasants' and Soldiers' Councils, 1905–1921* (New York, 1974), p. 222; also *Vpered* (Ufa), 24 March 1918.

18.  *Pravda*, 22 February 1918; *Kommunist*, 10 March 1918.

19.  *Sed'moi ekstrennyi s"ezd R.K.P(b.), mart 1918 goda: stenograficheskii otchet* (Moscow, 1962), p. 343 (hereafter *Sed'moi s"ezd); Izvestiia Saratovskogo Soveta*, 26 February 1918; *Kommunist*, 5 March 1918.

20.  *Leninskii sbornik*, XI, pp. 59–60; *Kommunist*, 5 March 1918, where Lomov argued that Moscow, the Urals, Khar'kov, Ekaterinoslav, Tsaritsyn, Kostroma, Kazan', Viatka, Saratov, Ivanovo-Kineshma, Kolomna, Krasnoiarsk, Poltava, Kronstadt, Tver, Voronezh and Arkhangel had rejected peace.

21.  Lenin, *CW*, 27, p. 76; *Pravda*, 1 March 1918.

22.  *Minutes of the Central Committee*, pp. 218, 221.

23.  Ibid., pp. 223–4.

24.  Varlamov, *Razoblachenie*, pp. 99–100. In the CEC 116 votes were cast in favour of peace, eighty-five against, with twenty-five abstentions.

25.  *Kommunist*, 14 March 1918; *Sed'moi s"ezd*, pp. 347–8.

26. *Pravda*, 3, 7, 9, 12, 20 March 1918; *Kommunist*, 10, 14 March 1918; Shelavin, *Peterburgskogo Komiteta*, pp. 106–7.
27. *Sed'moi s"ezd*, p. 60; *Leninskii sbornik*, XI, p. 71; *Izvestiia Moskvy*, 14 March 1918, reported only thirty-six voted for the Left Communist position.
28. *Izvestiia Saratovskogo Soveta*, 22 March 1918; *Kommunist*, 14 March 1918; Tkachev, *Bor'ba s "levymi kommunistami"*, pp. 66–7.
29. *Izvestiia Moskvy*, 14 March 1918; *Sotsial-Demokrat*, 15 March 1918.
30. G. L. Nikol'nikov, *Vydaiushchaiasia pobeda leninskoi strategii i taktiki* (Moscow, 1968), pp. 59–60; P. Kenez, *Civil War in South Russia, 1918* (Berkeley, 1971), pp. 119, 126.
31. Service, *Bolshevik Party*, pp. 80–2; C. Duval, 'Iakov Mikhailovich Sverdlov: Founder of the Bolshevik Party Machine', in R. C. Elwood (ed.), *Reconsiderations on the Russian Revolution* (Cambridge, Mass., 1976), pp. 225–8; L. Schapiro, *The Communist Party of the Soviet Union* (London, 1970), p. 247; *Otchet*, p. 30, and pp. 65f. for similar critique of Sverdlov by the Social Revolutionary, Il'in.
32. 'Tezisy o tekushchem momente', *Kommunist*, 1 (1918), p. 6 (hereafter *Tezisy*).
33. Ibid., p. 7. Osinskii had argued in a prophetically similar vein during a session of the CC on 21 January. *Kommunist*, 14 March 1918, contains a version of the theses that he presented then. K. Radek, 'Posle piati mesiatsev', *Kommunist*, 1, p. 3. The conflicts over agriculture, industry and the State are discussed fully in Chapters 4, 5 and 6 below.
34. D. V. Oznobishin, *K voprosu o bor'be*, pp. 70–3; Varlamov, *Razoblachenie*, p. 230.
35. S. A. Oppenheim. 'The Supreme Economic Council, 1917–1921', *Soviet Studies*, 3–4 (1973), p. 13.
36. Ibid., pp. 15–16; *Ocherki istorii Kommunisticheskoi Partii Urala*, 1 (Sverdlovsk, 1971), p. 330 (hereafter *Ocherki KP Urala*).
37. Cohen, *Bukharin*, p. 65; W. Lerner, *Karl Radek* (Stanford, 1970), p. 69, where, to be fair, he also concedes that even with strong leadership 'the Left Communists . . . had slender prospects at best'. Service, *Bolshevik Party*, pp. 80–3, has effectively refuted the notion that a failure of leadership contributed that significantly to their defeat.
38. See A. G. Shliapnikov's now classic account, 'Conditions of the Railways Under Workers' Control', J. Bunyan, H. H. Fisher, *The Bolshevik Revolution, 1917–1918. Documents and Materials* (Stanford, 1965), pp. 654–5; S. A. Smith, *Red Petrograd. Revolution in the factories, 1917–1918* (Cambridge, 1983), pp. 250–1; Service, *Bolshevik Party*, p. 82.
39. *Minutes of the Central Committee*, p. 224; *Sed'moi s"ezd*, p. 22; *Pravda*, 8 March 1918.
40. *Izvestiia V.Ts.I.K.*, 22 May 1918. Ironically, as we shall see in Chapter 6 below, many Left Communists agreed that all was not well within the party and sought a purge of the 'non-proletarian' elements which had permeated it.

41. 'Itogi partiinoi konferentsii Tsentral'noi promyshlennoi oblasti', *Kommunist*, 4 (1918), p. 15.
42. Varlamov, *Razoblachenie*, p. 365.
43. *Leninskii sbornik*, XI, p. 78; also R. B. Day, *Leon Trotsky and the Politics of Economic Isolation* (Cambridge, 1973), p. 18. S. Malle, *The Economic Organisation of War Communism* (Cambridge, 1985), p. 56, has argued that Left Communist criticisms played some part in the eventual failure of Lenin's plans for collaboration with the capitalists.
44. Ibid., p. 347.
45. Lenin, *CW*, 27, p. 19; also his speech, *Sed'moi s"ezd*, p. 13.
46. Ibid., pp. 38–9.

CHAPTER 2: THE DEBATE ON IMPERIALISM

1. V. V. Oreshkin, *Voprosy imperializma v rabotakh bol'shevikov-lenintsev v dooktiabr'skii period* (Moscow, 1968), p. 162.
2. D. A. Baevskii, 'Bol'sheviki v bor'be za III Internatsional', *Istorik Marksist*, 11 (1929), p. 34; and his 'Partiia v gody imperialisticheskoi voiny', in M. N. Pokrovskii (ed.), *Ocherki po istorii oktiabr'skoi revoliutsii* (Moscow, 1927), p. 435.
3. Sorin, *Partiia i oppozitsiia*, pp. 40–2; Varlamov, *Razoblachenie*, pp. 17, 35, 60, 178.
4. Day, *Leon Trotsky*, pp. 13–16; R. Pipes, *The Formation of the Soviet Union* (Cambridge, Mass., 1964), pp. 46–9; Daniels, *Conscience*, pp. 31–2; and Schapiro, *Autocracy*, pp. 108, 132.
5. S. F. Cohen, 'Bukharin, Lenin and the Theoretical Foundations of Bolshevism', *Soviet Studies*, XXI (1969–70), passim; and his *Bukharin*, pp. 35ff.
6. N. Harding, *Lenin's Political Thought*, 2. *Theory and Practice in the Socialist Revolution* (London, 1981), pp. 64–5.
7. V. I. Lenin, *CW*, 26 (Moscow, 1964), pp. 163–4, emphasis added.
8. Ibid., pp. 164, also 169–74. Baevskii, *Partiia*, p. 450, aptly remarks that although an identifiable current of Left Bolshevism did exist during World War I it was not the coherent faction that Otzovism previously or Left Communism itself were. Moreover, many of the leading Left Communists of 1918, such as Radek, were not members of the Bolshevik Party all during the war. Hence the terms Left Communists or the Left are used for convenience to avoid more convoluted expressions.
9. T. Bottomore, 'Introduction', in R. Hilferding, *Finance Capital. A study of the latest phase of capitalist development* (London, 1981), p. 1; Oreshkin, *Voprosy imperializma*, pp. 95ff.; Cohen, *Bukharin*, pp. 25–7; and Harding, *Political Thought*, 2, pp. 98f. and 53 where he disputes Cohen's contention that Lenin in fact owed more to John Hobson. K. N. Tarnovskii, *Sovetskaia istoriografiia rossiiskogo imperializma* (Moscow, 1964), p. 14, points out that of the leading Bolshevik theoreticians M. N. Pokrovskii remained an exception in developing an

analysis of imperialism that owed nothing to Hilferding.
10. Cohen, *Bukharin*, p. 396; A. Brewer, *Marxist Theories of Imperialism. A Critical Survey* (London, 1980), p. 79, argues, over-simplistically, that 'Lenin's contribution . . . was primarily to popularise the theories of Hilferding and Bukharin'.
11. Hilferding, *Finance Capital*, pp. 227–30.
12. Ibid., p. 225.
13. Ibid., pp. 223–4.
14. Ibid., p. 235; and p. 367 where he reiterated that '[t]he socialising function of finance capital facilitates enormously the task of overcoming capitalism.'
15. Ibid., p. 367.
16. Cohen, *Bukharin*, p. 89.
17. Hilferding, *Finance Capital*, p. 368.
18. Ibid., pp. 307–9.
19. Ibid., pp. 315–16, 318.
20. Ibid., p. 310.
21. Ibid., pp. 223–4.
22. Ibid., pp. 342–6, 350.
23. Ibid., pp. 346–9, 365.
24. Ibid., pp. 368, 370.
25. Ibid., p. 336.
26. Ibid., pp. 334f.
27. Ibid., pp. 312–13, 321–2.
28. Harding, *Political Thought*, 2, p. 102, is one of the few to have recognised the importance of Hilferding's work as precursor of subsequent Bolshevik thinking on the state.
29. Hilferding, *Finance Capital*, pp. 322, 327–31.
30. Ibid., p. 331.
31. Ibid., p. 332.
32. Ibid., p. 366; also Bottomore, *Introduction*, pp. 8–10.
33. V. I. Lenin, *CW*, 22 (Moscow, 1964), pp. 188–90.
34. M. Haynes, *Nikolai Bukharin and the Transition from Capitalism to Socialism* (Beckenham, 1985), p. 11.
35. N. I. Bukharin, *Imperialism and World Economy* (New York, 1929), p. 36, emphasis added; also pp. 28, 41.
36. Hilferding, *Finance Capital*, pp. 322, 329; B. Warren, *Imperialism: Pioneer of Capitalism* (London, 1980), p. 84.
37. Bukharin, *Imperialism*, pp. 38–9.
38. Ibid., p. 107; also pp. 61, 136–7.
39. Haynes, *Nikolai Bukharin*, p. 53.
40. Bukharin, *Imperialism*, p. 138.
41. Ibid., p. 133.
42. Ibid., p. 39.
43. K. Kautsky, 'Ultra-Imperialism', *New Left Review*, January–February, 1970, pp. 41–6, translated from 'Der Imperialismus', *Die Neue Zeit*, Jahrgang XXXII (1914), Band II, No. 21, pp. 921–2.
44. Bukharin, *Imperialism*, pp. 135–6.
45. Ibid., p. 136.

46. Ibid., p. 139.
47. C. A. Barone, *Marxist Thought on Imperialism* (London, 1985), p. 44; also E. M. Winslow, *The Pattern of Imperialism* (New York, 1948), p. 187.
48. Bukharin, *Imperialism*, pp. 137–8.
49. O. Gankin, H. H. Fisher, *The Bolsheviks and the World War: the Origin of the Third International* (Stanford, 1940), p. 188. In early 1918 Vardin-Mgeladze repeated the essence of this argument: 'For a long time Europe has been a single economic centre, from which the conclusion flows that it must be united politically. We propose the immediate slogan: "Long live a republican United States of Europe".' *Saratovskii Sovet*, p. 345.
50. Bukharin, *Imperialism*, p. 167, emphasis added.
51. N. I. Bukharin, *Selected Writings on the State and the Transition to Socialism* (Nottingham, 1982), p. 27; also *Imperialism*, pp. 146–8.
52. Baevskii, *Partiia*, p. 517.
53. Ibid., pp. 514–16.
54. Cited in V. I. Lenin, *CW*, 23 (Moscow, 1964), p. 23. Piatakov repeated the essence of this analysis at the April Conference, *Sed'maia (Aprel'skaia) vserossiiskaia konferentsiia R.S.D.R.P.(b.), aprel' 1917 goda: stenograficheskii otchet* (Moscow, 1962), pp. 212–16 (hereafter *Sed'maia konferentsiia*).
55. Baevskii, *Partiia*, p. 519.
56. *Vos'moi s"ezd R.K.P.(b.), mart 1919 goda: stenograficheskii otchet* (Moscow, 1959), pp. 111–12.
57. Varlamov, *Razoblachenie*, ch. 1, passim; E. H. Carr, *The Bolshevik Revolution*, 3 (Harmondsworth, 1971), pp. 18–19.
58. Gankin, *The Bolsheviks*, p. 215.
59. Ibid., p. 336; V. I. Lenin, *CW*, 36 (Moscow, 1966), p. 405, singled out the ideological affinity between Radek and Bronskii.
60. Gankin, *The Bolsheviks*, pp. 508–9.
61. Viator [K. Radek], 'Vneshniaia politika sovetskoi respubliki', *Kommunist* (Moscow), 2 (1918), p. 3; M. A. Savel'ev implicitly had argued much the same at the Sixth Party Congress, *Shestoi s"ezd R.S.D.R.P.(b.), avgust 1917 goda: stenograficheskii otchet* (Moscow, 1958), p. 160.
62. *Sotsial-Demokrat*, 18 April 1917; and N. Osinskii, 'Shest' mesiatsev revoliutsii', *Spartak*, 6 (1917), p. 7.
63. *Sotsial-Demokrat*, 18 April 1917.
64. *Materialy po peresmotru partiinoi programmy* (Petrograd, 1917), p. 9, emphasis added.
65. Varlamov, *Razoblachenie*, p. 35.
66. N. I. Bukharin, 'K peresmotru partiinoi programmy', *Spartak*, 4 (1917), p. 6. Peter Beilharz's critique of Trotsky's vision of world revolution appears to be equally applicable to the Left Communists: 'Trotsky's sound analytical basis – "national capitalism cannot be . . . understood except as a part of world economy" – is translated into political necessity, as though national culture and politics simply wither with the internationalisation of production, distribution and

finance. Rather than taking a distance from the forces/relations
formula of the 1859 Preface, the theory of Permanent Revolution
universalises it, projecting it onto the world system and reinforcing
thereby the fictitious notion of "automatic" revolution. Trotsky's
profound understanding of the importance of the world system is
effectively denied by its association with the notion of world revolution.' P. Beilharz, *Trotsky, Trotskyism and the Transition to Socialism*
(London, 1987), p. 28.

67. As Osinskii also argued in *Sotsial-Demokrat*, 18 April 1918.
68. Bukharin, *Selected Writings*, p. 28.
69. Ibid., pp. 17f., 25, 29.
70. Ibid., p. 19.
71. Bukharin, *Imperialism*, pp. 148–9; also his speech, *Shestoi s"ezd*,
p. 100.
72. Gankin, *The Bolsheviks*, p. 174.
73. N. I. Bukharin, 'The Imperialist Pirate State', in Gankin, *The
Bolsheviks*, pp. 238–9; also his *Imperialism*, pp. 127–9. Earlier, in a
more embryonic manner, Skvortsov-Stepanov and Lukin had
pointed to the growth in the power of the state that had accompanied the development of finance capitalism. Oreshkin, *Voprosy
imperializma*, pp. 106, 127.
74. Cohen, *Theoretical Foundations*, p. 157.
75. Bukharin, *K peresmotru*, p. 6; also his 'Rossiiskaia revoliutsiia i ee
sud'by', *Spartak*, 1 (1917), p. 11.
76. V. Smirnov, 'Demokraticheskoe soveshchanie', *Spartak*, 4, p. 9;
A. Lomov, 'Ot parlamenta k diktature', *Spartak*, 3 (1917), p. 6; N. I.
Bukharin, 'Gosudarstvennyi kapitalizm i sotsialisticheskaia revoliutsiia', *Spartak*, 2 (1917), pp. 7–10.
77. N. Osinskii, *Stroitel'stvo sotsializma* (Moscow, 1918), p. 32; his speech,
*Shestoi s"ezd*, p. 159; and, more generally, Harding, *Political Thought*,
2, pp. 145–6, and V. A. Lavrin, *Bol'shevistskaia partiia v nachale pervoi
mirovoi voiny (1914–1915 gg)* (Moscow, 1972), p. 58.
78. N. Harding, *Lenin's Political Thought, vol. 1. Theory and Practice in the
Democratic Revolution* (London, 1977), p. 206.
79. J. Riddell (ed.), *Lenin's Struggle for a Revolutionary International
Documents: 1907–1916 – The Preparatory Years* (New York, 1984),
p. 250.
80. Bukharin, *Imperialism*, p. 86.
81. Ibid., p. 137.
82. Haynes, *Bukharin*, p. 51, claims that Bukharin changed his opinion
regarding the prospects of socialist revolution in Russia between the
February Revolution itself and Lenin's promulgation of his April
Theses.
83. *Shestoi s"ezd*, p. 103.
84. Bukharin, *Rossiiskaia revoliutsiia*, pp. 9–10; *Gosudarstvennyi kapitalizm*,
p. 11; *K peresmotru*, p. 5; and his 'Krushenie kapitalizma', *Spartak*, 10
(1917), p. 7.
85. *Shestoi s"ezd*, pp. 103–4.
86. Ibid., p. 138, also pp. 102, 104.

87. Bukharin, *K peresmotru*, pp. 6–7. Lomov had argued for the abandonment of the minimum programme whilst in Saratov and, later, in exile in Kachuga during World War I. V. P. Antonov-Saratovskii, *Pod stiagom proletarskoi bor'by. Otryvki iz vospominaniia o rabote v Saratove za vremia c 1915g do 1918g* (Moscow, Leningrad, 1925), pp. 63–4. The party programme, drawn up at the Second Congress of the R.S.D.W.P. in 1903, contained a certain duality. While aiming ultimately at socialist revolution, it conceded that in the specific case of Russia it was first necessary to support the completion of bourgeois-democratic revolution, to sweep away the 'very many survivals from the old feudal order', including the most important of them all, the autocracy. The so-called minimum programme was designed with the latter revolution in mind. *1903. Second Ordinary Congress of the Russian Social-Democratic Labour Party* (London, 1978), pp. 3–9. Lenin himself conceded that the minimum programme was not designed to go beyond the framework of capitalism: *CW*, 41 (Moscow, 1969), pp. 384–5.

88. G. I. Safarov, 'Dve diktatury', *Spartak*, 10 (1917), p. 27; also his *Natsional'nyi vopros i proletariat* (Petrograd, 1922), pp. 138–9, where he reiterated this argument.

89. V. Sm[irnov], 'Regulirovanie proizvodstva i kontr-revoliutsiia', *Spartak*, 5 (1917), pp. 16–17; 'Regulirovanie proizvodstv', *Spartak*, 4 (1917), p. 6; Oreshkin, *Voprosy imperializma*, pp. 147–8 for Lukin; *Shestoi s"ezd*, p. 157, where Osinskii stressed the impact of war in accelerating the organisation of the Russian economy.

90. Antonov-Saratovskii, *Pod stiagom*, pp. 63f., 73.

91. A. L. Lomov, *Razlozhenie kapitalizma i organizatsiia kommunizma* (Moscow, 1918), pp. 4, 21–6.

92. Osinskii, *Stroitel'stvo*, pp. 6–7.

93. Ibid., pp. 6–7, 9–10.

94. Ibid., pp. 10, 13.

95. Ibid., pp. 5, 18.

96. Ibid., p. 6.

97. Ibid., pp. 12, 19.

98. Ibid., p. 13.

99. Ibid., pp. 14, 17.

100. Ibid., pp. 19–20; see too his *Demokraticheskaia respublika i sovetskaia respublika* (Odessa, 1920), p. 4, where he insisted that a system of finance capitalism analogous to that of the West had existed in Russia before the October Revolution.

101. Osinskii, *Stroitel'stvo*, p. 23.

102. K. Radek, *Piat' let Kominterna* (Moscow, 1924), pp. 21, 23–4; *Sotsial-Demokrat*, 27 October 1917, for a similar prognosis of the permeation of socialist production by Bukharin; cf. the views of Hilferding, *Finance Capital*, pp. 367–8.

103. Radek, *Piat' let*, pp. 25–6.

104. So Bukharin argued, *Sotsial-Demokrat*, 27 October 1917.

105. Harding, *Political Thought*, 2, pp. 321–2, makes the point that Lenin too failed to define how a general European revolution would

facilitate the construction of socialism in Russia.
106. *Sotsial-Demokrat*, 27 October 1917, emphasis added.
107. N. I. Bukharin, *The Politics and Economics of the Transition Period* (London, 1979), pp. 168–9; also his *Pirate State*, pp. 236–9, and his speech, *Sed'moi s"ezd*, p. 26. For similar explanations of why revolution first erupted in Russia, Radek, *Pravda*, 23 January 1918 and *Piat' let*, pp. 25–6; and Lomov, *Razlozhenie*, p. 65. Cf. the later formulation of Gramsci to account for the resistance of the West to socialist revolution: 'In the East [Russia], the State was everything, civil society was primordial and gelatinous; in the West, there was a proper relationship between State and civil society, and when the State trembled a sturdy structure of civil society was at once revealed. The State was only an outer ditch, behind which there was a powerful system of fortresses and earthworks; more or less numerous from one State to the next, it goes without saying – but this precisely necessitated an accurate reconnaissance of each individual country.' A. Gramsci, *Selections from the Prison Notebooks* (New York, 1971), p. 238.
108. Cohen, *Bukharin*, p. 47; Daniels, *Conscience*, pp. 35–6, argues similarly.
109. Harding, *Political Thought*, 2, p. 48, emphasis added, p. 67.
110. Ibid., p. 150.
111. Ibid., p. 313.
112. Ibid., p. 147.
113. Ibid., p. 163, also p. 59; but see p. 67 where Harding argues that in 1916 Lenin believed that socialist revolution 'would occur first in those advanced countries where the objective and subjective conditions had fully matured and where the national democratic revolution had long been accomplished'.
114. Ibid., pp. 320–2.
115. Ibid., p. 163.
116. Lenin, *CW*, 36, pp. 299, 302; and *CW*, 21 (Moscow, 1964), p. 126 where he claimed that 'bourgeois states, with their national boundaries, have outlived themselves ...'
117. Ibid., p. 345.
118. Ibid., p. 379.
119. Ibid., p. 279, also pp. 402f., 418f.
120. Lenin, *CW*, 23, pp. 307, 324, 340–1, 371.
121. Ibid., especially pp. 371–2, also pp. 297, 340.
122. V. I. Lenin, *CW*, 35 (Moscow, 1966), p. 298.
123. V. I. Lenin, *CW*, 24 (Moscow, 1964), p. 238.
124. Ibid., p. 305.
125. V. I. Lenin, *CW*, 25, (Moscow, 1964), p. 384; this appears to be the first explicit reference by Lenin to the concept of weak links in imperialist chains.
126. Lenin, *CW*, 26, pp. 74–7, also pp. 38, 40, 182.
127. Lenin, *CW*, 24, pp. 416–17; he repeated this argument at the Seventh Party Congress, *Sed'moi s"ezd*, p. 12.
128. S. V. Tiutiukin, *Voina, mir, revoliutsiia. Ideinaia bor'ba v rabochem*

*dvizhenii Rossii 1914–1917gg.* (Moscow, 1972), p. 172.
129. Lenin, *CW*, 21, p. 236
130. Lenin, *CW*, 22, p. 144; also *CW*, 21, p. 408.
131. Lenin, *CW*, 23, p. 60.
132. Lenin, *CW*, 21, p. 342; *CW*, 22, p. 245.
133. Ibid., p. 258, where he used this argument to explain the defeat of the Irish rebellion of 1916.
134. Lenin, *CW*, 25, p. 79; also *CW*, 21, p. 342.
135. Lenin, *CW*, 35, 253.
136. Lenin, *CW*, 23, pp. 58–9.
137. Lenin, *CW*, 24, pp. 66–7.
138. Lenin, *CW*, 26, p. 171, emphasis added.
139. Lenin, *CW*, 22, pp. 150–1, emphasis added.
140. Lenin, *CW*, 21, p. 33.
141. Ibid., pp. 259, 277, 306, 419–20; also *CW*, 22, pp. 134–5, 143, 154.
142. Ibid., p. 194.
143. Ibid., p. 205.
144. Ibid., p. 232.
145. Ibid., p. 259.
146. V. I. Lenin, *CW*, 39 (Moscow, 1968), p. 41.
147. Lenin, *CW*, 23, p. 59.
148. Lenin, *CW*, 35, p. 249.
149. Lenin, *CW*, 23, pp. 273–6.
150. Ibid., p. 308.
151. Ibid., pp. 340–1. Lenin's conversion on the question of the state can more appropriately be examined in detail in Chapter 6 below.
152. Harding, *Political Thought*, 2, p. 145; N. Sukhanov, *The Russian Revolution 1917. A Personal Record* (Princeton, 1984), pp. 280, 283.
153. Lenin, *CW*, 24, p. 22.
154. Sukhanov, *Revolution*, p. 284.
155. Ibid., p. 289.
156. Cited in ibid., p. 286; *Sed'maia konferentsiia*, pp. 106–7.
157. Lenin, *CW*, 24, pp. 462, 465.
158. Lenin, *CW*, 25, p. 44.
159. Ibid., p. 172 and p. 202 where he appears to have overcome any lingering doubts about the capitalist character of Russia.
160. Ibid., p. 358.
161. Ibid., p. 359.
162. Lenin, *CW*, 26, p. 94.
163. Ibid., pp. 105–6.
164. N. Maiorskii, N. El'vov, 'K voprosu o kharaktere i dvizhushchikh silakh Oktiabr'skoi revoliutsii', *Proletarskaia revoliutsiia*, no. 11 (1927), p. 35, claim that Lenin was able to defend the propriety of socialist revolution in Russia on the grounds that once a certain 'minimum level of capitalist development' had been achieved the transition to socialism was possible.
165. Harding, *Political Thought*, 2, pp. 199–201, 220, 324–5.
166. Lenin, *CW*, 27, p. 163; at the Seventh Party Congress he had begun to modify his view that state capitalism was the 'rung on the ladder of

history' immediately below that of socialism, arguing that '[w]e do not know and cannot know how many stages of transition to socialism there will be', ibid., p. 136.

167. Ibid., pp. 334, 338.
168. Ibid., p. 342; N. Valentinov, *Novaia ekonomicheskaia politika i krizis partii posle smerti Lenina* (Stanford, 1971) p. 6, claims that Lenin conceded after the October Revolution that the material base for socialism had not existed in Russia.
169. Lenin, *CW*, 26, pp. 470–1, also p. 443.
170. Ibid., p. 482.
171. Ibid., pp. 291–2, 386, 493.
172. Lenin, *CW*, 27, pp. 369, 377.
173. Ibid., pp. 372–3.
174. Daniels, *Conscience*, pp. 36–7.
175. Harding, *Political Thought*, 2, p. 3.
176. Remington, *Building Socialism*, p. 53; R. Service, *Lenin, a Political Life, 1: The Strengths of Contradiction* (London, 1985), p. 164.
177. Cohen, *Bukharin*, p. 64, lays great stress on the 'generational issue'.
178. R. B. Day, 'Introduction', Bukharin, *Selected Writings*, p. xxxix.
179. Harding, *Political Thought*, pp. 201, 205–8.

CHAPTER 3:   BREST-LITOVSK

1. Farnsworth, *Alexandra Kollontai*, p. 106.
2. W. H. Chamberlin, *The Russian Revolution*, 1 (New York, 1965), pp. 389, 397, 411–12. For Lenin, *CW*, 27, pp. 25–6, 36–7, 62, 92–4, 177, 231.
3. Chamberlin, *Revolution*, 1, p. 396.
4. V. Serge, *Year One of the Russian Revolution* (London, 1972), pp. 156, 175.
5. Schapiro, *Communist Party*, pp. 187–8; Daniels, *Conscience*, p. 72.
6. Cohen, *Bukharin*, pp. 64–5; for Lenin, *CW*, 27, pp. 92, 108.
7. Cited in J. W. Wheeler-Bennett, *Brest-Litovsk. The Forgotten Peace, March 1918* (London, 1968), p. 125. Sorin, *Partiia i oppozitsiia*, p. 52, lays great stress on emotional factors at the root of the Left Communists' opposition to peace.
8. *Minutes of the Central Committee*, p. 215. L. D. Trotsky, *My Life* (New York, 1960), p. 389. Of the Left Communists at this session of the CC, only Lomov supported Bukharin's unequivocal rejection of any aid from the Allies, *Minutes*, p. 213.
9. W. H. Rosenberg, 'Russian Labor and Bolshevik Power After October', *Slavic Review*, 2 (1985), p. 228; and *Sotsial-Demokrat*, 28 February 1918. For opposition from Polish and Baltic revolutionaries, *Minutes of the Central Committee*, p. 203; *Sotsial-Demokrat*, 28 February 1918; *Izvestiia Permskogo Gubernskogo Ispolnitel'nogo Komiteta*, 28 February 1918; *Izvestiia Saratovskogo Soveta*, 21 February 1918, reports Polish and Latvian delegates present at the session of

the Soviet on February 19 bitterly denounced the prospect of a separate peace with Germany; see too A. Ezergailis, *The Latvian Impact on the Bolshevik Revolution* (New York, 1983), pp. 292–4.

10. Cohen, *Bukharin*, p. 65; also Bukharin's speech, *Sed'moi s"ezd*, pp. 25, 38–9.

11. Schapiro, *Autocracy*, pp. 108–9, 132. Daniels, *Conscience*, p. 71, has also conceded that the Left Communists' opposition 'went much deeper [than emotions], to questions of basic political philosophy and the general prospects for the workers' revolution in Russia and the world'.

12. Schapiro, *Autocracy*, p. 100; Daniels, *Conscience*, pp. 71–2.

13. Lenin, *CW*, 21, pp. 403–4, emphasis added. In an earlier letter to A. G. Shliapnikov, on 23 August 1915, Lenin had expressed his preparedness to wage such a war: *CW*, 35, p. 205.

14. Lenin, *CW*, 23, p. 79.

15. Ibid., p. 370, also p. 338.

16. R. Service, 'The Bolsheviks On Political Campaign In 1917: A Case Study Of The War Question' (hereafter *War Question*) (unpublished CREES seminar paper, University of Birmingham, March 1988), pp. 7–9; Schapiro, *Autocracy*, p. 90, too remarked upon Lenin's waning commitment to revolutionary war during 1917.

17. Lenin, *CW*, 24, p. 165. He argued in the same vein before the Soldiers' Section of the Petrograd Soviet on 12 April: *CW*, 41 (Moscow, 1969), p. 406.

18. Lenin, *CW*, 24, pp. 237, 300.

19. Ibid., p. 394; Lenin, *CW*, 25, pp. 26–7, 56, 289; Lenin, *CW*, 26, p. 25.

20. Lenin, *CW*, 25, pp. 22, 34, 38, 41, 86, 109, 157; *CW*, 41, pp. 406, 432.

21. Ibid., *CW*, 26, 317–18.

22. Service, *War Question*, pp. 12–13.

23. Lenin, *CW*, 26, p. 136.

24. Lenin, *CW*, 25, p. 86; also *CW*, 26, p. 40.

25. Lenin, *CW*, 25, p. 315; also *CW*, 26, p. 63.

26. *Shestoi s"ezd*, pp. 104–5, 197, 202.

27. *KPSS v bor'be za pobedu velikoi oktiabr'skoi sotsialisticheskoi revoliutsii, 5 iiulia – 5 noiabria 1917g* (Moscow, 1957), pp. 208–9, 237, 330, 341, 397, 401.

28. For example, the resolution of the Executive Committee of the Petersburg Committee of 15 January 1918, *Minutes of the Central Committee*, p. 190; Preobrazhenskii argued similarly, *Pravda*, 3 January 1918, as did Bubnov, *Sed'moi s"ezd*, p. 49. Neither resolution in fact unequivocally committed the party to wage a revolutionary war. For the April Conference resolution, Lenin, *CW*, 24, pp. 270–3. Point 9 of the resolution on the current situation and the war adopted by the Sixth Party Congress read: 'The liquidation of imperialist rule sets before the working-class of that country which first realises the dictatorship of the proletariat and semi-proletariat the task of supporting by any means (including armed force) the struggling proletariat of other countries. In particular, such a task stands before Russia if, as is very likely, the new and unavoidable

upsurge of the Russian Revolution brings to power the workers and the poorer peasants before revolution takes place in the capitalist countries of the West'. *KPSS v bor'be*, p. 4.

29. For example, the 9 July resolution of the Siberian Regional Bureau and the Krasnoiarsk Committee, the resolution adopted by the Fifth Congress of Latvian Social Democrats in July, and the 10 August resolution of the Perm' Committee, *KPSS v bor'be*, pp. 201, 208, 281.
30. *Sotsial-Demokrat*, 12 January 1918; Dingel'shedt, *Iz vospominanii*, pp. 65–6.
31. *Leninskii sbornik*, XI, pp. 40–1.
32. *Minutes of the Central Committee*, pp. 175–80.
33. Ibid., p. 192.
34. For the debate over the structure of the new army, see Chapter 6 above, pp. 37–40.
35. For example, Bukharin in *Kommunist*, 5 March 1918; Vardin–Mgeladze in *Izvestiia Saratovskogo Soveta*, 21 January 1918; Varlamov, *Razoblachenie*, pp. 156ff., 162f. For the similarity between the Left Communists and the SRs, *Pravda*, 9 March 1918; elsewhere, *Donetskii Proletarii*, 15 March 1918, they were equated with the Mensheviks by their opponents in the party.
36. Bukharin's speech, *Sed'moi s"ezd*, p. 31, emphasis added; Osinskii reiterated this warning, ibid., p. 85.
37. J. H. L. Keep, *The Debate on Soviet Power* (Oxford, 1979), p. 10.
38. Carr, *Revolution*, 3, p. 32.
39. Lenin, *CW*, 26, p. 444.
40. The phrase is Radek's, *Pravda*, 25 January 1918; also ibid., 11, 23, 26 January 1918.
41. M. Phillips Price, *My Reminiscences of the Russian Revolution* (London, 1921), p. 232. A. Rhys Williams, *Journey into Revolution. Petrograd, 1917–1918* (Chicago, 1969), p. 213, bears out Price's recollection. *Moskovskii metallist*, 2–3 (1918), reported that in the light of events in Europe in early 1918 faith in imminent revolution had remained high.
42. Anxieties were expressed by Radek and Stukov, *Pravda*, 16, 19 February 1918.
43. *Sed'moi s"ezd*, pp. 50, 94.
44. Grigorii Usievich argued so, *Izvestiia Moskvy*, 31 January 1918, and Vandin-Mgeladze in *Izvestiia Saratovskogo Soveta*, 21 January 1918; Bukharin reiterated this argument, *Sed'moi s"ezd*, p. 28.
45. Radek and Pokrovskii argued so, *Pravda* 23 and 28 February 1918.
46. *Sed'moi s"ezd*, p. 26. The previous August Osinskii had sketched a similar picture of the demoralising impact of a revolutionary war on the opposing army. N. Osinskii, 'Vtoraia stepen'', *Spartak*, 4 (1918), p. 3.
47. *Sed'moi s"ezd*, p. 44.
48. *Minutes of the Central Committee*, pp. 175–6. S. Avineri, commenting on M. Rubel, 'The Relationship of Bolshevism and Marxism', in R. Pipes (ed.), *Revolutionary Russia* (New York, 1969), p. 420, gives credence to such a view, alleging that 'Brest-Litovsk was to deal a

death blow to any universalist or internationalist ideology still slumbering within the German Social Democratic Party'.

49. *Kommunist*, 7, 10 March 1918.
50. *Shestoi s"ezd*, p. 101.
51. *Pravda*, 3 January 1918. I. Liteinyi repeated this argument, *Zvezda. Organ Ekaterinoslavskago Komiteta RS-DRP*, 19 February 1918.
52. Carr, *Revolution*, 3, p. 35; also I. Deutscher, *The Prophet Armed* (Oxford, 1970), p. 356.
53. *Minutes of the Central Committee*, p. 209; *Sed'moi s"ezd*, p. 27.
54. *Otchet*, p. 64.
55. *Tezisy*, p. 5; Viator [K. Radek], 'Vneshniaia politika Sovetskoi respubliki', *Kommunist*, 2 (1918), p. 3.
56. Bukharin argued so, *Kommunist*, 5 March 1918.
57. Radek, Bronskii and Usievich argued so, *Pravda*, 16 February, 2, 5 March 1918; also Smirnov and Pokrovskii, *Kommunist*, 5 March 1918, Osinskii, ibid., 14 March 1918, Bukharin, *Sed'moi s"ezd*, p. 31. For German designs, M. Kitchen, *The Silent Dictatorship. The Politics of the German High Command Under Hindenburg and Ludendorff* (London, 1976), pp. 160, 172; also F. Fischer, *Germany's Aims in the First World War* (London, 1967), pp. 483–4, 491–2.
58. A. Lomov, 'Mirnyi dogovor i narodnoe khoziaistvo Rossii', *Biulleteni V.S.N.Kh.*, No. 1 (1918), pp. 4–10.
59. Ibid., pp. 11–13; for the views of Radek and Kossior, *Trudy 1 vserossiiskago s"ezda Sovetov Narodnogo Khoziaistva, 25 maia – 4 iiunia 1918g.* (Moscow, 1918), pp. 19–20, 31 (hereafter *Trudy SNKh*).
60. Ibid., pp. 23–4.
61. Ibid., pp. 57–60; and his argument, *Kommunist*, 14 March 1918. Earlier, I. I. Skvortsov-Stepanov, *Izvestiia Moskvy*, 10 March 1918, had warned against accepting aid of any sort from the Allies as this would merely re-establish Russia's subordination to international capitalism.
62. Bukharin, Pokrovskii and Smirnov argued so, *Kommunist*, 5 March 1918.
63. Bronskii and Radek so argued, *Pravda*, 2, 23 March 1918; also Osinskii, *Sed'moi s"ezd*, pp. 83–5, *Kommunist*, 14 March 1918.
64. Bronskii in *Pravda*, 2 March 1918. For the German demands see articles 13–16 of the Legal-Political Treaty Supplementary to the Treaty of Peace between Russia and the Central Powers, ratified on 29 March 1918, in *The Inquiry Handbooks*, 19 (Wilmington, 1974), pp. 124–6.
65. Osinskii in *Kommunist*, 12 March 1918.
66. *Izvestiia Saratovskogo Soveta*, 26 February 1918.
67. C. Sirianni, *Workers' Control and Socialist Democracy. The Soviet Experience* (London, 1982), p. 81.
68. *Sotsial-Demokrat*, 28 February 1918; *Izvestiia Moskvy*, 27 January 1918, reported very high levels of militancy amongst young workers in the Sokol'niki and Basmannyi districts; for the front and the south, Il'ia Ionov's report, *Kommunist*, 5 March 1918.
69. Fedotoff-White, *Red Army*, pp. 30–1; G. A. Tsypkin, R. G. Tsypkina,

*Krasnaia gvardiia – udarnaia sila proletariata v Oktiabr'skoi revoliutsii* (Moscow, 1977), p. 272, claim that in Moscow 20 000 workers volunteered for the Red Army, a figure that seems rather exaggerated as in the more militant Petrograd the corresponding figure was only 10 000. See too Chapter 7 above, pp. 152–3.

70. *Sotsial-Demokrat*, 7 March 1918.
71. Shelavin's report in *Sed'moi s"ezd*, p. 90; *Krasnaia gazeta*, 26 February 1918; Phillips Price, *Reminiscences*, p. 249.
72. So many of the delegates assembling in Moscow for the Fourth All-Russian Congress of Soviets reported, *Izvestiia Moskvy*, 14 March 1918; *Sotsial-Demokrat*, 15 March 1918; also Ia. Iankovskii's evaluation, *Petrogradskaia Pravda*, 3 April 1918, cited in Varlamov, *Razoblachenie*, pp. 88–9.
73. Speeches of Bukharin and Uritskii, *Sed'moi s"ezd*, pp. 35, 37, 41; *Kommunist*, 7 March 1918.
74. 'Iz protokolov zasedanii Moskovskogo Oblastnogo Biuro 1917 goda', *Proletarskaia Revoliutsiia*, 10 (1922), p. 179. A. K. Wildman, *The End of the Russian Imperial Army. The Road to Soviet Power and Peace*, II (Princeton, 1987), pp. 380ff., claims that the appeal of 9 November 1917, issued by Lenin and N. V. Krylenko, calling upon the troops at the front line themselves to initiate negotiations for an armistice, was the critical turning-point in the disintegration of the army.
75. Lenin, *CW*, 27, p. 44, emphasis added, also pp. 20, 57; *CW*, 26, p. 447.
76. Ibid., pp. 448, 523; *CW*, 27, p. 178.
77. Ibid., pp. 84, 115, 160–2.
78. Lenin, *CW*, 36, p. 469; *Minutes of the Central Committee*, pp. 174–5.
79. Lenin, *CW*, 27, pp. 71–2.
80. Ibid., p. 64, also pp. 62, 89–92, 166, 176–7.
81. Ibid., p. 367; also *CW*, 26, pp. 449, 513.
82. Lenin, *CW*, 27, pp. 45, 92–3.
83. Ibid., p. 237, also pp. 367–9.
84. Ibid., p. 64; also *CW*, 26, pp. 446, 448–9.
85. Lenin, *CW*, 27, pp. 76–7, 102, 108, 160–1, 210–17, 335–51.
86. Lenin, *CW*, 26, p. 269, also p. 447.
87. Lenin, *CW*, 27, p. 105.
88. *Leninskii sbornik*, XI, pp. 41–2; *Sotsial-Demokrat*, 8 March 1918.
89. *Minutes of the Central Committee*, p. 209; *Sed'moi s"ezd*, p. 52.
90. *Leninskii sbornik*, XI, p. 42.
91. *Tezisy*, p. 6.

## CHAPTER 4:   THE AGRARIAN QUESTION

1. Daniels, *Conscience*, p. 81.
2. As V. Meshcheriakov commented during the debate preceding the implementation of the law on land socialisation, *Pravda*, 24 January 1918.

3. Bukharin, *Selected Writings*, p. 4; and *Sotsial-Demokrat*, 27 October 1917.
4. Bukharin, *Rossiiskaia revoliutsiia*, p. 9; V. S[mirnov], 'O vserossiiskoi konferentsii', *Spartak*, 1 (1917), p. 32. Lomov apparently had lectured in a similar vein whilst in exile in Saratov during World War I. Antonov-Saratovskii, *Pod stiagom*, p. 62.
5. I. I. Skvortsov-Stepanov, *Ot rabochego kontrolia k rabochemu upravleniiu* (Moscow, 1918), pp. 107–8.
6. *Sotsial-Demokrat*, 20 April 1917; also his *Ot rabochego kontrolia*, p. 108; see too E. A. Preobrazhenskii in *Pravda*, 31 December 1917, for an analogous argument.
7. Bukharin, *Rossiiskaia revoliutsiia*, pp. 9–11; S[mirnov], *Konferentsii*, p. 32.
8. *Shestoi s"ezd*, p. 138; see too Chapter 2, p. 39.
9. Ibid., p. 103; also In. Stukov, 'Krest'ianstvo i organizatsiia vlasti', *Spartak*, 8 (1917), pp. 7–10.
10. E. Kingston-Mann, *Lenin and the Problem of Marxist Peasant Revolution* (Oxford, 1983), p. 42.
11. J. L. H. Keep, *The Russian Revolution: a study in mass mobilisation* (London, 1976), p. 391.
12. Lenin, *CW*, 24, p. 23.
13. Ibid., pp. 284, 290–1.
14. Ibid., pp. 291–2; F. Bystrykh, 'Razvitie vzgliadov Lenina po agrarnomu voprosu', *Proletarskaia Revoliutsiia*, 1 (1928), pp. 28–9.
15. Lenin, *CW*, 24, p. 242.
16. Ibid., p. 72; in 1906, in his 'Revision of the Agrarian Programme of the Workers' Party' he concluded with a warning against 'small scale ownership, which cannot, so long as commodity production exists, abolish poverty among the masses...', *CW*, 10 (Moscow, 1962), p. 195; in article on Karl Marx, completed in the autumn of 1914, he repeated the essence of this argument, *CW*, 21, p. 70; also Kingston-Mann, *Peasant Revolution*, pp. 108–9.
17. Lenin, *CW*, 24, pp. 168–9; *CW*, 25, p. 125.
18. Lenin, *CW*, 24, pp. 292–3, 487, 502; *CW*, 36, p. 441; Chamberlin, *The Russian Revolution*, 1, p. 249; E. H. Carr, *The Bolshevik Revolution*, 2 (Harmondsworth, 1966), p. 33.
19. Lenin, *CW*, 24, pp. 501–5; *CW*, 25, pp. 280.
20. Lenin, *CW*, 24, p. 440; *CW*, 25, pp. 280, 344.
21. Kingston-Mann, *Peasant Revolution*, pp. 149–50; *Sed'maia konferentsiia*, pp. 106–7, 191.
22. *Shestoi s"ezd*, p. 118; Kingston-Mann, *Peasant Revolution*, p. 151.
23. Lenin, *CW*, 25, p. 280. R. Service, 'Lenin and Agrarian Economics' (unpublished conference paper, London, 1988), pp. 13–15, has recently argued that Lenin began to shift his ground after attending the Congress of Peasant Deputies in May.
24. Lenin, *CW*, 25, pp. 275–6, 281.
25. Ibid., p. 275. Days before the revolution, he again charged that the peasants sought 'the conversion of land tracts farmed on a highly efficient level (orchards, plantations, etc.) into "model farms", their

transfer to "the exclusive use of the state and the communes" ...'
Lenin, *CW*, 26, p. 229. *The Peasant Mandate* is reprinted in full, ibid.,
pp. 258–60. I am grateful to Maureen Perrie for drawing my
attention to the specific references to model farms in *The Peasant
Mandate* and Lenin's own citing of them.

26. Lenin, *CW*, 26, p. 64.
27. Ibid., p. 269.
28. Ibid., pp. 334–5.
29. Bunyan, *Bolshevik Revolution*, p. 674.
30. Lenin, *CW*, 27, p. 138.
31. R. G. Wesson, *Soviet Communes* (New Brunswick, 1963), pp. 92–3.
32. Summary by M. D-skii, *Izvestiia*, 20 February 1918.
33. Ibid., 26 January 1918.
34. Ibid.
35. Ibid.; M. I. Vasil'ev pointed to same consequences of land division at
    the session of the Saratov Soviet on 29 January 1918, *Saratovskii
    Sovet*, p. 356, and again in *Izvestiia Saratovskogo Soveta*, 6 April 1918.
36. *Sotsial-Demokrat*, 27 January 1918; also his *Ot rabochego kontrolia*, pp.
    80–2, 87–8.
37. *Pravda*, 31 December 1917; N. I. Bukharin, *Historical Materialism*
    (Ann Arbor, 1969), p. 289, argued: 'In other words, the peasantry –
    for instance – lack several elements necessary to make them a
    communist class: they are bound down by property, and it will take
    many years to train them to a new view, which can only be done by
    having the state power in the hands of the proletariat; also, the
    peasantry are not held together in production, in social labour and
    common action; on the contrary, the peasant's entire joy is in his own
    bit of land; he is accustomed to individual management, not to
    cooperation with others.'
38. T. V. Sapronov argued in these terms, *Izvestiia Moskvy*, 30 May 1918.
39. Preobrazhenskii's argument, *Pravda*, 31 December 1917.
40. Preobrazhenskii's argument, *Izvestiia*, 13 January 1918; also Skvor-
    tsov-Stepanov, *Ot rabochego kontrolia*, pp. 100–1.
41. Conclusion of M. D-skii, *Izvestiia*, 20 February 1918.
42. *Tezisy*, p. 9.
43. *Izvestiia*, 13 January 1918; M. I. Vasil'ev too unequivocally defended
    the preservation of the large estates and the formation of artels,
    *Izvestiia Saratovskogo Soveta*, 6 April 1918; Klementii's summary, in
    *Izvestiia*, 14 February 1918.
44. Klementii's argument, ibid., 30 January 1918, 14 February 1918;
    *Pravda*, 8 March 1918.
45. *Sotsial-Demokrat*, 27 October 1917; see Chapter 2, p. 27.
46. *Pravda*, 31 December 1917; also G. I. Safarov, *Donetskii Proletarii*, 21
    February 1918.
47. So Safarov argued, ibid.; also Preobrazhenskii in *Pravda*, 31 Decem-
    ber 1917.
48. *Izvestiia*, 20 February 1918.
49. K. Radek, 'Posle piati mesiatsev', *Kommunist*, 1 (1918), p. 3.
50. S. Malle, *War Communism*, p. 324; S. Benet, *The Village of Viriatino*

(New York, 1970), pp. 169–70; T. Shanin, *The Awkward Class* (Oxford, 1972), pp. 151–2; A. A. Antsiferov, *Russian Agriculture During the War* (New Haven, 1930), p. 376; Keep, *Revolution*, pp. 417–18; L. Kritsman, *Geroicheskii period russkoi revoliutsii* (Moscow, n.d.), p. 45; and V. P. Danilov, *Rural Russia under the New Regime* (London, 1988), p. 304.

51. Antsiferov, *Agriculture*, p. 375; Shanin, *Class*, pp. 137, 145, 153–4;: Danilov, *Rural Russia*, pp. 87–8.

52. Varlamov, *Razoblachenie*, p. 248; Keep, *Revolution*, p. 412; Malle, *War Communism*, p. 327; J. Channon, 'The Bolsheviks and the Peasantry: the Land Question During the first Eight Months of Soviet Rule', *Slavonic and East European Review*, 4 (1988), pp. 610–12, 624.

53. Lenin, *CW*, 27, p. 430, also pp. 356, 363–4, 421–39.

54. Ibid., p. 356.

55. Ibid., pp. 401.

56. Lenin, *CW*, 35, p. 343.

57. Lenin, *CW*, 27, pp. 523, 527–8; Malle, *War Communism*, p. 347.

58. Lenin, *CW*, 27, p. 526.

59. Klementii, in *Izvestiia*, 30 January 1918; also Danilov, *Rural Russia*, pp. 87–8.

60. Bunyan, *Bolshevik Revolution*, pp. 684–5; also his article in *Pravda*, 24 January 1918.

61. D. Koenker, *Moscow Workers and the 1917 Revolution* (Princeton, 1981), p. 345.

CHAPTER 5:  THE ORGANISATION OF INDUSTRY

1. *Trudy SNKh*, p. 343.

2. Osinskii, *Stroitel'stvo sotsializma*, p. 34.

3. Lenin, *CW*, 26, p. 173.

4. Ibid., p. 365.

5. Smith, *Red Petrograd*, p. 211.

6. Ibid., p. 213; Carr, *Bolshevik Revolution*, 2, p. 80.

7. Cohen, *Bukharin*, pp. 53–4, and p. 402 where he alleges that 'the party's program in 1917 was really no more than Lenin's April Theses'.

8. Bukharin, *Gosudarstvennyi kapitalizm*, p. 8.

9. See Chapter 2 above, pp. 38–43.

10. Malle, *War Communism*, p. 297; V. Sm[irnov], *Regulirovanie proizvodstva*, p. 11; Lomov's speech, *Shestoi s"ezd*, p. 156.

11. N. I. Bukharin, 'Ekonomicheskii razval i voina,' *Spartak*, 3 (1917), pp. 5–6; also Sm[irnov], *Regulirovanie proizvodstva*, p. 11.

12. Cohen, *Bukharin*, p. 72.

13. N. Osinskii, 'Iz itogov s"ezda," *Spartak*, 5 (1917), p. 4; and his speech at the Sixth Party Congress, *Shestoi s"ezd*, pp. 157–8.

14. Bukharin, *Razval*, pp. 5–6.

15. *Sotsial-Demokrat*, 17 October 1917.

16. N. I. Bukharin, *Rossiiskaia revoliutsiia*, p. 11; S[mirnov], *Konferentsii*, p. 32.
17. *Sotsial-Demokrat*, 15 December 1917.
18. Sirianni, *Workers' Control*, p. 299.
19. Lenin, *CW*, 26, p. 170.
20. Lenin, *CW*, 25, pp. 20–1, 44; Harding, *Political Thought*, 2, pp. 71–2, 75–6.
21. M. Brinton, *The Bolsheviks and Workers' Control, 1917–1921* (London, 1970), pp. ii, 12; Smith, *Red Petrograd*, p. 228; Sirianni, *Workers' Control*, p. 260.
22. Lenin, *CW*, 26, p. 365.
23. Ibid., pp. 468, 500.
24. *Tezisy*, p. 8.
25. Lenin, *CW*, 25, pp. 329–31.
26. Ibid., pp. 324, 329–31, 360–1; Lenin, *CW*, 26, pp. 106–7.
27. Lenin, *CW*, 27, p. 297.
28. Lenin, *CW*, 26, pp. 109–11.
29. Ibid., p. 113.
30. Ibid., p. 116.
31. *Kommunist*, 12 March 1918, where Osinskii asserted that this was the case; Radek argued similarly, ibid., 14 March 1918; also *Tezisy*, p. 4. V. N. Brovkin, *The Mensheviks After October. Socialist Opposition and the Rise of the Bolshevik Dictatorship* (Ithaca, 1987), p. 71, has argued that '[t]he key lesson that Lenin drew from the crisis over the peace treaty was that Bolshevik economic policy had to be changed'.
32. Lenin, *CW*, 26, p. 409, also pp. 364ff. *State and Revolution* will be discussed in detail in Chapter 6 below.
33. Lenin, *CW*, 27, p. 118.
34. *Leninskii sbornik*, XI, p. 70.
35. Lenin, *CW*, 27, p. 210.
36. Ibid., pp. 211–12, 214, 248.
37. Ibid., p. 211; V. V. Anikeev, *Deiatel'nost' Ts.K. R.S.D.R.P.(b) – 1917–1918 godakh* (Moscow, 1974), p. 244.
38. Lenin, *CW*, 27, pp. 294–5.
39. Ibid., pp. 258, 299f.
40. Ibid., p. 295.
41. Ibid., p. 339.
42. A. Lomov, 'Ekonomicheskie zametki,' *Kommunist*, 1, 1918, p. 19.
43. Osinskii, *Stroitel-stvo*, p. 32.
44. N. I. Bukharin, 'Nekotorye osnovnye poniatiia sovremennoi ekonomiki', *Kommunist*, 3 (1918), p. 10.
45. N. Osinskii, 'O stroitel'stve sotsializma, I', *Kommunist*, 1, 1918, p. 15. For continuing rank-and-file antipathy to the capitalists, and even their *spetsy*, *Izvestiia Permskogo*, 28 February 1918; the worker Borisov's article, *Izvestiia Saratovskogo Soveta*, 2 April 1918; and *Izvestiia Moskvy*, 11 May 1918.
46. Osinskii, *Stroitel'stvo*, p. 32.
47. Ibid.
48. Osinskii, *O stroitel'stve*, I, p. 16; a recent critique of the Taylor system

can be found in N. P. Mouzelis, *Organisation and Bureaucracy. An Analysis of Modern Theories* (London, 1975), pp. 79–87.
49. Osinskii, *O stroitel'stve*, I, p. 16; Sirianni, *Workers' Control*, p. 143.
50. N. Osinskii, 'O stroitel'stve sotsializma II', *Kommunist*, 2 (1918), p. 6. See too Lomov, *Zametki*, p. 19.
51. Kritsman, *Geroicheskii period*, p. 86.
52. Ibid., pp. 86–7.
53. Bukharin, *Gosudarstvennyi kapitalizm*, p. 9.
54. Osinskii, *O stroitel'stve*, I, p. 16.
55. Radek, *Posle piati mesiatsev*, p. 3; also R. I. Kowalski (ed.), *Kommunist* (New York, 1990 reprint), note 1 to p. 41 of text.
56. *Trudy SNKh*, p. 64.
57. Osinskii, *O stroitel'stve*, II, pp. 5–6; Lomov, *Zametki*, p. 19; Vasil'ev's argument, *Izvestiia Saratovskogo Soveta*, 6 April 1918; and later, Bukharin, *Transition Period*, pp. 102–4; for the lack of enthusiasm of the *spetsy* for the Bolsheviks, K. Bailes, *Technology and Society under Lenin and Stalin* (Princeton, 1978), pp. 23–4.
58. N. Osinskii, 'Priamye otvety', *Kommunist*, 2, p. 17; *Tezisy*, p. 9.
59. *Trudy SNKh*, p. 65.
60. F. I. Kaplan, *Bolshevik Ideology and the Ethics of Soviet Labour. 1917–1920: The Formative Years* (New York, 1968), p. 127, and P. Avrich, 'The Bolshevik Revolution and Workers' Control in Russian Industry', *Slavic Review*, 1 (1963), pp. 54–7, stress the extent of anarchist and syndicalist currents among Russian workers; Smith, *Red Petrograd*, pp. 235–6, has posited that Anarchist influence was much more limited among the Russian workers than previous studies would suggest.
61. Osinskii, *O stroitel'stve*, II, p. 6.
62. N. I. Bukharin, 'Anarkhizm i nauchnyi kommunizm', *Kommunist*, 2, 1918, pp. 12–13; Bukharin, *Osnovye poniatiia*, p. 11.
63. Osinskii, *Stroitel'stvo*, p. 77; *Trudy SNKh*, p. 65.
64. Osinskii, *Stroitel'stvo*, pp. 73–7; *O stroitel'stve*, II, p. 8; *Trudy SNKh*, pp. 67–8.
65. Osinskii, *Stroitel'stvo*, p. 74.
66. Ibid., p. 81.
67. A. Nove, *The Economics of Feasible Socialism* (London, 1983), pp. 18, 30, 35, develops this issue.
68. *Sotsial-Demokrat*, 6 January 1918; *Izvestiia Ural'skogo Oblastnogo Soveta*, 1 June 1918, reported conflicts between the economic committees, 'representing the interests of the state entrepreneur' and the trades unions, 'representing the interests of the workers in the enterprises'.
69. Osinskii, *Stroitel'stvo*, pp. 72–4.
70. Brinton, *Workers' Control*, p. 43; Kaplan, *Bolshevik Ideology*, p. 275.
71. *Trudy SNKh*, p. 360.
72. R. Selucky, *Marxism, Socialism, Freedom* (London, 1979), p. 45; see too Nove, *Economics*, p. 52.
73. See Chapter 3, pp. 72–3.
74. *Tezisy*, pp. 6, 9; *Trudy SNKh*, p. 60; Sh[ternberg], 'Delovye zametki', *Kommunist*, 4 (1918), p. 15.

75. Carr, *Bolshevik Revolution*, 2, p. 149.
76. V. Smirnov, 'Finansovaia programma i "gosudarstvennyi kapitalizm"', *Kommunist*, 4, 1918, pp. 5–6; his speech in *Trudy SNKh*, pp. 147–9.
77. A. L[omov], 'Ekonomicheskie zametki: Programma finansovykh reform komissara Gukovskago', *Kommunist*, 2, p. 21; for Bukharin's critique, Varlamov, *Razoblachenie*, p. 281; for Lenin's more orthodox approach, R. W. Davies, *The Development of the Soviet Budgetary System* (Cambridge, 1958), pp. 16, 18.
78. Smirnov, *Finansovaia programma*, p. 6.
79. Bukharin, *Transition Period*, pp. 129, 228.
80. Carr, *Bolshevik Revolution*, 2, p. 95.
81. Smith, *Red Petrograd*, p. 229.
82. Ibid.
83. M. Vajda, *The State and Socialism* (London, 1981), pp. 4, 39–40, for a general discussion of this issue.
84. Smith, *Red Petrograd*, p. 227.
85. N. Osinskii, 'Polozhenie Donetskoi kamennougol'noi promyshlennosti i nashi zadachi', *Biulleteni Vysshago Soveta Narodnago Khoziaistva*, 1, 1918, pp. 17–18.
86. A. Lomov, 'Ch'e bankrotstvo? (K voprosu o padenii proizvoditel'nosti truda', *Narodnoe Khoziaistvo*, 5 (1918), pp. 17–18; and his *Razlozhenie kapitalizma*, pp. 77–8.
87. *Trudy SNKh*, p. 80.
88. Lomov, *Bankrotstvo*, p. 18; Osinskii's speech, *Trudy SNKh*, p. 66, where he claimed that questions of food and finance had been crucial in determining the success or failure of experiments in workers' management; also Carr, *Bolshevik Revolution*, 2, p. 77.
89. Smith, *Red Petrograd*, pp. 236–9, 248–51, 260; Sirianni, *Workers' Control*, pp. 111–18.
90. L. Krassin, *Leonid Krassin: His Life and Work* (London, 1929), p. 86.
91. 'Conditions of the Railways', in Bunyan, *Bolshevik Revolution*, pp. 664–5.
92. 'Conditions on the Railroads', in J. Bunyan, *Intervention, Civil War and Communism in Russia, April–December, 1918: Documents and Materials* (New York, 1976), p. 384.
93. For example, the circular of the Central Committee of the Metal Workers' Union, *Metallist*, 1 (1918), pp. 83–4; Smith, *Red Petrograd*, pp. 242, 260.
94. Sirianni, *Workers' Control*, pp. 331–2.
95. Nove, *Economics*, pp. 11–12; Malle, *War Communism*, pp. 22–3, 30.
96. Osinskii, *Stroitel'stvo*, p. 46; also Kritsman, *Geroicheskii period*, p. 59.
97. Nove, *Economics*, pp. 18, 30, 37, 44, 59.
98. Ibid., p. 34; also Selucky, *Marxism*, pp. 85–7.
99. Nove, *Economics*, p. 50.
100. Ibid., p. ix.

CHAPTER 6:   POLITICS AND THE STATE

1. Daniels, *Conscience*, p. 87.
2. A. J. Polan, *Lenin and the End of Politics* (London, 1984), p. 6; and T. Wohlforth, 'The Transition to the Transition', *New Left Review*, 130 (1981), p. 67.
3. K. Marx, F. Engels, 'The Communist Manifesto', in R. C. Tucker (ed.), *The Marx-Engels Reader* (New York, 1972), p. 352; E. H. Carr, *The Bolshevik Revolution*, 1 (Harmondsworth, 1966), p. 244; F. Claudin, 'Democracy and Dictatorship in Lenin and Kautsky', *New Left Review*, 106 (1977), pp. 64–6.
4. Marx, *Manifesto*, p. 352.
5. Ibid., p. 332.
6. K. Marx, 'The Civil War in France', in Tucker, *Reader*, pp. 554–5.
7. R. N. Hunt, *The Political Ideas of Marx and Engels*, II (Pittsburgh, 1984), p. 130.
8. Marx, *Civil War*, pp. 554–5.
9. Ibid., p. 555; Hunt, *Marx*, II, p. 155.
10. Polan, *Lenin*, pp. 6–7.
11. Marx, *Civil War*, p. 537.
12. Ibid., pp. 536–7.
13. R. N. Hunt, *The Political Ideas of Marx and Engels*, I (Pittsburgh, 1974), p. 328. Marx's article is reprinted in K. Marx, F. Engels, *Collected Works*, 22 (London, 1986), p. 634.
14. Marx, *Civil War*, p. 557.
15. Wohlforth, *Transition*, pp. 67–70.
16. Hunt, *Marx*, II, p. 155.
17. Harding, *Political Thought*, 2, p. 84; Cohen, *Bukharin*, p. 55.
18. See Chapter 2, p. 37.
19. Haynes, *Bukharin*, p. 43; also Bukharin, *K peresmotru*, p. 6.
20. *Shestoi s"ezd*, pp. 132–3, 114–16; N. I. Bukharin, 'Sovety prezhde i teper', *Spartak*, 9, pp. 7–8; A. Rabinowitch, *The Bolsheviks Come to Power. The Revolution of 1917 in Petrograd* (New York, 1976), pp. 87–8; Answeiler, *The Soviets*, p. 173.
21. Bukharin, *Selected Writings*, p. 13; also his *Anarkhizm i nauchnyi kommunizm*, pp. 12–13; and Safarov, *Dve diktatury*, p. 7.
22. Bukharin, *Rossiiskaia revoliutsiia*, p. 11.
23. Ibid., p. 11; Bukharin, *Gosudarstvennyi kapitalizm*, pp. 8–9; and Smirnov, *Regulirovanie proizvodstva*, p. 17.
24. Bukharin, *Ekonomicheskii razval*, p. 5.
25. Bukharin, *Osnovye poniatiia*, p. 11; also S[mirnov], *Konferentsii*, p. 32.
26. Bukharin, *Sovety*, p. 7.
27. *Tezisy*, p. 8.
28. Ibid., p. 19; see also his speech, *Sed'moi s"ezd*, p. 160.
29. Harding, *Political Thought*, 2, p. 84.
30. Among many others, Sirianni, *Workers' Control*, pp. 266–7.
31. Lenin, *CW*, 21, p. 342. In his *Several Theses* of October, 1914, Lenin made a passing reference to 'Soviets of Workers' Deputies and

similar institutions . . . as organs of insurrection, of revolutionary
rule', but this notion remained undeveloped before 1917. Ibid.,
p. 402.

32. Lenin, *CW*, 35, pp. 213, 228, 230–1.
33. Lenin, *CW*, 23, pp. 165–6.
34. Lenin, *CW*, 25, p. 368.
35. A. B. Evans, 'Rereading Lenin's State and Revolution', *Slavic Review*,
    1 (1987), pp. 5–7.
36. Lenin, *CW*, 25, p. 383.
37. Lenin, *CW*, 23, pp. 290, 304, 325–6.
38. Lenin, *CW*, 24, pp. 23, 33, 142, 239; Anweiler, *The Soviets*, p. 151.
39. Lenin, *CW*, 25, p. 189.
40. Evans, *State and Revolution*, pp. 1–3; Harding, *Political Thought*, 2,
    p. 84.
41. Lenin, *CW*, 25, p. 409. For his earlier ideas, among a myriad of
    references, *CW*, 24, pp. 39, 100–1, 150, 169, 181–2, 278, 323, 537–8.
42. Lenin, *CW*, 25, pp. 388, 406–9, 418–19, 420–3, 426.
43. Ibid., pp. 420–1, 473.
44. Lenin, *CW*, 24, p. 323.
45. Ibid., pp. 242–3, 429; also *CW*, 25, pp. 53, 368–70. Kingston-Mann,
    *Peasant Revolution*, pp. 141–3, 173–5, 183, has argued that during
    1917 Lenin repeatedly emphasised the role for popular initiative on
    the part of the peasantry as well as of the workers.
46. Lenin, *CW*, 24, p. 33.
47. Lenin, *CW*, 25, pp. 429–30, 447.
48. Ibid., pp. 404, 436, 463.
49. Ibid., p. 404; for earlier references, ibid., pp. 111, 129. Harding,
    *Political Thought*, 2, pp. 71–2, 119, emphasises this strand in Lenin's
    thinking in 1917.
50. Lenin, *CW*, 25, pp. 413, 419–20.
51. Ibid., pp. 402, 406.
52. Ibid., pp. 457, 462–3, 468–9. At the Seventh Party Congress, in
    March 1918, Lenin repeated this message, although he then rather
    optimistically added that after two further congresses it would be
    possible to see 'how our state is withering away'. *Sed'moi s"ezd*, pp.
    160, 167.
53. Lenin, *CW*, 25, pp. 425–6.
54. Ibid., p. 473, also pp. 421, 451.
55. Evans, *State and Revolution*, pp. 17–18.
56. Anweiler, *The Soviets*, p. 222; also Chamberlin, *The Russian Revolu-
    tion*, 1, p. 416.
57. Carr, *Bolshevik Revolution*, 1, p. 141.
58. Lenin, *CW*, 26, pp. 481–2; also pp. 409, 412, 415, 455.
59. Ibid., p. 498.
60. Lenin, *CW*, 27, pp. 118, 135.
61. Ibid., pp. 213, 218.
62. Ibid., p. 233.
63. Ibid., pp. 302–5, 352–4.
64. Lenin, *CW*, 26, p. 113.

65. Ibid., pp. 115–18.
66. Ibid., pp. 113–14.
67. Lenin, *CW*, 27, pp. 265, 453; Sirianni, *Workers' Control*, pp. 291ff., for Lenin's continuing concerns regarding the 'timidity' of the working people; Harding, *Political Thought*, 2, pp. 196–7, for Lenin's renewed emphasis on the leading role of the party in the revolutionary state.
68. Sirianni, *Workers' Control*, p. 208.
69. Lenin, *CW*, 27, pp. 248–9, also pp. 310–11, 315–16, and *CW*, 26, p. 110.
70. Carr, *Bolshevik Revolution*, 1, pp. 253–4; also T. H. Rigby, *Lenin's Government: Sovnarkom 1917–1922* (Cambridge, 1979), pp. 13–15, 229–30.
71. *Tezisy*, pp. 8–9; also speech of A. Lomov at the Ivanovo-Voznesensk city party conference of 28 April 1918, *Kommunist*, 4 (1918), p. 16.
72. Vl. Sorin, 'K voprosu sovetskoi vlasti', ibid., p. 7.
73. Ibid.
74. Ibid., pp. 7–8; D. Dallin, 'The Outbreak of the Civil War', in L. H. Haimson (ed.), *The Mensheviks* (Chicago, 1974), pp. 159–60. Earlier, in the debate over peace, Vardin-Mgeladze had resisted efforts to muzzle the Mensheviks and SRs, *Izvestiia Saratovskogo Soveta*, 26 February 1918.
75. Bukharin's speech, *Sed'moi s"ezd*, pp. 25, 35–8; *Tezisy*, p. 6; Radek, *Posle piati mesiatsev*, p. 3; Mandel, *Petrograd Workers*, pp. 400–1.
76. Bukharin's speech, *Sed'moi s"ezd*, p. 39; Wohlforth, *Transition*, p. 78, observes more generally that the promotion of workers to hold administrative positions is no solution to the problem of controlling the state bureaucracy as they become transformed into bureaucrats themselves, no longer with firm links to the shop floor.
77. So R. Sakwa contends, incorrectly in my view, in 'The Commune State in Moscow in 1918', *Slavic Review*, 46 (1987), p. 446.
78. See Chapter 1, p. 21.
79. *Tezisy*, p. 8.
80. Anweiler, *The Soviets*, p. 228.
81. Carr, *Bolshevik Revolution*, 3, pp. 72–3; J. H. Erickson, *The Soviet High Command* (London, 1962), pp. 21, 27; J. H. Erickson, 'The Origins of the Red Army', in Pipes (ed.), *Revolutionary Russia*, pp. 301–3, 306–7; Fedotoff-White, *Red Army*, pp. 16, 30–1, 41.
82. Erickson, *High Command*, pp. 21, 25, and 'Origins', pp. 303–6; Fedotoff-White, *Red Army*, pp. 37–8. *Rabochaia revoliutsiia na Urale. Epizody i fakty* (Ekaterinburg, 1921), pp. 110–11, describes the multiplicity of military detachments in the Urals alone, the lack of clear lines of command and the lack of military *nous* prevalent among their leaders.
83. Carr, *Bolshevik Revolution*, 3, pp. 74–6; Erickson, *High Command*, pp. 28–34; Fedotoff-White, *Red Army*, pp. 38, 41.
84. *Tezisy*, p. 8; A. F. Il'in-Zhenevskii, *Bol'sheviki u vlasti. Vospominaniia o 1918 gode* (Leningrad, 1929), pp. 58–60, 64, 77–8, 141–2. Iaroslavskii also criticised conscription and especially the use of former tsarist

officers at a meeting of the Moscow Soviet on 19 March, *Pravda*, 20 March 1917.

85. *Kommunist* (Petrograd), 7 March 1918.
86. Ibid., 14 March 1918; Varlamov, *Razoblachenie*, pp. 155–6.
87. I.T.S., 'V bor'be s kontr-revoliutsiei', *Kommunist*, 4, p. 3.
88. K. Radek, 'Krasnaia armiia', *Kommunist*, 2, pp. 14–16; also *Tezisy*, pp. 12–13; I.T.S., *V bor'be*, pp. 3–4.
89. Lenin, *CW*, 27, p. 529. The target of his outburst on this occasion was the Left SRs, but his argument is equally applicable to the Left Communists.
90. Erickson, *High Command*, p. 46.
91. Sirianni, *Workers' Control*, pp. 207–8; D. Koenker, 'Urbanisation and Deurbanisation in the Russian Revolution and Civil War', *Journal of Modern History*, 57 (1985), pp. 440–2.
92. See Chapter 5, pp. 111–14; Evans, *State and Revolution*, pp. 3, 14–15.
93. E. P. Thompson, 'Eighteenth-century English Society: class struggle without class', *Social History*, 3 (1978), p. 147.
94. Vajda, *The State*, pp. 17–18, 23, 26–7, 30, 61.
95. Sirianni, *Workers' Control*, p. 267.
96. Polan, *Lenin*, p. 77.
97. Sirianni, *Workers' Control*, p. 278.
98. R. Miliband, 'The State and Revolution', in *Class Power & State Power* (London, 1983), pp. 159–60; M. Ferro, *The Bolshevik Revolution. A Social History of the Russian Revolution* (London, 1985), p. 214.
99. Polan, *Lenin*, pp. 128–9; also Remington, *Building Socialism*, pp. 17–18.
100. Polan, *Lenin*, p. 140.
101. Bukharin, *Transition Period*, pp. 162–4; Malle, *War Communism*, pp. 5–6.
102. Sakwa, *Commune State*, p. 444.

CHAPTER SEVEN:    THE STRENGTH OF THE LEFT COMMUNIST MOVEMENT

1. Schapiro, *Communist Party*, p. 188, and his *Autocracy*, pp. 109, 130; Cohen, *Bukharin*, p. 65.
2. Daniels, *Conscience*, pp. 76–7, 88, 98–9; Schapiro, *Autocracy*, pp. 135, 140–1; Service, *Bolshevik Party*, pp. 79–80, 83.
3. See n. 34 to Introduction.
4. Serebriakova, *Oblastnye ob"edineiia Sovetov*, p. 91. Until the spring of 1918 the Moscow region encompassed the provinces of Iaroslavl', Kaluga, Kostroma, Moscow, Nizhegorod, Orel', Riazan', Smolensk, Tambov, Tula, Tver, Vladimir and Voronezh. V. Iakovleva, 'Partiinaia rabota v Moskovskoi oblasti v period fevral' – oktiabr' 1917g.', *Proletarskaia Revoliutsiia*, 3 (1923), p. 197.

5. *Ocherki istorii Moskovskoi organizatsii KPSS*, II (Moscow, 1983), pp. 50ff.; *Sed'moi s"ezd*, pp. 312–13; *Sotsial-Demokrat*, 17 January 1918; *Pravda*, 21 January 1918; Varlamov, *Razoblachenie*, p. 82.
6. *Izvestiia Moskvy*, 16, 17, 31 January 1917.
7. *Sed'moi s"ezd*, pp. 313–14; *Ocherki*, II, p. 57.
8. Daniels, *Conscience*, p. 76; the City Committee passed a similar resolution of no confidence on 28 February, Chubar'ian, *Brestskii mir*, p. 41.
9. *Sotsial-Demokrat*, 8 March 1918, where it reported that delegates from Iaroslavl', Smolensk, Voronezh, Nizhnii Novgorod, the Okrug Committee, Sormovo, Aleksandrov, Teikovo, Bobrov, Guchkovo-Tushino, Naro-Fominsk, Bogorod-Glukhovo, Rodnikov and Venev were present at the 2 March session, together with Bolsheviks from Samara, Saratov and Simferopol'; Berlina, *Brestskii mir'*, p. 41.
10. *Izvestiia Moskvy*, 26 February 1918.
11. Ibid., 21, 24, 26 January 1918; *Sotsial-Demokrat*, 27 January 1918.
12. *Izvestiia Moskvy*, 26 February, 3 March 1918. K. Ukhanov, I. Borisov, *Iz zhizni i deiatel'nosti Soveta R i K D Rogozhko-Simonovskogo raiona g. Moskvy (mart 1917g – ianvar' 1921g)* (Moscow, 1921), p. 21. *Sotsial-Demokrat*, 5 March 1918 carries a report sketching the same picture of militancy in the districts of the city at the end of February.
13. *Pravda*, 23 February 1918.
14. *Sotsial-Demokrat*, 20 February 1918; *Izvestiia Moskvy*, 23, 27 February 1918.
15. *Sotsial-Demokrat*, 28 February 1918; *Izvestiia Moskvy*, 27 January 1918, for the militancy of the young workers of the Basmannyi and Sokol'niki districts. I am grateful to Richard Sakwa for bringing this point to my attention.
16. *Izvestiia Moskvy*, 2, 3 March 1918. Other resolutions of support for revolutionary war in late February came from the workers of the Moscow-Kazan' railway, the Abrikosov factory, the Shrader factory, the Volk i Vaterpruf works, the Levenson printing works, the Riazan' tram park, the Motor plant and many more, ibid., 28 February, 2 March 1918. For the Postavshchik, Provodnik AMO plants, among others, *Sotsial-Demokrat*, 28 February, 3, 5 March 1918.
17. *Izvestiia Moskvy*, 14 March 1918.
18. *Sed'moi s"ezd*, pp. 300–2; *Istoricheskii arkhiv*, 3 (1958), p. 28; Chubar'ian, *Brestskii mir*, p. 221, claims that many local organisations, including the important ones in Liudvinsk and Zhidra, opposed peace; and *Pravda*, 20 January 1918.
19. *Istoricheskii arkhiv*, 3 (1958), pp. 21–2, 29; *Sotsial-Demokrat*, 28 February 1918; *Otchet*, pp. 124, 127.
20. *Istoricheskii arkhiv*, 4 (1958), p. 27; Chubar'ian, *Brestskii mir*, pp. 223–4; *Pravda*, 27 February 1918; and *Izvestiia Moskvy*, 28 February 1918.
21. *Istoricheskii arkhiv*, 4 (1958), p. 37; *Otchet*, pp. 115, 118; Chubar'ian, *Brestskii mir*, pp. 222–3.
22. Ibid., pp. 225, 228; *Pravda*, 5 March 1918. The Smolensk party

organisation had abandoned revolutionary war as early as 23 February, *Sed'moi s"ezd*, p. 343.

23. *Izvestiia Moskvy*, 5, 6 March 1918; *Sotsial-Demokrat*, 5, 6 March 1918; *Pravda*, 6 March 1918.
24. *Izvestiia Moskvy*, 5, 6 March 1918; *Istoricheskii arkhiv*, 3 (1958), p. 31.
25. *Sotsial-Demokrat*, 7 March 1918.
26. Ibid.
27. Ibid., 15 March 1918; *Izvestiia Moskvy*, 14 March 1918; *Istoricheskii arkhiv*, 4 (1958), p. 27; Chubar'ian, *Brestskii mir*, pp. 223–4, 227; *Professional'nyi vestnik*, 5–6 (1918), pp. 19–20.
28. M. N. Pokrovskii, *Oktiabr'skaia revoliutsiia* (Moscow, 1921), p. 17; Service, *Bolshevik Party*, p. 81.
29. Vindzberg, '1-i Moskovskoi revoliutsionnyi dobrovol'cheskii otriad po bor'be s kontr-revoliutsiei', *Put' k Oktiabriu*, 3 (Moscow, 1923), p. 119.
30. *Izvestiia Moskvy*, 14 March 1918; *Sotsial-Demokrat*, 15 March 1918.
31. *Izvestiia Moskvy*, 14 March 1918.
32. Oznobishin, *K istorii bor'by*, p. 34; *Sed'moi s"ezd*, pp. 318–19; *Uprochenie sovetskoi vlasti v Moskve i moskovskoi gubernii* (Moscow, 1958), pp. 408–9.
33. *Izvestiia Moskvy*, 29 March 1918; the rank-and-file in Klin and Kolomna, and the Mozhaisk and Bronnitsy Soviets also issued declarations in support of peace, *Uprochenie*, pp. 153–7, *Sed'moi s"ezd*, p. 319.
34. Serebriakova, *Oblastnye ob"edineniia*, p. 92.
35. *Itogi partiinoi konferentsii*, p. 15.
36. R. Sakwa, *Soviet Communists in Power. A Study of Moscow during the Civil War, 1918–21* (London, 1988), pp. 138–9, accepts that the re-registration of party members may have been directed against the Left Communists but concludes that the available evidence permits no definitive judgment to be made regarding the impact of this process.
37. *Pravda*, 25 April 1918.
38. *Kommunist*, 3, 1918, pp. 17–18.
39. Varlamov, *Razoblachenie*, pp. 242–3; Nikol'nikov, *Pobeda leninskoi strategii*, p. 155.
40. *Kommunist*, 3, 1918, pp. 18–19; *Ocherki po istorii revoliutsionnogo dvizheniia i bol'shevistskoi organizatsii v Baumanskom raione* (Moscow, 1928), p. 173.
41. *Leninskii sbornik*, XI, p. 87.
42. *Pravda*, 15 May 1918.
43. Ibid., 19 May 1918.
44. *V Baumanskom raione*, p. 173. This is the last instance that I have been able to discover of a Left Communist resolution being adopted, at least outside of the Ukrainian party.
45. *Kommunist*, 4 (1918), p. 16. At the conference of the district party the fairly strong organisations in Ivanovo-Voznesensk itself, Kineshma, Kovrov and Rodniki were represented, as well as those of Teikovo, Sereda, Shuia, Kokhma, Vichuga and Iuzha.

46. Ibid., pp. 16–18.
47. *Professional'nyi Vestnik*, 9–10 (1918), p. 14; *Vestnik Metallista*, 3 (1918), pp. 75–8.
48. *Sed'moi s"ezd*, pp. 189–90, 327–9; *Vpered* (Ufa), 27 February 1918.
49. *Ocherki KP Urala*, pp. 131–3; *Istoricheskii arkhiv*, 3 (1958), pp. 23–4.
50. O. H. Radkey, *The Sickle under the Hammer. The Russian Socialist Revolutionaries in the Early Months of Soviet Rule* (New York, 1963), pp. 121–3, 154, 300; J. Keep, 'October in the Provinces', in Pipes (ed.), *Revolutionary Russia*, pp. 248–9; *Pravda*, 26 April 1918, reported that at the Congress of Soviets of Perm' province in April the Left SRs outnumbered the Bolsheviks 307 to 211.
51. *Otchet*, p. 118.
52. *Pravda*, 26 February 1918; *Vpered*, 6 March 1918.
53. *Izvestiia Permskogo*, 28 February 1918.
54. *Vpered*, 27 February, 7 March 1918; Markova, *Bor'ba V. I. Leninym*, pp. 65–6; *Otchet*, pp. 115–16; *Ocherki KP Urala*, p. 331; *Izvestiia Permskogo*, 28 February 1918; *Pravda*, 3 February 1918. Lomov, *Kommunist*, 5 March 1918, appears to have been mistaken in alleging the worker-dominated Nizhnii Tagil' Soviet had supported peace.
55. *Vpered*, 6, 7, 20 March 1918; *Otchet*, p. 115; *Istoricheskii arkhiv*, 3 (1958), pp. 23–4; *Natsionalizatsiia promyshlennosti na Urale (oktiabr' 1917 – iiul' 1918gg)* (Sverdlovsk, 1958), p. 237; *Pravda*, 25 April 1918, claimed Menshevik and SR influence in Zlatoust.
56. *Kommunist*, 10 March 1918; for the resolution of the meeting *Izvestiia Permskogo*, 28 February 1918.
57. *Vpered*, 8, 9 March 1918. The resolution is reprinted in *Sed'moi s"ezd*, p. 329.
58. Berlina, *Brestskii mir'*, p. 43.
59. *Vpered*, 14, 19 March 1918.
60. *Sed'moi s"ezd*, p. 330; for Usievich, M. P. Khil'chenko, 'Inostrannye gruppy RKP(b) na Urale', *Iz istorii partiinykh organizatsii Urala* (Sverdlovsk, 1966), p. 4.
61. *Sed'moi s"ezd*, pp. 330–2; *Ocherki KP Urala*, p. 333; *Pravda*, 25 April 1918.
62. *Otchet*, p. 111; Chubar'ian, *Brestskii mir'*, p. 231; *Vpered*, 27 March 1918; *Ocherki KP Urala*, p. 333.
63. Oznobishin, *K istorii bor'by*, pp. 37–8; *Sed'moi s"ezd*, pp. 332–4; *Bol'sheviki Ekaterinburga vo glave mass* (Sverdlovsk, 1962), p. 272; for accusations levelled against the Ekaterinburg Bolsheviks, *Vpered*, 15, 16, 25 May 1918.
64. E. Preobrazhenskii, 'S"ezd neobkhodim', *Kommunist*, 4 (1918), p. 13; *Pravda*, 8 May 1918; *Sed'moi s"ezd*, p. 334; *Ocherki KP Urala*, pp. 333–4.
65. Oznobishin, *K istorii bor'by*, p. 38; Berlina, *Brestskii mir*, p. 42.
66. *Kommunist*, 4 (1918), pp. 18–19.
67. Berlina, *Brestskii mir*, p. 46; Oznobishin, *K voprosu o bor'be*, p. 71; Varlamov, *Razoblachenie*, pp. 376–8; *Ocherki KP Urala*, p. 334.
68. *Kommunist*, 4 (1918), p. 19; *Izvestiia Ural'skogo Oblastnogo Soveta*, 18 May 1918.

69. Erickson, 'Origins', p. 304.
70. P. S. Flenley, 'Workers' Organisations in the Russian Metal Industry, February 1917–August 1918' (Ph.D., Birmingham, 1983), p. 491; Sirianni, *Workers' Control*, pp. 115–16.
71. *Natsionalizatsiia promyshlennosti*, pp. 42–4, 51–3, 93–7.
72. Ibid., pp. 145–7, and p. 263 for Nev'iansk; *Izvestiia Ural'skogo Oblastnogo Soveta*, 18 May 1918 for the Ekaterinburg Soviet.
73. *Izvestiia Moskvy*, 18 May 1918.
74. *Trudy SNKh*, pp. 219ff., especially pp. 364ff.
75. *Rabochii klass Urala v gody voiny i revoliutsii*, 1 (Sverdlovsk, 1927), p. vii; Keep, *Russian Revolution*, pp. 285, 364. Anweiler, *The Soviets*, pp. 48–9, for Soviets in the mining districts of the Urals in 1905 prepared to engage in armed struggle.
76. *Rabochii klass*, pp. xv–xvi; J. H. Bater, R. A. French (eds), *Studies in Russian Historical Geography*, 2 (Orlando, 1983), pp. 380f.
77. S. Berk, 'The "Class Tragedy" of Izhevsk: Working-Class Opposition to Bolshevism in 1918', *Russian History*, 2 (1975), p. 177; *Rabochii klass*, pp. 21–3; M. Vladimirov, 'Ural'skaia metallurgiia i rabochii klass do i vo vremia voiny', *Vestnik Metallista*, 1 (1917), pp. 28–32; and Baevskii, *Partiia*, p. 457.
78. *Rabochii klass*, pp. 18–21, 26, 29–30; *Proletarskii Golos*, 4 (1916).
79. Preobrazhenskii, *S"ezd neobkhodim*, p. 14.
80. *Natsionalizatsiia promyshlennosti*, p. 7.
81. Ibid., pp. 8, 62–3; *Rabochaia revoliutsiia na Urale*, pp. 133–4, 157; Lenin, *CW*, 36, p. 459.
82. Andronnikov's report, *Trudy SNKh*, pp. 221–7; *Natsionalizatsiia promyshlennosti*, pp. 204–5; Flenley, 'Workers' Organisations', pp. 364–7, 398–401.
83. Ibid., p. 525.
84. J. Bushnell, 'G. L. Piatakov', in J. L. Wieczynski (ed.), *Modern Encyclopedia of Russian and Soviet History*, 28 (Gulf Breeze, 1982), p. 67.
85. *Otchet*, p. 33; R. Pipes, *Formation*, pp. 128–9.
86. For the narrow definition adopted by the Provisional Government, R. P. Browder, A. F. Kerensky (eds), *The Russian Provisional Government*, 1 (Stanford, 1961), p. 396. The *Rada* staked its claim in its Third Universal, Bunyan, *Bolshevik Revolution*, pp. 435–8.
87. E. Bosh, *God bor'by* (Moscow, 1925), pp. 25–6; Pipes, *Formation*, ppl. 128–9; J. Borys, *The Sovietisation of the Ukraine, 1917–1923* (Edmonton, 1980), pp. 134, 141–2.
88. Nikol'nikov, *Pobeda leninskoi strategii*, p. 55. Bosh, *God bor'by*, p. 2, stresses that this antipathy had existed throughout 1917.
89. V. Zatonskii, 'K piatletiiu KP(b)U', *Pervyi s"ezd KP(b)U, 5–12 iiulia 1918 goda* (Khar'kov, 1923), p. 14; also E. Kviring, 'Nashi raznoglasiia', ibid., p. 7.
90. Ibid., pp. 62, 73.
91. Pipes, *Formation*, p. 132; Daniels, *Conscience*, p. 98; Kviring, *Raznoglasiia*, p. 6; A. E. Adams, *Bolsheviks in the Ukraine. The Second Campaign, 1918–1919* (New Haven, 1963), pp. 18–19; S. Mazlakh, V. Shakhrai,

*On the Current Situation in the Ukraine* (Ann Arbor, 1970), pp. 36, 192.
92. Bosh, *God bor'by*, pp. 251-3; 'K osveshcheniiu voprosov istorii Kommunisticheskoi partii Ukrainy', *Kommunist Ukrainy*, 6 (1959), p. 43.
93. *Otchet*, p. 130; *Bol'shevistskie organizatsii Ukrainy (noiabr' 1917 – aprel' 1918gg.)* (Kiev, 1962), pp. 596-7.
94. *Otchet*, p. 125.
95. Ibid., pp. 116-17.
96. *Bol'shevistskie organizatsii*, pp. 667-8.
97. The following account casts doubt on the view that the Left Communists in the Ukraine can be equated simply with the Kievan Bolsheviks, as suggested, for example, by Pipes, *Formation*, p. 131.
98. *Donetskii Proletarii*, 1 March 1918. For similar support for a more radical economic policy adopted by the Fourth Congress of Soviets of the Donets and Krivoi Rog basins, *Zvezda*, 19 February 1918.
99. Ibid.; *Pravda*, 17 March 1918; *Bol'shevistskie organizatsii*, pp. 93-5, 316-17, 360-1, 374-5, 461; Sirianni, *Workers' Control*, pp. 102-4.
100. *Donetskii Proletarii*, 3 March 1918.
101. Ibid., 8 March 1918.
102. Ibid., 1 March 1918.
103. *Otchet*, p. 123.
104. *Sed'moi s"ezd*, pp. 335-6; *Bol'shevistskie organizatsii*, pp. 378-9; *Istoricheskii arkhiv*, 3 (1958), p. 25; but Stozhok may have exaggerated the support for war since the local Soviet agreed, by the substantial margin of twenty-three to six, to accept peace, *Otchet*, p. 111.
105. Ibid., pp. 117, 119-20, 131; *Bol'shevistskie organizatsii*, pp. 377-8.
106. Iaglov [A. S. Bubnov], 'Mirnaia politika i voenniia porazheniia', *Kommunist. Organ Org. Biuro po sozyva Konferentsii Part. Organizatsii Kommunistov (b) Ukrainy, 3-4* (1918), pp. 2-3 (thereafter *Kommunist Ukrainy*); N. A. Skrypnik's report of conditions in the Ukraine, *Izvestiia VTsIK*, 3 April 1918, reprinted in *Bol'shevistskie organizatsii*, pp. 73-8.
107. *Kommunist*, 12 March 1918.
108. *Sed'moi s"ezd*, pp. 334-5; *Bol'shevistskie organizatsii*, pp. 666, 690-1.
109. Berlina, *Brestskii mir*, p. 42; for Artem's claims, *Istoricheskii arkhiv*, 3 (1958), p. 26.
110. *Istoricheskii arkhiv*, 3 (1958), p. 27, 4 (1958), p. 31.
111. *Otchet*, p. 108.
112. *Bol'shevistskie organizatsii*, pp. 305-7; *Donetskii Proletarii*, 8 March 1918.
113. *Bol'shevistskie organizatsii*, pp. 303-5, 308-9.
114. *Donetskii Proletarii*, 16, 22 March 1918.
115. Ibid., 15 March 1918. Testimony to the bitterness of the intra-party conflict in the Ukraine can be gauged from the unsigned editorial which viciously attacked the Left Communists for succumbing to 'the Menshevik symphony of revolutionary resistance' which, it continued, was quite unrealistic at the present time. Also *Bol'shevistskie organizatsii*, pp. 136-7.
116. Ibid., pp. 214-15.

117. Ibid., pp. 212–13; *Izvestiia Moskvy*, 26 March 1918.
118. *Bol'shevistskie organizatsii*, pp. 215–16, 384.
119. Skrypnik's report, ibid., p. 76.
120. *Sotsial-Demokrat*, 15 March 1918; *Bol'shevistskie organizatsii*, pp. 692–3.
121. Ibid., pp. 79–81.
122. I.T.S., 'V bor'be s kontr-revoliutsiei', *Kommunist*, 4 (1918), p. 2; I. Kulik, 'Revoliutsionnoe dvizhenie na Ukraine', *Zhizn' Natsional'nostei*, 4 (1919).
123. Skrypnik's report, *Bol'shevistskie organizatsii*, p. 76. Collin Ross, of the German Ministry of Foreign Affairs, who was present in the Ukraine in March 1918, had warned that any policy of plunder would provoke widespread resistance, *Arkhiv russkoi revoliutsii*, 1 (1922), p. 293. Also Cohen, *Bukharin*, p. 69; and Deutscher, *The Prophet Armed*, pp. 399–400.
124. Bosh, *God bor'by*, pp. 217–18; Borys, *Sovietisation*, p. 146. *Ocherki istorii KP Ukrainy* (Kiev, 1977), alleges seventy-one delegates were present.
125. Kviring, *Raznoglasiia*, pp. 6–7; Pipes, *Formation*, p. 132; Bosh, *God bor'by*, p. 219; V. Bilinsky, 'The Communist Take-over of the Ukraine', in T. Hunczak (ed.), *The Ukraine, 1917–1921: A Study in Revolution* (Cambridge, Mass., 1977), p. 114.
126. *Kommunist Ukrainy*, 1–2 (1918), pp. 19–20.
127. Ibid., pp. 20–1.
128. Ibid., 3–4 (1918), pp. 9–10.
129. Ibid., pp. 26–30. At the conference itself the Kievan delegate complained that the rank-and-file in the Ukraine had no knowledge of the proceedings and decisions of the Seventh Party Congress. Kulik, *Revoliutsionnoe dvizhenie*, exaggerated the extent of Bolshevik revival in the summer of 1918.
130. *Kommunist Ukrainy*, 3–4 (1918), p. 25.
131. *Pervyi s"ezd*, p. 184. Four organisations failed to reply to the question on factional allegiance. Of the Left organisations, seven were from the Kiev district, three from Odessa, two from Ekaterinoslav and one from Khar'kov. Two of the Right organisations were centred on Ekaterinoslav, and four on Khar'kov. Of the seven Centrist organisations, five were from the Ekaterinoslav district and two from Khar'kov.
132. Ibid., pp. 103ff., 132–5.
133. Ibid., p. 170.
134. Ibid., pp. 35–7.
135. 'Iz deiatel'nosti TsK KP(b)U i TsVRK v period mezhdu I i II s"ezdami KP(b)U', *Letopis' revoliutsii* (Khar'kov), 1 (1927), pp. 155–6.
136. *Pervyi s"ezd*, p. 177.
137. *Iz deiatel'nosti*, p. 122.
138. Ibid., p. 141.
139. Adams, *Bolsheviks in the Ukraine*, pp. 124–35; J. E. Mace, *Communism and the Dilemmas of National Liberation. National Communism in the Soviet Ukraine, 1918–1933* (Cambridge, Mass., 1983), pp. 34–5.

CONCLUSION

1. R. Luxemburg, 'The Russian Revolution', *Rosa Luxemburg Speaks* (New York, 1970), p. 376.
2. Preobrazhenskii, *S"ezd neobkhodim*, p. 15.
3. Sirianni, *Workers' Control*, p. 148.
4. Luxemburg, *Russian Revolution*, p. 390.
5. *Kommunist*, 3 (1918), p. 19; Haynes, *Bukharin*, p. 49.
6. R. Bahro, *The Alternative in Eastern Europe* (London, 1978), pp. 103–4.
7. Remington, *Building Socialism*, p. 140.
8. E. Haberkern, 'Machajski: A Rightfully Forgotten Prophet', *Telos*, 71 (1987), p. 111.
9. Daniels, *Conscience*, p. 91.
10. Sirianni, *Workers' Control*, p. 1.
11. M. S. Gorbachev, *Perestroika. New Thinking for Our Country and the World* (London, 1988), pp. 90–1; A. Aganbegyan, *Moving the Mountain. Inside the Perestroika Revolution* (London, 1989), pp. 9–10, 15, 99–100; and M. Lewin, *The Gorbachev Phenomenon* (London, 1988), pp. 129–44.

# Bibliography

NEWSPAPERS, JOURNALS AND PERIODICAL PUBLICATIONS

*Biulleteni V.S.N.Kh.*
*Donetskii Proletarii*
*Istoricheskii arkhiv*
*Istorik Marksist*
*Izvestiia Permskogo Gubernskogo Ispolnitel'nogo Komiteta*
*Izvestiia Saratovskogo Soveta*
*Izvestiia Sovetov Rab., Sold., i Krest. Deputatov goroda Moskvy i Moskovskoi oblasti*
*Izvestiia Ural'skogo Oblastnogo Soveta*
*Izvestiia V.Ts.I.K.*
*Kommunist* (Petrograd)
*Kommunist* (Moscow) (reprinted as *Kommunist* (New York, 1990) ed. R. I. Kowalski)
*Kommunist. Organ Org. Biuro po sozyva Konferentsii Part. Organizatsii Kommunistov (b) Ukrainy*
*Kommunist Ukrainy*
*Krasnaia gazeta*
*Krasnaia Letopis'*
*Letopis' revoliutsii* (Khar'kov)
*Metallist*
*Moskovskii metallist*
*Narodnoe khoziaistvo*
*New Left Review*
*Pravda*
*Professional'nyi vestnik*
*Proletarskaia Revoliutsiia*
*Proletarskii golos*
*Radical History Review*
*Russian History*
*Slavic Review*
*Slavonic and East European Review*
*Sotsial-Demokrat*
*Soviet Studies*
*Spartak*
*Telos*
*Vestnik metallista*
*Voprosy Istorii*
*Voprosy Istorii K.P.S.S.*
*Vpered* (Ufa)
*Zhizn' Natsional'nostei*
*Zvezda*

## DOCUMENTARY MATERIALS

Where no author's name is given, the work is listed alphabetically under
the first word of the title.

*Arkhiv russkoi revoliutsii* (1922–)

*Bol'shevistskie organizatsii Ukrainy*

Bone, A. (ed.), *The Bolsheviks and the October Revolution, Minutes of the Central
Committee* (London, 1974)

Browder, R. P., Kerensky, A. F., *The Russian Provisional Government*
(Stanford, 1961)

Bunyan, J., Fisher, H. H., *The Bolshevik Revolution, 1917–1918. Documents
and Materials* (Stanford, 1965)

Bunyan, J., *Intervention, Civil War and Communism in Russia, April–December,
1918: Documents and Materials* (New York, 1976)

*Deiateli S.S.S.R. i Oktiabr'skoi Revoliutsiia* (Moscow, 1927–9)

Gankin, O., Fisher, H. H., *The Bolsheviks and the World War: the Origin of the
Third International* (Stanford, 1940)

*The Inquiry Handbooks* 19 (Wilmington, 1974)

*'Iz deiatel'nosti TsK KP(b)U i TsVRK v period mezhdu I i II s"ezdami KP(b)U',
Letopis' revoliutsii*, I (1927)

Keep, J. H. L. (ed.), *The Debate on Soviet Power* (Oxford, 1979)

*KPSS v bor'be za pobedu velikoi oktiabr'skoi sotsialisticheskoi revoliutsii, 5 iiulia-5
noabria 1917g* (Moscow, 1957)

*Leninskii sbornik*, XI (Moscow, Leningrad, 1929)

*Natsionalizatsiia promyshlennosti na Urale (Oktiabr' 1917-iiul' 1918gg)* (Sverdlovsk, 1958)

*1903. Second Ordinary Congress of the Russian Social-Democratic Labour Party*
(London, 1978)

*Pervyi s"ezd KP(b)U, 5–12 iiulia 1918 goda* (Khar'kov, 1923)

*Rabochii klass Urala v gody voiny i revoliutsii*, I (Sverdlovsk, 1927)

Riddell, J. (ed.), *Lenin's Struggle for a Revolutionary International. Documents:
1907–1916 – The Preparatory Years* (New York, 1984)

*Saratovskii sovet rabochikh deputatov, 1917–1918: Sbornik dokumentov* Antonov-Saratovskii, V. P. (ed.), (Moscow, Leningrad, 1931)

*Sed-maia (Aprel'skaia) vserossiiskaia konferentsiia R.S.D.R.P.(b.), aprel' 1917
goda: stenograficheskii otchet* (Moscow, 1962)

*Sed'moi ekstrennyi s"ezd R.K.P.(b.), mart 1918 goda: stenograficheskii otchet*
(Moscow, 1962)

*Shestoi s"ezd R.S.D.R.P.(b.), avgust 1917 goda: stenograficheskii otchet* (Moscow,
1958)

*Stenograficheskii otchet 4-ogo Chrezvychainogo S"ezda Sovetov Raboch., Soldatsk.,
Krest'iansk i Kazach'ikh Deputatov* (Moscow, 1920)

*Uprochenie sovetskoi vlasti v Moskve i moskovskoi gubernii* (Moscow, 1958)

*Trudy Sovetov Narodnogo Khoziaistva 1-ogo vserossiiskogo s"ezda Sovetov Narod-
nogo Khoziaistva. 25 maia-4 iiunia 1918gg. Stenograficheskii otchet* (Moscow,
1918)

*Vos'moi s"ezd R.K.P.(b.), mart 1919 goda: stenograficheskii otchet* (Moscow,
1959)

## SECONDARY WORKS IN RUSSIAN

Anikeev, V. V., *Deiatel'nost' Ts.K. R.S.D.R.P.(b) – 1917–1918 godakh* (Moscow, 1974)

Antonov-Saratovskii, V. P., *Pod stiagom proletarskoi bor'by. Otryvki iz vospominaniih o rabote v Saratove za vremia c 1915g do 1918g* (Moscow, Leningrad, 1925)

Baevskii, D. A., 'Bol'sheviki v bor'be za III Internatsional', *Istorik Marksist*, 11 (1929)

Baevskii, D. A., 'Partiia v gody imperialisticheskoi voiny', in Pokrovskii, M. N. (ed.), *Ocherki po istorii oktiabr'skoi revoliutsii* (Moscow, 1927)

Berlina, Z. I., Gorbunova, N. T., 'Brestskii mir i mestnye partiinye organizatsii', *Voprosy Istorii K.P.S.S.*, 9 (1963)

*Bol'sheviki Ekaterinburga vo glave mass* (Sverdlovsk, 1962)

Bosh, E., *God bor'by* (Moscow, 1925)

Bubnov, A. S., *VKP(b)* (Moscow, 1931)

Bystrykh, F., 'Razvitie vzgliadov Lenina po agrarnomu voprosu', *Proletarskaia Revoliutsiia*, 1 (1928)

Chubar'ian, A. O., *Brestskii mir* (Moscow, 1964)

Dingel'shtedt, F. N., 'Iz vospominaniia agitatora Petersburgskogo Komiteta RSDRP(b). (S sentiabria 1917g po mart 1918g.), *Krasnaia Letopis'*, 1 (1927)

Gaisinskii, M. G., *Bor'ba s uklonami ot general'noi linii partii. Istoricheskii otchet vnutripartiinoi bor'by posle oktiabr'skoi revoliutsii* (Moscow, 1931)

Gorelov, I. E., *Nikolai Bukharin* (Moscow, 1988)

Iakovleva, V., 'Partiinaia rabota v Moskovskoi oblasti v period fevral'-oktiabr' 1917g.', *Proletarskaia Revoliutsiia*, 3 (1923)

Iaroslavskii, Em., *Istoriia VKP(b)*, 2 (Moscow, 1933)

Ignat'ev, G. S., *Moskva v pervyi god proletarskoi diktatury* (Moscow, 1975)

Il'in-Zhenevskii, A. F., *Bol'sheviki u vlasti. Vospominaniia o 1918 godu* (Leningrad, 1929)

*Istoriia KPSS* (Moscow, 1967)

Khil'chenko, M. P., 'Inostrannye gruppy RKP(b) na Urale', in *Iz istorii partiinykh organizatsii Urala* (Sverdlovsk, 1966)

'K osveshcheniiu voprosov istorii Kommunisticheskoi partii Ukrainy', *Kommunist Ukrainy*, 6 (1959)

Kritsman, L., *Geroicheskii period russkoi revoliutsii* (Moscow, n.d.)

Kulik, I., 'Revoliutsionnoe dvizhenie na Ukraine', *Zhizn' Natsional'nostei*, 4 (1919)

Lomov, A., 'Mirnyi dogovor i narodnoe khoziaistvo Rossii', *Biulleteni V.S.N.Kh.*, 1 (1918)

Lomov, A. L. *Razlozhenie kapitalizma i organizatsiia kommunizma* (Moscow, 1918)

Maiorskii, N., El'vov, N., 'K voprosu o kharaktere dvizhushchikh silakh Oktiabr'skoi revoliutsii', *Proletarskaia revoliutsiia*, 11 (1927)

Markov, R. I., 'Bor'ba V. I. Leninym s trotskistami i "levymi kommunistami" v period Bresta', *Voprosy Istorii K.P.S.S.*, 5 (1959)

*Materialy po peresmotru partiinoi programmy* (Petrograd, 1917)

Nikol'nikov, G. L., *Vydaiushchaiasia pobeda leninskoi strategii i taktiki* (Moscow, 1968)

*Ocherki istorii Moskovskoi organizatsii KPSS*, II (Moscow, 1983)

*Ocherki istorii KP Ukrainy* (Kiev, 1977)

*Ocherki istorii Kommunisticheskoi Partii Urala*, 1 (Sverdlovsk, 1971)

*Ocherki po istorii revoliutsionnogo dvizheniia i bol'shevistskoi organizatsii v Baumanskom raione* (Moscow, 1928)

Oreshkin, V. V., *Voprosy imperializma v rabotakh bol'shevikov-lenintsev v dooktiabr'skii period* (Moscow, 1968)

Osinskii, N., *Demokraticheskaia respublika i sovetskaia respublika* (Odessa, 1920)

Osinskii, N., *Stroitel'stvo sotsializma* (Moscow, 1918)

Oznobishin, D. V., 'K istorii bor'by partii protiv "levykh kommunistov" posle VII s"ezda RKP(b)', *Voprosy Istorii K.P.S.S.*, 10 (1969)

Oznobishin, D. V., 'K voprosu o bor'be s fraktsiei "levykh kommunistov"', *Voprosy Istorii*, 9 (1971)

Pokrovskii, M. N. (ed.), *Ocherki po istorii oktiabr'skoi revoliutsii* (Moscow, 1927)

Pokrovskii, M. N., *Oktiabr'skaia revoliutsiia* (Moscow, 1921)

*Put' k Oktiabriu*, 3 (Moscow, 1923)

*Rabochaia revoliutsiia na Urale. Epizody i fakty* (Ekaterinburg, 1921)

Radek, K., *Piat' let Kominterna* (Moscow, 1924)

Safarov, G. I., *Natsional'nyi vopros i proletariat* (Petrograd, 1922)

Serebriakova, Z. L., *Oblastnye ob"edineniia Sovetov Rossii, mart 1917–dekabr' 1918* (Moscow, 1977)

Shelavin, K. I., 'Iz istorii Petersburgskogo Komiteta bol'shevikov v 1918g', *Krasnaia Letopis'*, 2 (1927)

Skvortsov-Stepanov, I. I., *Ot rabochego kontrolia k rabochemu upravleniiu* (Moscow, 1918)

Sorin, V., *Partiia i oppozitsiia. Iz istorii oppozitsionnykh techenii, 1. Fraktsiia levykh kommunistov* (Moscow, 1925)

Taranev, I. M., 'Diskussii v RSDRP(b)-RKP(b). Mart 1917–1920gg. i novye podkhody') *Voprosy Istorii K.P.S.S.*, 10 (1989)

Tarnovskii, K. N., *Sovetskaia istoriografiia rossiiskogo imperializma* (Moscow, 1964)

Tiutiukin, S. V., *Voina, mir, revoliutsiia. Ideinaia bor'ba v rabochem dvizhenii Rossii 1914–1917gg.* (Moscow, 1972)

Tkachev, V. I., 'Bor'ba s "levymi kommunistami" v period Brest-Litovskikh peregovorov. (Na materialakh partiinykh organizatsii Povolzh'ia') *Voprosy Istorii K.P.S.S.*, 6 (1986)

Tsypkin, G. A., Tsypkina, R. G., *Krasnaia gvardiia – udarnaia sila proletariata v Oktiabr'skoi revoliutsii* (Moscow, 1977)

Ukhanov, K., Borisov, I., *Iz zhizni i deiatel'nosti Soveta R i K D Rogozhko-Simonovskogo raiona g. Moskvy (mart 1917g-ianvar' 1921g)* (Moscow, 1921)

Valentinov, N., *Novaia ekonomicheskaia politika i krizis partii posle smerti Lenina* (Stanford, 1971)

Varlamov, K. I. Slamikhin, N. A., *Razoblachenie V. I. Leninym teorii itaktiki 'levykh kommunistov'* (Moscow, 1964)

Vindzberg, '1-i Moskovskoi revoliutsionnyi dobrovol'cheskii otriad po bor'be s kontr-revoliutsiei', in *Put' k Oktiabriu*, 3 (Moscow, 1923)

SECONDARY WORKS IN ENGLISH

Adams, A. E., *Bolsheviks in the Ukraine. The Second Campaign, 1918–1919* (New Haven, 1963)

Aganbegyan, A., *Moving the Mountain. Inside the Perestroika Revolution* (London, 1989)

Antsiferov, A. A., *Russian Agriculture During the War* (New Haven, 1930)

Anweiler, O., *The Soviets: The Russian Workers, Peasants and Soldiers Councils, 1905–1921* (New York, 1974)

Avrich, P., 'The Bolshevik Revolution and Workers' Control in Russian Industry', *Slavic Review*, 1 (1963)

Bahro, R., *The Alternative in Eastern Europe* (London, 1978)

Bailes, K., *Technology and Society under Lenin and Stalin* (Princeton, 1978)

Barone, C. A., *Marxist Thought on Imperialism* (London, 1985)

Bater, J. H., French, R. A. (eds), *Studies in Russian Historical Geography*, 2 (Orlando, 1983)

Beilharz, P., *Trotsky, Trotskyism and the Transition to Socialism* (London, 1987)

Benet, S., *The Village of Viriatino* (New York, 1970)

Berk, S., 'The "Class Tragedy" of Izhevsk: Working-Class Opposition to Bolshevism in 1918', *Russian History*, 2 (1975)

Borys, J., *The Sovietisation of the Ukraine, 1917–1923* (Edmonton, 1980)

Bottomore, T., 'Introduction', in Hilferding, R., *Finance Capital* (London, 1981)

Brewer, A., *Marxist Theories of Imperialism. A Critical Survey* (London, 1980)

Brinton, M., *The Bolsheviks and Workers' Control, 1917–1921* (London, 1970)

Brovkin, V. N., *The Mensheviks after October. Socialist Opposition and the Rise of the Bolshevik Dictatorship* (Ithaca, 1987)

Bukharin, N. I., *Historical Materialism. A System of Sociology* (Ann Arbor, 1969)

Bukharin, N. I., *Imperialism and World Economy* (New York, 1929)

Bukharin, N. I., *The Politics and Economics of the Transition Period* (London, 1979)

Bukharin, N. I., *Selected Writings on the State and the Transition to Socialism* (Nottingham, 1982)

Bushnell, J., 'G. L. Piatakov', in Wieczynski, J. L. (ed.), *Modern Encyclopaedia of Russian and Soviet History*, 28 (Gulf Breeze, 1982)

Carr, E. H., *The Bolshevik Revolution, 1917–1921*, 1–3 (Harmondsworth, 1966)

Chamberlin, W. H., *The Russian Revolution*, 1 (New York, 1965)

Channon, J., 'The Bolsheviks and the Peasantry: the Land Question During the first Eight Months of Soviet Rule', *Slavonic and East European Review*, 4 (1988)

Claudin, F., 'Democracy and Dictatorship in Lenin and Kautsky', *New Left Review*, 106 (1977)

Clements, B., *Bolshevik Feminist. The Life of Alexandra Kollontai* (Bloomington, 1979)

Cohen, S. F., *Bukharin and the Bolshevik Revolution. A Political Biography* (Oxford, 1980)

Cohen, S. F., 'Bukharin, Lenin and the Theoretical Foundations of Bolshevism', *Soviet Studies*, 4 (1969–70)

Crowe, D. M., Jr., 'Preobrazhenskii, Evgenii Alekseevich', in Wieczynski, J. L. (ed.), *Modern Encyclopaedia of Russian and Soviet History*, 29 (Gulf Breeze, 1982)

Dallin, D., 'The Outbreak of the Civil War', in Haimson, L. H. (ed.), *The Mensheviks: from the revolution of 1917 to the second world war* (Chicago, 1974)

Daniels, R. V., *The Conscience of the Revolution. Communist Opposition in Soviet Russia* (Cambridge, Mass., 1980)

Danilov, V. P., *Rural Russia under the New Regime* (London, 1988)

Davies, R. W., *The Development of the Soviet Budgetary System* (Cambridge, 1958)

Day, R. B., 'Introduction', in Bukharin, N. I., *Selected Writings on the State and the Transition to Socialism* (Nottingham, 1982)

Day, R. B., *Leon Trotsky and the Politics of Economic Isolation* (Cambridge, 1973)

Deutscher, I., *The Prophet Armed* (Oxford, 1970)

Dotsenko, P., *The Struggle for Democracy in Siberia, 1917–1921* (Stanford, 1983)

Duval, C., 'Iakov Mikhailovich Sverdlov: Founder of the Bolshevik Party Machine', in Elwood, R. C. (ed.), *Reconsiderations on the Russian Revolution* (Cambridge, Mass., 1976)

Erickson, J. H., 'The Origins of the Red Army', in Pipes, R. (ed.), *Revolutionary Russia* (New York, 1969)

Erickson, J. H., *The Soviet High Command* (London, 1962)

Evans, A. B., 'Rereading Lenin's *State and Revolution*', *Slavic Review*, 1 (1987)

Ezergailis, A., *The Latvian Impact on the Bolshevik Revolution* (New York, 1983)

Farnsworth, B., *Alexandra Kollontai. Socialism, Feminism and the Bolshevik Revolution* (Stanford, 1980)

Fedotoff-White, D., *The Growth of the Red Army* (Princeton, 1944)

Ferro, M., *The Bolshevik Revolution. A Social History of the Russian Revolution* (London, 1985)

Fischer, F., *Germany's Aims in the First World War* (London, 1967)

Flenley, P. S., 'Workers' Organisations in the Russian Metal Industry, February 1917–August 1918', Ph.D. thesis (Birmingham, 1983)

Getzler, I., *Kronstadt 1917–1921: the fate of a Soviet democracy* (Cambridge, 1983)

Gorbachev, M., *Perestroika. New Thinking for Our Country and the World* (London, 1988)

Gramsci, A., *Selections from the Prison Note-books* (New York, 1971)

Haberkern, E., 'Machajski: A Rightfully Forgotten Prophet', *Telos*, 71 (1987)

Harding, N., *Lenin's Political Thought*, vol. 1. *Theory and Practice in the Democratic Revolution* (London, 1977)

Harding, N., *Lenin's Political Thought*, vol. 2. *Theory and Practice in the Socialist Revolution* (London, 1981)

Haynes, M., *Nikolai Bukharin and the Transition from Capitalism to Socialism* (Beckenham, 1985)

Hilferding, R., *Finance Capital* (London, 1981)

*History of the CPSU(b)* (Moscow, 1938)

Hunczak, T. (ed.), *The Ukraine, 1917–1921: A Study in Revolution* (Cambridge, Mass., 1977)

Hunt, R. N., *The Political Ideas of Marx and Engels*, I, II (Pittsburgh, 1974, 1984)

Kaplan, F. I., *Bolshevik Ideology and the Ethics of Soviet Labour. 1917–1920: The Formative Years* (New York, 1968)

Kautsky, K., 'Ultra-Imperialism', *New Left Review*, 59 (1970)

Keep, J. L. H., 'October in the Provinces', in Pipes, R. (ed.), *Revolutionary Russia* (New York, 1969)

Keep, J. L. H., *The Russian Revolution: A Study in Mass Mobilisation* (London, 1976)

Kenez, P., *Civil War in South Russia* (Berkeley, 1971)

Kingston-Mann, E., *Lenin and the Problem of Marxist Peasant Revolution* (Oxford, 1983)

Kitchen, M., *The Silent Dictatorship. The Politics of the German High Command Under Hindenburg and Ludendorff* (London, 1976)

Koenker, D., *Moscow Workers and the 1917 Revolution* (Princeton, 1981)

Krassin, L., *Leonid Krassin: His Life and Work* (London, 1929)

Lenin, V. I., *Collected Works* (London, 1960–70)

Lerner, W., *Karl Radek* (Stanford, 1970)

Lewin, M., *The Gorbachev Phenomenon* (London, 1989)

Luxemburg, R., 'The Russian Revolution', in *Rosa Luxemburg Speaks* (New York, 1970)

McClelland, J. C., 'The Utopian and the Heroic: Divergent Paths to the Communist Educational Ideal', in Gleason, A. *et al.* (eds), *Bolshevik Culture: Experiment and Order in the Russian Revolution* (Bloomington, 1985)

McClelland, J. C., 'Utopianism versus Revolutionary Heroism in Bolshevik Policy: The Proletarian Culture Debate', *Slavic Review*, 3 (1980)

Mace, J. E., *Communism and the Dilemmas of National Liberation. National Communism in the Soviet Ukraine, 1918–1933* (Cambridge, Mass., 1983)

Malle, S., *The Economic Organisation of War Communism* (Cambridge, 1985)

Mandel, D., *The Petrograd Workers and the Soviet Seizure of Power* (London, 1984)

Marx, K., Engels, F., *Collected Works*, 22 (London, 1986)

Mazlakh, S., Shakhrai, V., *On the Current Situation in the Ukraine* (Ann Arbor, 1971)

Miliband, R., *Class Power & State Power* (London, 1983)

Mouzelis, N. P., *Organisation and Bureaucracy. An Analysis of Modern Theories* (London, 1975)

Nove, A., *The Economics of Feasible Socialism* (London, 1983)

Oppenheim, S. A., 'The Supreme Economic Council, 1917–1921', *Soviet Studies*, 3–4 (1973)

Phillips Price, M., *My Reminiscences of the Russian Revolution* (London, 1921)

Pipes, R., *The Formation of the Soviet Union. Communism and Nationalism 1917–1923* (Cambridge, Mass., 1964)

Polan, A. J., *Lenin and the End of Politics* (London, 1984)

Rabinowitch, A., *The Bolsheviks Come to Power. The Revolution of 1917 in Petrograd* (New York, 1976)

Radkey, O. H., *The Sickle under the Hammer. The Russian Socialist Revolutionaries in the Early Months of Soviet Rule* (New York, 1963)

Remington, T. F., *Building Socialism in Bolshevik Russia. Ideology and Industrial Organisation* (Pittsburgh, 1984)

Rhys Williams, A., *Journey into Revolution. Petrograd, 1917–1918* (Chicago, 1969)

Rigby, T. H., *Lenin's Government: Sovnarkom 1917–1922* (Cambridge, 1979)

Rosenberg, W. H., 'Russian Labor and Bolshevik Power After October', *Slavic Review*, 2 (1985)

Rubel, M., 'The Relationship of Bolshevism and Marxism', in Pipes, R. (ed.), *Revolutionary Russia* (New York, 1969)

Sakwa, R., 'The Commune State in Moscow in 1918', *Slavic Review*, 3/4 (1987)

Sakwa, R., *Soviet Communists in Power. A Study of Moscow during the Civil War, 1918–1921* (London, 1988)

Schapiro, L. B., *Communist Party of the Soviet Union* (London, 1970)

Schapiro, L. B., *The Origins of the Communist Autocracy. Political Opposition in the Soviet State. First Phase: 1917–1922* (Cambridge, Mass., 1955)

Selucky, R., *Marxism, Socialism, Freedom* (London, 1979)

Serge, V., *Memoirs of a Revolutionary* (Oxford, 1963)

Serge, V., *Year One of the Russian Revolution* (London, 1972)

Service, R., *The Bolshevik Party in Revolution, 1917–1923* (London, 1979)

Service, R., *Lenin, A Political Life, 1: The Strengths of Contradiction* (London, 1985)

Service, R., *The Bolsheviks On Political Campaign In 1917: A Case Study of the War Question* (Paper presented to Soviet Industrialisation Project seminar, CREES, Birmingham, March 1988)

Service, R., *Lenin and Agrarian Economics in 1917* (Unpublished conference paper, London, 1988)

Shanin, T., *The Awkward Class* (Oxford, 1972)

Siegelbaum, L. H., 'Historical Revisionism in the USSR', *Radical History Review*, 44 (1989)

Sirianni, C., *Workers' Control and Socialist Democracy. The Soviet Experience* (London, 1982)

Smith, S. A., *Red Petrograd. Revolution in the factories, 1917–1918* (Cambridge, 1983)

Snow, R., *The Bolsheviks in Siberia, 1917–1918* (London, 1977)

Sochor, Z. A., *Revolution and Culture. The Bogdanov-Lenin Controversy* (Ithaca, 1988)

Sukhanov, N., *The Russian Revolution 1917. A Personal Record* (Princeton, 1984)

Thompson, E. P., 'Eighteenth-century English Society: class struggle without class', *Social History*, 3 (1978)

Trotsky, L. D., *My Life* (New York, 1960)

Tucker, R. C., Cohen, S. F. (eds), *The Great Purge Trial* (New York, 1965)

Tucker, R. C. (ed.), *The Marx-Engels Reader* (New York, 1972)

Warren, B., *Imperialism: Pioneer of Capitalism* (London, 1980)

Wesson, R. G., *Soviet Communes* (New Brunswick, 1963)

Wheeler-Bennett, J. W., *Brest-Litovsk. The Forgotten Peace, March 1918* (London, 1968)

Wildman, A. K., *The End of the Russian Imperial Army. The Road to Soviet Power and Peace* (Princeton, 1987)

Winslow, E. M., *The Pattern of Imperialism* (New York, 1948)

Wohlforth, T., 'The Transition to the Transition', *New Left Review*, 130 (1981)

# Glossary of Russian terms and abbreviations used in text

| | |
|---|---|
| **ARCWC** | All-Russian Council of Workers' Control |
| *batrak* | farm labourer |
| **CC** | Central Committee [of Communist Party] (*Tsentral'nyi Komitet*) |
| **CEC** | Central Executive Committee [of Soviets] (*Tsentral'nyi Ispolnitel'nyi Komitet*) |
| **CP(b)U** | Communist Party of the Ukraine (Bolsheviks) |
| *dessiatina* | measure of land = 2.7 acres |
| *duma* | city or town council |
| *kollegiia* | board [of administration of factory or plant] |
| *kulak* | rich peasant |
| **MRC** | Military Revolutionary Committee (*Voenno-revoliutsionnyi Komitet*) |
| *muzhik* | peasant |
| *obshchina* | peasant commune |
| *otriad* | (military) detachment |
| *oblast'* | region |
| *okrug* | administrative unit between a region (*oblast'*) and a district (*raion*) |
| **Orgburo** | *Organizatsionnoe biuro* (Organisation Bureau [of party]) |
| *pomeshchik* | landowner, noble |
| *Rada* | council, legislative body of Ukraine |
| *raion* | city district |
| **SDKPiL** | Social Democracy of the Kingdom of Poland and Lithuania |
| **SR** | Social Revolutionary (*sotsialist-revoliutsioner*) |
| *samodeiatel'nost* | self-activity, self-creativity [of working class] |
| *smychka* | union, or alliance [of workers and peasants] |
| **Sovnarkhoz** | *Sovet Narodnogo Khoziaistva* (Economic Council) |
| **Sovnarkom (SNK)** | *Sovet Narodnykh Komissarov* (Council of People's Commissars) |
| *spetsy* | (bourgeois) specialists (*spetsialisty*) |
| *uezd* | rural district |
| **Vesenkha (VSNKh)** | *Vysshii Sovet Narodnogo Khoziaistva* (Supreme Council of National Economy) |
| *volost'* | small rural district |
| *zemstvo* | district council |

# Index